Sonic Mosaics

Conversations with Composers

Sonic

PAUL STEENHUISEN

Mosaics

Conversations with Composers

 THE UNIVERSITY OF ALBERTA PRESS

Published by

The University of Alberta Press
Ring House 2
Edmonton, Alberta, Canada   T6G 2E1

Copyright © 2009, Paul Steenhuisen.

LIBRARY AND ARCHIVES CANADA CATALOGUING IN PUBLICATION

Steenhuisen, Paul Brendan Allister, 1965-
    Sonic mosaics : conversations with composers / Paul Steenhuisen.

Includes index.
ISBN 978-0-88864-474-9

    1. Composition (Music). 2. Composers—Interviews. I. Title.

ML430.S814 2008   781.3   C2008-907119-0

The University of Alberta Press is committed to protecting our natural environment. As part of our
efforts, this book is printed on Enviro Paper: it contains 100% post-consumer recycled fibres and is
acid- and chlorine-free.

The University of Alberta Press gratefully acknowledges the support received for its publishing
program from The Canada Council for the Arts. The University of Alberta Press also gratefully
acknowledges the financial support of the Government of Canada through the Book Publishing
Industry Development Program (BPIDP) and from the Alberta Foundation for the Arts for its
publishing activities.

Dedicated to Tara

Contents

Acknowledgements

SINCE I STARTED doing these interviews in the summer of 2001, I've
learned something new about each composer. I didn't really expect to
agree with so many completely different composers. In some ways I find
that disconcerting—I don't want to agree that much. The interviews have
also deepened my perspectives of other composers' work. Other books are
either too old or absent for those revelations to be present. I've also had
the opportunity to hear diametrically opposed people state overlapping
ideas, and provide convincing arguments on troublesome musical topics.
Doing the interviews has made available first-hand information from
composers, but it's also made things less clear, and more layered. It's been
both humbling and fascinating.

I would like to thank the Society of Composers, Authors and Music
Publishers of Canada (SOCAN) Foundation for its generous support. Also,
without the assistance of Toronto's new music groups, this book might
not exist. Their work as presenters facilitated many of the discussions

within these pages, and I would like to thank them and several others for their assistance, including David Olds, Robert Aitken, Alex Pauk, Elisabeth Bihl, Lawrence Cherney, Allison Cameron, Eve Egoyan, Gayle Young, David Parsons, Jean-François Denis, David Jaeger, Larry Lake, and Peter Hatch. As well, my thanks to the musicians who perform our music and to the support staff at these organizations. Thanks to David Perlman for proposing the first interview and printing many of the others. As well, my appreciation goes to Keith Hamel for his support over the years and to Bob Pritchard for his thoughts and enthusiasm. Thank you to the Toronto Symphony for necessitating my move to Toronto, and through that, the many good people I met there. I am indebted to Laurie Brown, who helped and encouraged me immeasurably, and to all members of The Morningstars Hockey Club for the sport, humour, and camaraderie we share.

Composition involves the daily awareness of inner life and death, the compression and distillation of thousands of hours of thought and commitment. My deepest appreciation and thanks to each of the interviewed composers for sharing their ideas, opinions, and music, and to their partners, husbands, wives, and loves, whose compassion often goes unheralded.

Introduction

CANADA HAS MULTIPLE GENERATIONS of musical tradition and
a repertoire of high quality compositional work, yet it doesn't have
adequate information available for the music to be deeply considered by
audiences, performers, researchers, critics, and even other composers. By
interviewing Canadian artists and several from other countries (France,
Germany, England, and the United States) over the span of approximately
three years, I hope that this firsthand information will address the situation, and increase knowledge about contemporary music activity around
the time of the millennium. By documenting artists' words, ideas, plans,
and recollections, I hoped that readers would develop a greater sense of
the cultural context and creative milieu in which the music is made.
Given that the interviewed composers also range in age between their
early thirties and nineties, and come from diverse ethnic, educational,
and economic backgrounds, the collection inevitably contains, as

a subtopic, aspects of how contemporary music developed from World War II until the present, both in North America and Europe.

Primary reference points for contemporary music remain the scores, recordings, broadcasts, and concerts of the pieces, yet critical support material or pre-listening material in the form of information directly from the composers has been surprisingly absent.

Andrew Ford's book *Composer to Composer* (originally published in 1993) is a significant compilation, with engaging interviews from many important international figures, and the majority of published international figures in contemporary music have well-written monograph interview texts available. Interviews with Canadian composers, however, were only available piecemeal. Prior to this collection, a large set of interviews with Canadian composers has not been available. Follow-up material is available largely through the Canadian Music Centre, which disseminates scores, recordings, and information on Canadian composers.

From west to east, the geographical distribution of composers is somewhat diverse, though by no means comprehensive within Canada or internationally. Based on current place of residence, the list reveals the expected concentration of contemporary music in major centres, especially Toronto, Montreal, and Vancouver. It also shows that despite the large landmass that is Canada, many of the composers included here have migrated from their place of birth or undertaken many years of travel for study or work. The geographic trends exhibited by the composers on this list also reveal the interconnectedness of creative work in Canada, and its antennae outward to many international locations.

The majority of my interview opportunities arose from concert activities in Toronto and were facilitated by Toronto's new music presenters. As a result, this book provides a strong reflection of new music aesthetics, composition, and concert activity in Toronto at the time. When interviewed, only thirteen of the artists in the collection resided full-time in the Greater Toronto Area, and fourteen lived in other parts of Ontario or elsewhere in Canada (with the remaining six resident in other countries). As a result, the book also provides a reasonable, though not comprehensive, view of contemporary music activity in Canada. The primary reason for the focus on Toronto was straightforward and practical. Almost all of the interviews were conducted for first publication in Toronto's *Wholenote*

Magazine, a monthly, small-run publication (approximately twenty-five thousand copies) that is distributed primarily in the Greater Toronto Area. The overriding constraint when selecting a composer for an interview was that in most cases there was a link to concert activity during month of publication. Some of the interviews are not connected to a specific live performance, but to a CD release. In two cases, the interview included in the book is different from the original printing. The Butterfield and Arnold interviews were first published in *MusicWorks*, and shorter, differently-edited versions appeared there. The last ten interviews were compiled following a move to Edmonton, Alberta.

The idea for the series originally came from *Wholenote* editor David Perlman. In the summer of 2001, he asked if I would consider interviewing R. Murray Schafer about his upcoming instalment of the *Patria* series. Initially, I was reluctant to do the interview, thinking such things should be the work of musicologists, but clearly they were neglecting the task. With a bit of urging, I agreed to interview Schafer. I was pleased that he, one of Canada's senior composers, was so open to discussing his ideas, and soon realized that composers were speaking candidly and openly to me about their work for two main reasons: first, I'm a composer, I know their work, and while being critical, I asked questions as an "insider"; second, I happened to be talking to them about two of their favourite subjects—themselves and their work!

I wish to make it clear that I am, first and foremost, a composer, which, as an interviewer, provides a unique perspective into the work. As a so-called "insider" in the field, the reader will be aware that an objective, journalistic approach to the questions and line of conversation would not be possible. My affiliations and activities in new music are longstanding, as is my service work for the Canadian League of Composers Executive Council, the Canadian Music Centre, and the International Society for Contemporary Music, among others. While trained in neither journalism nor interviewing techniques, I am instead a self-taught critic, and approached the interviews as an interested professional, with the goal that my own interests and perspectives on the work of the interviewee would overlap with those of other listeners. I did spend a great deal of time, however, reading and writing about music. Living in Amsterdam for a year, I was fortunate to attend concerts several nights a week. I assigned myself the task of writing a review of every concert I attended. Having studied and taught music academically, as well as working as a professional composer since the late 1980s, that training also no doubt influences the nature of the questions. The goal is not for my artistic awareness and history to be a primary subject in the text, but for this subtopic to be acknowledged from the outset. Ultimately, the interviews are not formal, theoretical analyses or basic research, but streams of conversation in which I began with a predetermined set of questions, yet freely followed the direction of discussion as it emerged.

Wholenote readers found my perspective as an "insider" in the contemporary music scene a compelling factor in the interviews, and in all cases, my effort was toward a pertinent line of questioning regardless of my personal relationship with the composers. On some level, I am sympathetic to every composer included here, and hope that the ideas in these pages are accurate representations of them. The decision and commitment to making contemporary art music is a courageous one, replete with difficulty and hardship on creative and personal levels. The vast timeframe necessary for the creation of these works is little known in our culture of quick production and turnover. Meanwhile, many of the artists here spend weeks, months, and years on a single piece, honing, developing, and refining it into what it needs to be. In all cases, I respect that necessity, and the commitment to achieve it. My obligation to the work, to discuss it in detail, and explore the concepts and intents of that artist, in my opinion, should be stronger than my allegiance to the individual. Fair, necessary, and difficult questions supersede any other connection that may or may not exist. In most cases, there is active, unstated agreement on this matter between the interviewee and me. It is this agreement that enables James Rolfe, Juliet Palmer, Chris Paul Harman, Keith Hamel, Howard Bashaw, myself, and others to engage in informal, lengthy, and sometimes heated discussions over the course of an evening and bottles of wine.

Also included after the interviews is an *Afterword*, in which I describe my own work as a composer, so the reader can examine how my creative inclinations influenced the questions. There is also a discography containing a maximum of five recordings per composer. Compiling the lists was a revealing exercise, as it demonstrated a comparative lack of representation for Canadian composers. At the same time as acknowledging the historical significance and quality of work from the interviewed European composers (Boulez, Kagel, Lachenmann), it behooves the reader to recognize the significantly more advanced recording and publishing industry structures that exist to propagate their work. No less than four recordings of Boulez conducting *one* of his works (*Le marteau sans maître*) are available, meanwhile for several other talented and important Canadian artists, it is difficult to find a *total* of four of their works that are available on CD. Despite the existence of the CMC's Centrediscs, CBC Records, and the whole range of small and independent labels, there are far fewer recordings of Canadian new music than there are for European and American composers. The issue is not generational, artistic, or aesthetic, but economic and exemplary of both support and investment in the arts, as well as the reality of making recordings of contemporary orchestral, choral, and chamber music in Canada compared with abroad. In each of the above instrumental categories (though to a lesser extent with chamber music and in a relatively minor way with electroacoustic music), the cost of recording, union fees, manufacturing, distribution, and promotion limit the opportunity for a work to be heard beyond its premiere.

The situation is increasingly distressing when the current tone of Canadian public broadcasting is factored in. The CBC has been a significant force in the careers of many composers, myself included. However, at the beginning of the twenty-first century, their representation of diversity of contemporary Canadian music creation is diminishing, along with their budget and relevance. Canadian composers under thirty years of age used to look forward to the CBC Young Composers Competition, *Two New Hours* (the only CBC program devoted exclusively to contemporary Canadian Music), and a greater proportion of commissioning funds. In addition to the obvious ignorance of their mandate, as outlined in the Broadcast Act of 1991, the decline of the CBC affects composers negatively in a complex trickle-down.[1] As the primary organization that recorded new Canadian music (for broadcast), we now have fewer professional recordings of our work performed by dedicated practitioners. Composers have fewer recordings of our work even for promotional purposes, and fewer opportunities to propagate our work amongst a wide-ranging international field of artists. At this point, we run the risk of losing touch with at least one generation of Canadian composers, because the machinery working *for* the music does not match its quality and artistry. As John Weinzweig regularly reminded us, we *have* a Canadian musical heritage—the problem is that it's not known.

※

In my experience, readers are also interested in knowing the practicalities of life as a composer—what we know as the norm of a life in music is in some areas quite different from that of other artistic avenues and occupations. Composers working freelance gain their (usually very modest) musical incomes through four or five economic paths: commissions, performance royalties, broadcast royalties, discussing their music at publicly- and/or academically-funded talks, and through sales of their music in recorded or written formats. The most significant source of income for a composer is the commission, the process through which performers and ensembles request and seek funding to pay the composer to write a new work. Most often, fifty per cent of the fee is paid in advance, and the remainder upon delivery of the work. Content restrictions and stylistic guidelines are rarely part of the contract, while the instrumentation and approximate duration of the work is. From time to time the commissioning organization might request a conceptual link to other works or an overriding programming idea, but usually they are already very aware of the artist's work and thus know the general aesthetic of the music they will receive. Similarly, the composer is usually well aware of what the organization does, may know the performers personally, and can consult with the musicians as needed while composing. In the case of works for smaller groups and soloists, composer and performer sometimes work very closely. If a premiere date is set in the organization's concert schedule, a completion date is also part of the commission agreement.

Funding sources include the Canada Council for the Arts, provincial arts councils, city arts councils, foundations, and a few private sources. As diverse as that may appear, the reality is much different. At the beginning of the twenty-first century, the success rate for commission applications at the Canada Council is approximately one in seven (whereas it used to be approximately one in four). For every project that is supported, six are declined due to lack of funds. Provincial arts councils have a miniscule budget compared to the Canada Council, and the existence of city arts councils that commission music is not consistent throughout the country. The Canadian League of Composers establishes minimum commissioning fees, on a per-minute basis, depending upon the instrumentation of the work. However, not every work is commissioned. The Canada Council has two commission juries per year, and other arts councils function independently. In British Columbia, the small amount of funds devoted to commissioning music through the provincial government will, as a rule, cover only fifty per cent of the fee, with the assumption that matching funds will be gathered elsewhere. It usually means that composers work at fifty per cent of the set minimum fee established by the Canadian League of Composers.

Music takes a great deal of time and concentration to compose. Depending upon the piece and instrumentation, often it takes months. There is no rule as to the speed a work can be produced, and often, the challenges of the musical material and ideas—the project—dictate the speed at which it can be written. This amount varies from composer to composer and, paraphrasing Morton Feldman, I have often said that it takes eighteen hours to get four hours of work done. The fastest I have produced a work is two weeks, and the longest amount of time I have spent is a year. I used to try to compose a minute a week, meanwhile Michael Finnissy once told me he couldn't write more than two minutes in a day! It could conceivably take a day to compose major sections of a work, while it could take weeks to settle on a single detail. Some composers work on several pieces at once, while others work on one at a time. Equally diverse is what part of the work is written first, and the order the sections are composed in. Some composers engage in significant pre-compositional research, while others start writing and sort out challenges as they occur.

Composers receive a fee for the performance of their work, and another fee for the broadcast. Depending upon the venue, royalties for performance are rarely more than a few dollars, and for broadcast, they can range between a few cents and thousands of dollars, depending where the music is broadcast. On average, however, royalty payments are meagre, unpredictable amounts, and none of the interviewed Canadian composers makes their living exclusively from the combination of commissions, live performance of their works, and broadcast royalties. Secondary occupations or sideline musical activities are the norm for Canadian composers. A number of composers are also involved in improvisation and performance (Oswald, Couroux, Arnold, Finnissy, Kasemets, Wolff). Several are also conductors (Boulez, Kulesha, Finnissy, Kagel, Butterfield). Many others are involved in teaching at post-secondary institutions, either as full-time faculty, or as sessional instructors. The list of full-time instructors includes Normandeau and Piché (Université de Montréal), Daniel (University of Western Ontario), Finnissy (Sussex University), Hamel (University of British Columbia), Bashaw, (University of Alberta), Hatch (Wilfrid Laurier University), Harley (University of Guelph), Kulesha (University of Toronto), Rea (McGill University), and Butterfield (University of Victoria). Retired faculty members include Weinzweig and Beckwith (University of Toronto), Kasemets (Ontario College of Art & Design), Christian Wolff (Harvard University, where he taught Classics), Crumb (University of Pennsylvania), and Francis Dhomont (Université de Montréal). The list of those who have taught previously on a full-time or part-time basis, and those who are teaching sessionally (including those who have done teaching in the past) consists of Linda C. Smith, Alexina Louie, Juliet Palmer, Martin Arnold, Barbara Croall, Hildegard Westerkamp, and R. Murray Schafer. It should be highlighted that the life of a composer varies from country to country. While Canada is a rich nation, its new music composers aren't. The choice of a life in art is fraught with difficulty and instability, while also being one of profound beauty and growth.

Despite the chronological presentation of the interviews, it is informative to parse the material in such a way that this collection reveals trends in the artistic activity taking place between 2001 and 2004. New Music Concerts, under the artistic direction of Robert Aitken and with the hard work of General Manager David Olds, provided the impetus for many of the interviews. Robert Normandeau, Chris Paul Harman, Pierre Boulez, George Crumb, Helmut Lachenmann, Mauricio Kagel, Keith Hamel, and Howard Bashaw had works presented by New Music Concerts between

2001 and 2004. Presenting the most European and international collection of composers, New Music Concerts also maintains regular working relationships with some of the most significant senior composers of the late twentieth and early twenty-first centuries.

One of the interviews came about through a link with Soundstreams Canada—that with Omar Daniel, on the topic of his piece *The Flaying of Marsyas*. Only one interview here was connected with Arraymusic (Christian Wolff). Many other composers that I've interviewed have also enjoyed strong ties to Arraymusic, including Linda Smith, Martin Arnold, Christopher Butterfield, Udo Kasemets, James Rolfe, Juliet Palmer, and James Harley. Although none of the interviews is specifically linked with a Continuum Contemporary Music concert, Jennifer Waring was a strong supporter of the project, and many of the composers also have links with Continuum. Alex Pauk's Esprit Orchestra was liaison for two interviews, one with John Rea, and the other with Yannick Plamondon and Marc Couroux. The Gary Kulesha interview, published over two issues of *Wholenote Magazine*, also came about through an orchestral connection, in this case the Toronto Symphony. Three interviews were related to operatic works: the Canadian Opera Company's unstaged performance of Alexina Louie's work *The Scarlet Princess*; Queen of Puddings Music Theatre's commissioning of a new opera from James Rolfe; and the University of Toronto Opera Program's performance of John Beckwith's *Taptoo!* Sometime after our interview, Linda Smith had her opera *Facing South* performed, continuing the trend of opera commissioning and production by smaller, chamber music-sized companies. The largest of the operas, Alexina Louie's *The Scarlet Princess,* was not staged, and was performed once.

Five of the composers (Normandeau, Oswald, Dhomont, Piché, and Westerkamp), are primarily or solely electroacoustic composers, while another four have significant or ongoing links with electroacoustic/computer music and sound art (Boulez, Daniel, Hamel, and Harley). In total, ten involve electronic media in their work to varying degrees and with divergent artistic goals. Some compose solely for tape (performance without live instrumentalists) while others work with mixed media (instruments and electronics—either live electronics or fixed sound files). Of those involved with new media, some also make installation works, as opposed to works for the concert hall (Oswald, Palmer, Couroux, and Butterfield). The instrumentation of the works discussed reveals that the majority of contemporary art music composed in Canada at this time is for chamber music configurations, or, in the case of electroacoustic music, without performers, in the traditional sense (diffusion, or sound projection of electroacoustic pieces is performance). Only three interviews were prompted directly by orchestral music performances. Many of the other composers, however, have written a significant amount of music for orchestra. While the Esprit Orchestra maintained its activity (at this time with a statistically large amount of Dutch music), at the Toronto Symphony there was a relative drought. The other composers interviewed who have written many orchestral pieces include R. Murray Schafer, Chris Paul Harman, John Weinzweig, Pierre Boulez, Mauricio Kagel, and John Rea. Almost all others have written at least one orchestral work. In the cases of Boulez, Kagel, and Lachenmann, their mature orchestral music is, unfortunately, never performed in Toronto.

❊

The interview process was straightforward, and usually followed the same method. Questions were prepared in advance, but not viewed by the composer. Conversation usually strayed from the ordered line of questioning on paper, following the line of thought presented by the composer. While my preference was to record our conversations via telephone, some composers, particularly senior composers, preferred to speak in person. I fondly recall arriving at Udo Kasemets's apartment in Toronto, setting up my equipment, and being told, "No, we have to share a pot of tea before we can do the interview." John Beckwith and John Weinzweig also preferred to meet, in the case of Beckwith in his house in the Annex area of Toronto, and Weinzweig in the boardroom at the Canadian Music Centre's national office on St. Joseph Street. Christopher Butterfield and Keith Hamel also stated that it was necessary to have our discussion in person, since neither considered themselves a "phone person." In June 2004, I drove from Edmonton to Victoria to meet Butterfield at his house, only to find myself doing some pre-interview gardening. Following the lengthy drive I had just completed, I was happy to oblige and force large boulders into new locations before chatting at length. Having spoken with Keith Hamel by phone many times over the years, it was clear that a trip to Vancouver was required. In late September 2004, I flew to my hometown and had a pleasant day talking about his work at his office and house in Point Grey. With James Rolfe, I went over to his new home near High Park in Toronto, as I had done on numerous other occasions, and we talked throughout the afternoon while his baby daughter played and conducted her own cackling brand of interview simultaneously. While many of the composers interviewed found it entirely acceptable to follow my own preference to work over the phone (even Linda C. Smith, who lived about a thirty-second walk from my apartment at the time), in many cases it was a practical matter, due to distance. Michael Finnissy, Pierre Boulez, Helmut Lachenmann, and Mauricio Kagel all live in the UK or Europe. With Boulez, who maintains a busy conducting schedule, the process of finding a suitable time was complicated, and I nearly went to Paris to meet him there. My feeling is that the offer to do so clarified the commitment to the interview, and he ultimately became available for more time than I had expected. Chris Harman and I tended to meet for coffee about once a month in those years, but confining our talk to the telephone enabled us to focus on the task at hand and bypass the usual hijinks. Schafer, Normandeau, Daniel, Croall, Plamondon, Couroux, Crumb, Hatch, and Dhomont all lived far enough away to warrant interviews by phone.

When I began the interviews, they were recorded onto the mini tape recorder of my phone/fax machine, which only held twenty-minute tapes. After those twenty minutes, I would have to transcribe the rest while the composer spoke. By the time of the fifth interview, I was recording the interviews onto mini-disk. Our recorded conversations usually lasted ninety minutes, and in some cases up to two hours (Weinzweig, Boulez, and Kulesha). I then transcribed the interviews word-for-word and edited them numerous times before presenting them to the composers. Transcription and editing usually took one day, depending upon the diction, clarity, and verbosity of the composer. Since the timeframe for completion of the interviews was often very tight, I offered the composers a twenty-four hour window to read their interview and make comments. It was my goal to represent the ideas of each person as clearly as possible. My stating this in advance of the interview was always pleasantly received and likely established a comfort level for the process. Not one of the composers requested a major change be made or expressed concern with the content. In most cases, the composers provided a backup to my own editing, and made very few changes to the text. Otherwise, the only changes that were made were infrequent stylistic revisions.

The offer to review the texts and make minor edits in advance of publication did nothing to limit my line of questioning, however. None of the interviewed composers refused a question, and even with the infrequently pointed questions, those revealing my personal biases, or those moments in the interviews that became a little more heated, and no one requested removal of material. Since the goal of the project has been to learn more and present the ideas of current composers, I felt an obligation to be critical, analytical, and creative in my line of questioning. Almost all of the composers would have known this about me in advance of my interview request, so there were no surprises. That same critical nature, I suppose, was the reason that one composer refused to be interviewed altogether. In addition, only one composer (after the window of editing possibility had expired, and after the publication date), was frustrated with the material published in *Wholenote*. What I had done, I later realized, was to remove the self-congratulatory statements and focus instead on the content and ideas and how they related to the work in question. While at first there was concern about the removal of career-oriented statements, the composer capitulated shortly after, when so many friends and colleagues were supportive of the statements made and how they offered a different view of this serious artist.

☀

Specific to this text, I have met, known, worked with, studied with, or have been close friends with each contributing composer prior to commencing the interview project. The only exceptions are George Crumb and Christian Wolff, whose work I was familiar with, but whom I had not met in person or previously spoken. Rather than make false claims of objectivity, I have elected to disclose my relationships with those present in this collection, and allow those relationships to function as a subtext to the reader. I have met R. Murray Schafer a number of times, and have studied his work over many years. The same can be said for Robert Normandeau. Chris Paul Harman and Linda Catlin Smith are both friends of mine, and I've known each of them for nearly a decade. When I first met him, Chris and I, along with composer Melissa Hui, tended to be grouped together in concerts, panel discussions, interviews, et cetera. I met Linda in 1996 at the first Vancouver International New Music Festival, and despite the obvious differences in our music, I found myself agreeing with everything she said during our first panel discussion together.

Alexina Louie and Omar Daniel are active figures in Canadian new music and I have met them both on numerous occasions, primarily professionally; Alexina, by her connection to the Esprit Orchestra, and Omar on the executive of the Canadian League of Composers. I met Michael Finnissy through pianist James Clapperton while I was living in Amsterdam. I had heard his music often, and was fascinated by its physicality and complexity. Eventually, I wrote to him and asked for lessons. He refused to offer "composition lessons," instead offering "consultations," and for the remainder of my time in Amsterdam, I would travel to Hove, England (near Brighton), once a month and meet with him for half a day. I had met John Weinzweig and John Beckwith on occasion, usually through the Canadian League of Composers. Along with R. Murray Schafer, they are steadfast and valuable figures in the history of Canadian music, setting the groundwork for the contemporary musical culture the rest of us inhabit. I think about their varied and lengthy careers and recognize the strength of their commitment and contributions. Despite their perseverance and concentration on Canadian music, many of the composers of my generation consider theirs the time of relative prosperity and opportunity—a golden time in the formation of Canada's musical culture. Despite significant cutbacks and devastating changes at the Canadian Broadcasting Corporation, I suspect that each would disagree with the observation that they were some of the lucky ones.

I first met Udo Kasemets in 2001, when I was co-ordinating the Canadian Music Centre Ontario Region's "New Music for Young Musicians" project. Executive Director Elisabeth Bihl had entrusted me with commissioning composers to write pieces for young performers to play, and Udo wrote a spatialized, indeterminate piece that was beautifully performed by students from Toronto's Royal Conservatory of Music. For the students, Udo's piece was an ear-opening experience, and two of the three performers have continued to play contemporary music. Pierre Boulez is arguably one of the most significant contributors to post-war contemporary music. I met him in Amsterdam in 1990 when I snuck into the press conference surrounding the Ensemble InterContemporain's tour of his piece *Répons*. I spoke with him afterwards, and then a month later visited IRCAM (Institut de Recherche et Coordination Acoustique/ Musique, the Institute for the Research and Coordination of Acoustics and Music that he created and directed at the Centre Pompidou in Paris). Several years later, I went to IRCAM for one year, and although Boulez was then more distant from the facility, I had the opportunity to talk with him on occasion.

My professional connection with Barbara Croall began in 1998, when we both signed on as Composers in Residence with the Toronto Symphony Orchestra. The third party in this triumvirate was Gary Kulesha, the TSO's ongoing Composer Advisor. Jukka-Pekka Saraste was the Music Director at the time, although he was in the early stages of withdrawing from the orchestra. Without doubt, our contrasting natures made Kulesha, Croall, and me an interesting group. We didn't, however, have much contact. After the end of my affiliation with the orchestra in 2000, I didn't feel as though I knew Barbara very well. Due to the TSO's strike and the minimal amount of activity during my time there, there was little contact between us. I was pleased to have the opportunity to discuss her music and ERGO Projects in the interview forum, and have since also written a piece for the group. During my time with the orchestra, there was more contact with Composer Advisor Gary Kulesha, and I found him to be a shrewd member of an opaque administration. This, combined with my impatience and unwillingness to bend to the slow pace of orchestral business, made for a difficult time. Post-concert discussions with Kulesha were always pleasant and highly anecdotal, while the professional component was more tenuous. His interview solicited the largest number of private comments; a fact that I believe would neither concern nor displease him.

Yannick Plamondon and Marc Couroux are both friends and part of a then-tight group of Montrealers that included Michael Oesterle, Scott Godin, and Justin Mariner, among others. Yannick was less closely part of this group, but we met frequently when I was in Montreal, often having listening parties at the Oesterle or Couroux apartments. Beer flowing, we would guess pieces based on brief fragments of material, complain about everything imaginable (especially other composers), and without fail, end up with Oesterle and me in an escalating dispute about something artistic. They were all passionate communicators and well-informed artists, so I would look forward to my visits to Montreal, while not always enjoying the intensity to which it would progress. Thankfully, we have mellowed somewhat since then. Peter Hatch and I have many colleagues in common, and he has always been supportive of my work as a composer, including using my pieces in his teaching at Wilfrid Laurier University, and including the performance of my piece *Wonder* at his Open Ears festival. The John Oswald interview resulted from a previously failed attempt to review his CD. I've for a long time been interested in the subversive nature of his work, and was looking forward to exploring that more fully in a review, but complimentary review copies were not available. The cost of the CD exceeded the remuneration for a review, and at the time, I was unable to absorb the loss. Somewhat later, I decided that an interview was in order, so I approached him to do so. What started as a prickly communication receded and Oswald offered me an excellent interview.

As a composer, I am equally involved in acoustic and electroacoustic music, and am therefore well versed in the creative work of both Francis Dhomont and Jean Piché. One of the master's of the field, Dhomont was generous and outgoing, and Piché spoke with precision and clarity. At the time of the Martin Arnold interview, I was just getting to know him better, though I had always been sympathetic and supportive of his important role in the Toronto scene. He too was originally from the West, and had studied with Louis Andriessen, but our contact in Toronto had been limited. Juliet Palmer became known to me when she moved to Toronto, and we have been acquainted socially and professionally since then. My interviews with Helmut Lachenmann and Mauricio Kagel were highlights of the compilation process. I remember having met Kagel when I was a student at the Royal Conservatory of Music in The Hague, The Netherlands. He was a distinguished guest visitor during a festival devoted to his work, and I had a lesson with him. Students filed in one after the other (half an hour each), and Kagel sat nervously twitching a cigar in one hand, and a large felt pen in the other, his foot anxiously tapping a different tempo simultaneously. For a long time, the differently refined madness of Kagel and Lachenmann's music has been highly attractive to me, and both offered significant insight into their work.

John Rea was the first living composer I met. In 1984, as a nine-teen-year-old student at Douglas College in New Westminster, British Columbia, I was employed as the Student Assistant to the Music Department. I had an infant son, and school and work made for an excessively busy schedule. I fondly recall that Kathryn Cernauskas had commissioned John Rea to compose a piece for flute and string quartet, and it was my responsibility to tend to the concert and setup of the Purcell String Quartet. I was becoming increasingly engaged in contem-porary music and my conversation with John Rea helped make the possibility of being a composer seem more rich and valid. James Harley and I have been in contact off and on since approximately 1995, and he was an infrequent guest with the Montreal listening gang that eventually became Ensemble Kore. Having grown up in Vancouver, I met Hildegard Westerkamp quite early on in my musical studies. I have always appre-ciated her ideas, and enjoyed each opportunity I had to speak with her. I am a reluctant airline traveller and she was of assistance to me in what remains the most frightening flight I've ever experienced. Following the 1994 CBC Young Composers Competition, at which I was a prizewinner, the twenty-minute flight from Moncton to Saint John, New Brunswick (following a six-hour delay), was achieved in very rough weather. The CBC *Two New Hours* crew experienced it as a fun-filled bucking bronco ride, but I was green and ill and clung to my seat with all my strength.

The two composers I have the most history with among this group are Howard Bashaw and Keith Hamel. Bashaw was a senior student at UBC at the time I was emerging, and was a strong influence on many of us, including Melissa Hui, Bob Pritchard, Michael Oesterle, Douglas G. Smith, Jacqueline Leggatt, theorist Brenda Ravenscroft, musicologist Anna Ferenc, and others. Keith Hamel moved from Queen's University in Kingston, Ontario, to Vancouver in 1987, where he took over the task of developing UBC's electronic music studios. I studied with him for many years, and was greatly influenced by his thought as our relationship changed from student and teacher to friend and colleague. To this day, I still consult with him on matters of technology, and continue to learn from his research and programming. As individual creative personalities define, flow, and shift, these ties remain constant and the engagement in creative exploration continues.

The geographical movement of composers, and the interconnectedness of our lives and careers, describe also the flow of ideas and music
internationally, and more prominently across the Canadian musical
landscape. Almost every composer on this list has a significant educational or professional tie with at least one other interviewed composer.
Bashaw and Hatch were students together at UBC, while Martin Arnold,
Linda C. Smith, and Christopher Butterfield all studied with Rudolph
Komorous at the University of Victoria. Their musical connection
continued through Toronto's Arraymusic ensemble and organiza-
tion, a group that has performed music by Kasemets, Rolfe, Hatch,
Oswald, Arnold, Palmer, Hamel, Harley, and Wolff, if not more. One of
Martin Arnold's performing groups, The Burdocks (now defunct), was
named after the piece of the same name by Christian Wolff. Hildegard
Westerkamp worked at Simon Fraser University in Burnaby, British
Columbia, and was part of the World Soundscape Project started by
R. Murray Schafer. There are many other contributors to the development of the new music scene in British Columbia that I would like to
interview at some point, but Schafer, Westerkamp, Hamel, Bashaw, and
Butterfield make a strong start. Schafer studied briefly at the University
of Toronto with John Weinzweig, who taught many of the composers that
attended U of T and/or the Royal Conservatory of Music. John Beckwith
took lessons from Weinzweig, and he in turn taught Omar Daniel and
James Rolfe, to name two. John Rea also studied with Weinzweig, and
he has gone on to teach many successful composers graduating from
McGill University, including James Harley. In his multi-faceted education, Harley also attended seminars with Pierre Boulez. Rea also attended
Princeton University, though much earlier than James Rolfe and Juliet
Palmer. Barbara Croall spent time studying with Peter Maxwell Davies
in the Orkney Islands, as did Keith Hamel when Davies was a visiting
composer at Harvard many years earlier. Martin Arnold, James Rolfe,
and Juliet Palmer studied with Louis Andriessen. Hamel, Palmer, Rolfe,
and I also attended numerous master classes with Brian Ferneyhough.
Together with Michael Finnissy, Ferneyhough was a leading figure in
the New Complexity movement that was prevalent from the 1980s to
mid-1990s. Marc Couroux, in his initial incarnation as performer of

hyper-complex music, has performed the music of Bashaw, Finnissy, Harley, and others, as well as writing about Harley and Bashaw. With his Ensemble Kore (sharing the artistic direction with Michael Oesterle) Couroux has presented portrait concerts featuring the music of Hatch, Smith, Arnold, and many others.

Without trying to be comprehensive, the interconnectedness of the composers here is amply demonstrated, despite the diversity of musical output from those in question. The large pool and range of national and international influences has been differently ordered and applied in overlapping, personal ways amongst the broad sampling of composers interviewed. I hope that by exploring this text, readers will also be inspired to explore the music further, in its many forms. Although the series herein is finished, it is by no means complete. There are additional composers, in Canada and internationally, whose ideas require detailed exploration through performance, listening, and discussion.

NOTE

1. Steenhuisen was instrumental in the initial round of protests against CBC Radio changes beginning in 2005. A transcript of his meeting with them can be found at: <stopcbcpop.ca/CBC_New%20Music_Dec05.htm>. Steenhuisen continues to assist in materials provided at: <www.earsay.com/standonguardforcbc/>.

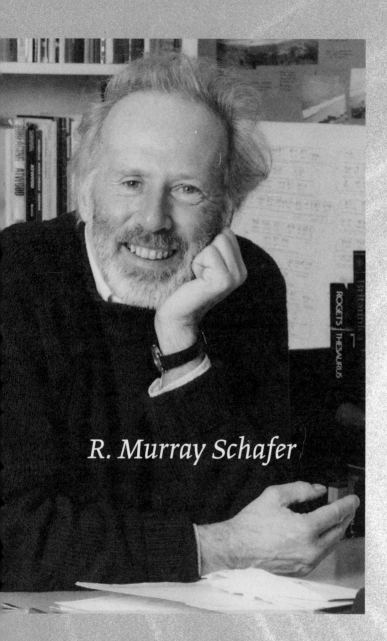

R. Murray Schafer

RENEGADE *Canadian composer R. Murray Schafer was born in Sarnia, Ontario, in 1933 and currently lives in a farmhouse near Indian River. He spent a decade in Vancouver, where he initiated the World Soundscape Project at Simon Fraser University. For more than thirty years, Schafer has been writing his twelve-part* Patria *cycle.* Patria *(meaning "homeland") traverses space, time, and knowledge to tell a circuitous story that, despite its breadth, remains uniquely Canadian. To me, Schafer's work propagates awareness of the vast intellectual and natural richness of the world, so it was a pleasure to talk with him, composer to composer. Our primary subject was his most recent* Patria *piece,* The Palace of the Cinnabar Phoenix (Patria 8), *which was premiered September 13 through 16, 2001, at Wolverton Hills on the Oak Ridges Moraine. A fantasy based in reality, the story is set in China during the Tang Dynasty (618–907 CE). Emperor Wei Lu bemoans the disappearance of the Cinnabar Phoenix and, with it, the loss of peace and harmony. The Emperor and his court have made their annual pilgrimage to the Lake of Dragons with the hope that the Sunken Palace and the Cinnabar Phoenix will appear once again and restore harmony to the realm.*

PS: In promotional materials for the piece, you're quoted as saying "This is my *Falstaff*." What do you mean?

RMS: With reference to Verdi's only enduring comic opera, *The Palace of the Cinnabar Phoenix* is lighter and more tuneful than some of the other *Patria* pieces, possibly the lightest.

PS: How would you describe the piece? Is it opera? Music theatre?

RMS: I call the *Patria* series "music dramas," because they have a lot of dramatic elements that most opera doesn't have—spoken material, and theatrical effects that are not really part of the domain of opera, although there is more continuous singing in *Cinnabar* than in some of the other *Patria* pieces. Perhaps this one is closer to opera, but I don't like using that term. I find it very confining. If we lived in Europe and got commissions for opera from the time we were thirty-five years old, we probably would have written operas, but thank God nobody ever commissioned me to write one, so I did what I wanted to do.

PS: Do you feel that you're developing a new genre?

RMS: Certainly some of the pieces are outside of the traditional genres. I don't think this one is—I think it's a more conventional piece— but *Princess of the Stars* is outside of the traditional genres, as are *The Greatest Show*, *Ra*, and *The Wolf Project*—they're way, way outside.

PS: Was it a pre-compositional decision that you would make this piece lighter?

RMS: Yes, in the sense that it fits into the whole cycle. The nadir of whole cycle is *Ra (Patria 6)*, and *Hysterium (Patria 7)*, which are the heaviest and the most difficult. After those, I wanted to have three lighter pieces, almost as if through some kind of levitation, you'd entered a world of fairy tales, and the *Cinnabar* is one of those, along with *The Enchanted Forest*, and *The Spirit Garden* closer to being family pieces.

PS: So you're shaping the cycle as a whole.

RMS: Yes. Not that I intend that the cycle ever be performed in sequence. Practically, it's not possible. For example, *Princess of the Stars* occurs at five o'clock in the morning, and *Ra* runs eleven hours, all night long. *The Wolf Project* runs for eight days. Each one of the works is totally self-contained, but there is a shaping in my own mind. The thing that connects them is that there are certain themes, contexts, and characters that keep recurring.

The main theme is of a man and a woman who are searching for one another, and they have been broken apart at the very beginning. The Princess of the Stars descended to earth and was wounded by Wolf. She escapes, and moves through various cultures and various societies under the earthly name of Ariadne, constantly pursued by Wolf, who wants to apologize to her. It's only when he does this finally, and is able to renounce his savagery that the conclusion comes about and the Princess is able to return to the stars. That basic theme unites the two. So Wolf and Ariadne reappear in the various pieces in many different guises, travelling to many parts of the world—Ancient Egypt, Crete, Medieval Europe, modern metropolis, and in this case China, in order to explore some of the philosophical ideas in that part of the world.

As well, there are material relations between the pieces. Though musically they are quite different, there's a *Patria* row in all of them. Not all the music is based on it, but a lot of it is. It's an all-interval tone row, on which the whole of *Princess of the Stars* is written.

PS: In addition to exploring different parts of the world in the *Patria* pieces, and a different time period/philosophical setting for each place, each work is multi-sensory—you describe it as "a feast for the senses."

RMS: All the *Patria* works are, in one way or another. Some use perfume—*Ra* uses perfume and incense all the way through it, every scene uses a different incense, and each god has a different perfume. Some of the other works, including this one, have food involved. There is a "Banquet of Celestial Harmony" in *Cinnabar* that the court will indulge in, as well as the audience. I thought that to leave audience out and have them watch while the puppets eat their food (*laughs*), would be unfortunate, so we decided we would have something for the audience. It's not going to be a feast, but we will have something for the audience. During this section of the piece, the audience will eat their morsels synchronized with music. It's part of a much, much larger idea that I've always had, that I tried to use in *The Spirit Garden*, in which the many different courses would all correspond to pieces of music that would be specially composed. The program would explain why the music and food were intended to go together. It's an interesting idea, and flies in the face of universal muzak that accompanies everything.

PS: It also breaks down the audience/performer barrier.

RMS: That's true. In all the *Patria* pieces, in one way or another, the audience is involved. In *The Enchanted Forest*, they accompany the children through the forest. The children are the protagonists, and the audience is protecting them from the malicious spirits. In *Cinnabar*, there isn't a great deal of audience participation, other than the banquet, and except for the fact that every time he Emperor speaks, the audience has to stand up and bow. I don't know if they actually will, and if they don't maybe the emperor won't speak; but it's just a few little things, to make them feel that somehow they're not just sitting slothfully in their fauteuil digesting their dinner.

PS: Given the type of audience involvement, you encourage the audience to be very aware of what's going on in the piece—and it becomes somewhat ceremonial.

RMS: Yes. In this case, it's fairly light, but it's definitely present. In other *Patria* works, the involvement is very ceremonial and ritualistic, but in this work, it's modestly present.

PS: You mentioned that this is more of a family work.

RMS: I think so. First of all, it involves puppets. When I initially thought of the work, I felt that with this incredibly magnificent Tang dynasty of China, you'd need to have chariots and pagoda boats, millions of warriors, and an orchestra of five thousand. There is no way we could get those sorts of resources, so I reversed the thing, and miniaturized the characters by turning them into puppets, making them distant and remote. They're dignified, and have a light-hearted, ceremonial quality. They are present near the water, and there's action in the water, on the water. There are dragons, and people who do tai chi on the water. It's festive, definitely festive.

PS: Describe the location of the performances. Why outdoors?

RMS: I like working outdoors, and wanted to set it near a small pond. With the miniaturization of the characters, I wanted a pond about a hundred metres long. I looked around Toronto for the right location, without finding anything quiet enough, or remote enough. Eventually I found this location, which is a private property, about two hundred acres.

PS: Is the piece site-specific?

RMS: Yes. I thought it might be able to be re-created indoors, if the lake components were filmed, but that wouldn't be as interesting. That might be something for after I'm gone.

PS: You live and work in a rural setting, placing many of your perform-ances directly on the land, in the trees, on or by a lake, yet a large portion of the people who come to hear your work live in an urban environment. Is there a particular idea you would like the audience to take away with them?

RMS: I want it to be an experience. I think it's terribly necessary not to lose touch with the land, and that consciousness. We don't have the respect for nature and the environment that is necessary if humanity is going to survive at all. Anything that gets people out into nature and incorporates natural elements into the work is important. With *The Enchanted Forest*, after the performance, people talked about the incredible moment when the clouds parted and the wolf howled—this could never be choreographed, but we created the opportunity for it to be appreciated and for people to become more aware of these things. If you know your environment, it's likely that things will happen. The soothsayer says that the wind in the trees and the way that the leaves are being blown is an indication of how the plot is going to develop. Also, with *Princess of the Stars*, she is imprisoned in the bottom of the lake—if the princess is in the lake, you're not going to pollute it. That may be what Native people everywhere in the world had in mind— why they were such good ecologists—because the land was full of spirits, and if you damage it, you may disturb the tree gods, and the gods of the land and water. These elements get into the work; being aware.

PS: With the current rate of land development and environmental erosion in Ontario, there is a very real risk that the trees of your performance landscape could be replaced by condos, the water will be a hazard, and the air unbreathably full of particulates. How do you think this process of decay can or should be reversed?

RMS: More needs to be done. Greenpeace, the Suzuki Foundation, Earthroots, and others do good work. Artists can participate, but many don't. They certainly aren't required to, but those that do perhaps don't understand that you have to go *with* nature. There's no point taking glossy pictures of trees and putting them on the internet, you have to work with nature itself. Whether or not my outdoor works endure, as Whitby becomes the core of an expanding Toronto, I don't know. Regardless, many of the *Patria* works are *engagé*, which used to mean "in a political sense," socialist. There's a message implicit in all of my outdoor pieces. There's a world out there that we're neglecting at our own peril. And it's a very beautiful world.

Robert Normandeau

ELECTROACOUSTICIAN *Robert Normandeau was born in Quebec City in 1955 and now lives in Montreal. He has spent significant periods at the Banff Centre for the Arts and in Belfast, Bourges, Paris, and Karlsruhe, Germany. Robert Normandeau has long been active on the international electroacoustic music scene, composing richly layered pieces based primarily on acoustic sounds. By stretching, contorting, mutating, bending, and morphing sounds we hear every day, he constructs imagined worlds in which we sense a million shades and nuances, re-hear, and remember ourselves in a deeply self-actualizing listening process. Beyond the highly refined techniques for developing the material (projected through a cornucopia of loudspeakers), what I find interesting about this music is the issue of the perspective of the listener—where are we in relation to this sonic landscape? If we listen passively, from a stationary, objective point, we remain engaged in* the sensuality of the sounds, yet when we allow ourselves to move with it, it is as though we have wings, and are projecting through a multidimensional field, in a manner specific to this genre of electroacoustic music. October 26, 2001, provided the rare opportunity to experience this first-hand in Toronto and, in preparation, I spoke directly with Normandeau, to learn more about his work and ideas.

PS: We walk into the performance space, sit in our chairs, cough, relax, look up and see...

RN: Nothing! *(Laughs)* Absolutely nothing! This is a main idea of acousmatic music, and *Rien à Voir* (Nothing to look at) is the name of the concerts we present in Montreal. It is a very strong statement from us to promote that kind of title. Often, when promoters realize there are not many people at their concerts, they try to turn them into more spectacular events. We decided to go in the opposite direction, to present a very pure musical point of view. There's no spectacle, but there is something VERY spectacular for the ears.

PS: You used the term *acousmatic* to describe your work. What is acousmatic art?

RN: "Acousmatic" defines an aesthetic genre in the electroacoustic music field, a genre described as music that uses the sound material as the source of musical inspiration. The acousmatic music composer is an experimental music composer, working very closely with sound material, listening to it, trying to learn from it what can be developed into the musical structure. This is very different from the classical instrumental writing process, where the music often has a form before the material comes into it. Every single piece of acousmatic music is different, since you're working with different sound materials and each of these materials tells you something new. The acousmatic music composer tries to explore the intrinsic nature of sounds.

PS: What is *cinema for the ear*?

RN: It's something I tried to develop in my Doctoral thesis eight or nine years ago, and doesn't apply to all acousmatic music. We share some essential elements with cinema, one of which is that we use a recorded medium. In some books about cinema, people wrote that one of the basic elements is editing, putting together pieces of film that in reality would never meet. In electroacoustic music, this is also a basic compositional technique, which allows you to put together very different elements that create their own environment. And with cinema we share sounds from reality—we go on the street with a tape recorder and later work with the material that people recognize from their own sonic landscape, and remind them of their own experience. Through these sounds, they can reach into their own memories.

PS: And at the same time, it's not a music that is about reality.

RN: Exactly. This is not a documentary, not at all.

PS: It seems that illusion and stepping beyond the fundamental qualities of sound materials are essential to the music.

RN: Absolutely. This is the main difference between the acousmatic music composition process and the sound ecology/soundscape point of view.

PS: Can we listen to your music in the same way that we listen to nineteenth century music? How do you want it to be heard?

RN: The listener has to be open-minded. This music is probably easier to listen to than contemporary instrumental music, and for a very simple reason. If you think about instrumental music, it has been evolving over a very long time, in a very complex way, and with a sophisticated and complicated language, which is at some point very difficult to understand. In acousmatic music, there is something that every single listener can relate to, because they can find something that is common to their own sonic experience on a day-to-day basis. People can establish a close relationship with the sounds because they recognize something about themselves. Because of these points of reference, a listener can enter into the work more easily.

PS: But this is by no means simple music...

RN: Since I work on my pieces over a very long time, if they are too simple, I myself would be bored, and I am my first listener. Because of that, I build many layers, so if people listen to it more than one time they will find more than just the basic level. Embedded in this is also my feeling that as contemporary composers we have to seduce the audience.

PS: Is this program music? Is there a narrative?

RN: At some point, for me as a composer, it is always related to program music. The listener doesn't have to know about a particular story or narrative, but it's a way of working, like the choice of sound materials.

The listener will notice that the piece is built around a limited collection of sound materials, but they will ultimately build their own story, it doesn't have to be mine. I want that openness, as it is also the way that I behave as a listener—I like it very much, and it brings me into a new, previously unheard musical world.

PS: Given the relative absence of pitch as a basic organizing principal, how do you maintain unity and cohesion in your pieces?

RN: That's a good question for an electroacoustician, because there is no censorship, you can use whatever sound you want, and there isn't a common language, or recipes for how to work. The acousmatic composer has to deal with the fact that at some point he must establish boundaries, limits on a specific work. Type of sounds, et cetera. In my case, I can't start working on a new piece without a title, because the title includes so much information about the basic material. Then when I'm in my studio working, I can stay close to my goal, and can make new sonic material and musical choices according to the chosen project.

PS: Helmut Lachenmann wrote that when he (infrequently) projects sound through a loudspeaker, it is always symbolic of the death of the sound. For you it's seems quite the opposite. How do you project sound and deal with the space of the concert hall?

RN: Over the centuries, composers dealt with different aspects of music: form, pitch, etc, and electroacoustic music deals so much with *space*. Acousmatic music is based on the idea that the space is essential to the structure or form—it's neither cosmetic, optional, nor superficial, but a basic element. When I present a piece that has been composed as a multi-channel piece, a stereo version is a reduction, but with the concert version, space is fundamental. If you go to a cinema and see a film by Fellini, you will have a strong aesthetic experience, but if you watch this film on your television, I'm not quite sure that some basic elements of the Fellini experience won't be compromised. So why go to a concert where there are only speakers? There is a very fundamental experience, a rich sonic experience—you are surrounded by speakers, and are in the concert space with many different people. The ritual of being seated with people who share with you the same time, space, and experience is very important. This is possibly the most musical experience you can have, as there is nothing interfering.

The aristocratic ritual of instrumental concert music is based on the star system, to see a soloist, and electroacoustic music experience has none of that.

PS: How did you select the pieces you've chosen for this concert?

RN: I was asked to present my own music—*Le rénard et la rose* (1995), *Malina* (2000), *Erinyes* (2001)— and different aspects of acousmatic music showing a broad range from the last ten years. I also wanted to include other music from Montreal, so there is music by Francis Dhomont—*Objets retrouvés* (1996), *Phonurgie* (1999). For me, he was a real master during my student years, and now he is my close friend. I also chose Louis Dufort—*Decap* (2000). When he came to the Université de Montréal, where I teach, we all knew he was at the right place, that he was a composer. He has done very good work over the years, and his music is quite challenging for us, since we have the feeling that the younger generation continues to produce good music, so we can't stay seated.

PS: Who comes to your concerts?

RN: Many different people—they're getting younger and younger, and there's more and more brightly coloured hair, et cetera. I think this is because of the *techno* scene. They're listening to music that is more like acousmatic music, though we don't have a beat. There is a cross between these genres, and I believe that it's because the electro-acoustic music scene is closer to the techno scene and the popular scene than to contemporary music.

Chris Paul Harman

OCTOBER 2001

CHRIS PAUL HARMAN *was born in Toronto, Ontario, in 1970 and lived there for most of his life. After a winter in the Netherlands, he returned to Toronto and, in the summer of 2005, moved to Montreal to begin teaching at McGill University. Since being awarded the Grand Prize at the* CBC *Young Composers Competition in 1990, Harman has maintained a high profile in Canadian music. November 2001 marked two significant signposts in his compositional career: the release of the first* CD *dedicated to his music (on the* CMC*'s Centrediscs label) and the presentation of the Jules Léger Prize for Chamber Music for his piece* Amerika *(awarded and performed at the NuMuFest on November 19, 2001, Massey Hall). Since we first met in 1995, in the heyday of the Winnipeg New Music Festival, Chris Paul Harman and I have maintained contact, sharing ideas, debating, and sparring on*

15

many musical issues, both privately and publicly. The prominence of his work made it an opportune time to interview him about his music and its complex array of inspirations.

PS: To my ears, the past two years have been critical for the development of your music. What would you identify as the primary areas of change in your music?

CPH: Most recently, the nature of the materials that I use is opening up and changing quite a bit. For example, in my work *Catacombs* (for flute and orchestra), the source material is drawn from a large number of orchestral and solo literature for the flute. By using an ever-growing number of source materials, I think my pieces are starting to become overloaded with the content itself, which is somewhat counter-intuitive to what many of us are taught about being economical and honing, clarifying, refining ideas. However, not just the quantity of materials has increased, but the emotional palette. Up until about three years ago, I didn't think that I could write humorous music, and I think the truth was that I had not found the way to express humour or whimsy in my music. It also interests me that the more one has put in, the more difficult it is to create an identity for what the work is. As such, I find that work in that vein has an innate ability to renew or refresh itself with repeated hearings, and it becomes a goal to build this element into the music in such a way that I can surprise myself even.

PS: Your music has also become increasingly fragmented. Isolated, seemingly dislocated textures and materials are begun and then dropped. Why fragments?

CPH: The impetus behind using fragments is to create a structure that is not easily foreseeable. I have mostly used fragments of roughly equal length, which sets up an expectation in terms of length of phrases and silences. In doing this, two opposing ideas are presented. On the one hand, ideas that are proposed and then abandoned prevent the establishment of a clear hierarchy of materials. On the other hand, the idea of using fragments makes me think of Mozart's faster movements, especially the rondos. The gestures are often encapsulated in tiny, energetic four-bar, even two-bar phrases. It's always going past you, and there's something kind of painful, kind of claustrophobic about the idea of concentrating so much energy into these little spaces.

PS: How do you want the pieces to be heard? Are they a series of variations, or more like puzzles with parts missing, that we have to piece together ourselves?

CPH: They could be either or both of these things—it depends upon the piece. For example, in my piece *Projections*, it is a set of variations with a lot of silences. In my piece *Amerika*, I like to think of it more like a comic book, where the action takes place within little boxes. In this particular instance, the implementation of fragments was inspired by the comic books of Robert, Charles, and Maxim Crumb. In the documentary *CRUMB*, they showed the young artist's talent test that Charles completed when he was eighteen. In his cartoon he developed a kind of wrinkle motif that was eventually extended to include every element of the comic—the grass, the skin, trees, the sky. It was carried to an absurd degree, and I sometimes think about this when I contemplate my own recent fragmentary pieces, because even though the material may be light or frivolous in one way, there is a slightly masochistic quality to the way everything is boxed.

PS: ...The difference being, though, that in a comic book there is a narrative that carries from window to window. Yours seem to be units, or music without transitions.

CPH: Yes. I think that this was because I wanted to suggest some of the programmatic elements of the source material (from Bernstein's *West Side Story*), while treating them in a non-contextual way. I wasn't trying to build a line or a bridge between these different impressions, but wanted to take these elements, which are somewhat popular, romantic, even schmaltzy, and treat them in a very abstract way.

PS: You mentioned that *Amerika* was built on music from *West Side Story*. Most of your pieces are based on material appropriated from other sources. Is there a sub-text to your choice of materials?

CPH: More often than not, the impetus is, surprisingly, sentimental or nostalgic. For example, my work *Midnight With the Stars and You* is based on a popular song from the 1930s, which is used at the end of the film *The Shining*. This film that has been a favourite of mine since I was a child *(laughter all around)* ...so for me, there was a humorous and perhaps slightly grotesque element to taking this material and treating it abstractly. I was taking it from one context, and placing it in another, or perhaps putting it into a situation with no context. As well, I like irony. When *Amerika* was commissioned by New Music Concerts, it was originally to be on a concert called "All Canadian, Eh," so I decided to look for material that was decidedly non-Canadian. I had previously been thinking about using material from *West Side Story* as the basis for a piece anyway, as there was some technical impetus for using this material. Bernstein's melodies transpose in ways that give them a free atonal structure, which, with a few more simple steps, could be quite easily serialized. Having done this, I found it interesting to maintain some of the gestures and feelings of the original music after restructuring the pitch material.

PS: Why don't you begin with material you compose yourself?

CPH: I don't trust myself. I find that looking at my own material is too difficult. When I look at material I've written myself, I feel that what I am looking at is not music. Perhaps because it is too transparent, too naked. However, when I look at somebody else's music, perhaps it is simply an aura of mystery that makes me feel more comfortable starting out with their material.

PS: So you're working this way to distance yourself?

CPH: Partly, but that isn't sufficiently explanatory. There are techniques and procedures that I use to manipulate musical material, and I find that when I cross-reference these systems with the basic material from another piece of music, the results vary wildly, depending on the nature of that other music. This often leads me toward musical sens-ibilities I might not have consciously been able to reach, or which I may have consciously avoided; so this is a way of reaching music I cannot hear, cannot yet understand, or cannot yet recognize as a viable representation of my creative self. A useful analogy is the cut-up writing approach of William S. Burroughs. By cutting up newspapers, shuffling the snippets, and pasting them together, Burroughs thought (somewhat supernaturally) that this was a way of predicting future events. More practically, he also felt it was a way of discovering things he did not know, or things he did not know that he knew.

PS: One could say that you're treating the material coldly and objectively to, ultimately, achieve an emotional result.

CPH: I would agree with that inasmuch as this is the way I begin to generate material. However, by no means does this imply that I keep everything that is generated. There is still a part of the process where I consciously and emotionally make choices about what to keep and how to order it.

PS: Are these equal partners in your compositional process?

CPH: These days, no. I think the emotional choices are becoming fewer.

PS: Why?

CPH: For reasons that I can't presently explain, I'm not comfortable getting too close to this material. I think that my music is going to change dramatically in the near future.

PS: Do you have a sense of how it will change?

CPH: I feel that the work I have done with fragment structures has not gone as far as I would have liked. At this point, I feel I have not been capable of working spontaneously with this kind of structure to obtain the most interesting results. One possible answer to the question may lie not with a purely linear juxtaposition of ideas or fragments but perhaps with a combination of linearity and superimpositions.

PS: You once told me that from time to time you consider composing other (for lack of a better word), more avant-garde music. To me, this implied that you're conscious of particular boundaries and limitations you have in your work, and perceive yourself in a certain way, aesthetically.

CPH: The issue of boundary and freedom is something I struggle with, and it is a difficult balance for me to find. What is important for me is to have a way of conceiving or approaching music, whether it be my own or somebody else's. I don't mean explicitly *labelling* the music; there may simply be some characteristics I can understand in a certain way. For me, writing music and listening to music is ninety-five per cent of the time an intensely analytical process.

PS: Describe the sound of your music.

CPH: At the moment that you asked, I saw a page of one of my scores, and I could see sections from *Amerika*, which look like sections in a comic book. I don't know what this signifies.

PS: What comes off the page?

CPH: A stain, an imprint of itself.

Linda Catlin Smith

COMPOSER Linda Catlin Smith was born in 1957 and raised in White Plains, New York. She attended the State University of New York (SUNY) in Stony Brook and the University of Toronto's Victoria College. Smith has been an active contributor in Toronto's new music scene since her move there in 1981. While developing a consistent oeuvre of pieces for diverse, sometimes unusual, instrumentations, she has also explored music as concert presenter, Artistic Director of Arraymusic, and as a member of the collaborative, multidisciplinary URGE ensemble. Whenever I speak with her, I leave thinking about topics I hadn't considered before, or having to reconsider an issue. With the release of her CD Memory Forms in 2001, I was compelled to attempt a more formal discussion, and glean some ideas to pass on and ponder.

PS: Scanning your CD, the titles of your pieces are very evocative. What is your intention when you name a piece?

LCS: It's usually just a name—you have to call it something. It's not really a huge clue, or mapping on of meaning, but the words are usually something that can resonate with the "tenor" of the piece in some way. Three of the pieces have titles that I borrowed from within novels by the American writer Cormac McCarthy. The titles just jumped out while I was reading those books at the time I was composing the music (*Among the Tarnished Stars, Through the Low Hills,* and *With Their Shadows Long*). The three pieces have similar instrumentations and something similar going on—perhaps tone—in fact, all the pieces have this aspect of tone, or what I might even call "mood," and are circumscribed within that mood, never venturing out. They are very interior.

PS: What is the tone of the pieces?

LCS: I think that's tricky, because then you're getting into adjectives. I find trying to describe music in words somewhat troubling. When I'm working, I'm finding a soundworld or an atmosphere that is compelling to me, one that draws me in, and keeps drawing me in. If there's a sensibility at work there, I'm not manipulating it, but rather observing it, staying within it. That's why there is a palette that one could refer as a tone, a mood, or a sensibility. In the realm of painting, you might have a kind of *glow* that you try to set up with what you're doing, and you take it right to the edges, without bringing in another kind of palette, you stick with that.

PS: Glow, or shadow, implies an essence emanating from or off something else... it's like the music is beside the figure.

LCS: I think I know what you're getting at. It's very difficult to talk about, and it's something that I don't quite understand yet. What I'm looking for is always something beyond what I actually know about, so when I'm working, I'm observing, and extending—often, I write material and then strip some of it back, or take some of it away. Each piece is how I understand the instrumental possibilities at that time, and how I could extend my thinking. It's my way of creating continuity, and this idea of glow, which just came up in this conversation, is something that comes out of the sounds I'm working with—it's the "something else" that happens beyond gesture, melody, and harmony.

PS: You often mention painters. Who has influenced you, and how?

LCS: A lot of times, what I look at are painters who do "still life," such as Giorgio Morandi, and my friend Nancy Kembry (whose painting is on the cover of the CD), also Chardin. More recently, I've become interested in the paintings of Mary Hiester Reid. It's the way they use the light around the objects, the shadows and the background—it's quite mysterious. I like the quality of sombre thought in this genre of painting. They're not action paintings, and they're not fully abstract either. I look at a lot of abstraction also, by painters like Agnes Martin, Mark Rothko, and Cy Twombly. What I get from painting is things to do with form, texture, layering, and transparency. Looking at painting is a kind of sustenance, just like listening to certain kinds of music—it's something I take into myself. Nature does the same thing for me. I like observing the small details.

PS: What music draws you in?

LCS: For a long time I was drawn to music of the Baroque era, people like Lully, Rameau, and Couperin, because of the transparency in the sound, and the emotional restraint. I've also been pretty fascinated by French music at the end of the fourteenth century, composers such as Solage and the music of the *ars subtilitas*. What I like about it is the kind of weave of the music. The music is quite continuous, and in its own way, complex. I like the sense of non-directedness. It's not about big moments—I'm not interested in big moments, I'm interested in being *within* an experience, staying with it for a while. I like when a composer or artist of any kind gets really caught up in something. The deeper someone goes with something, sticking with it, I want to go with them, with their concentration. I've been trying to look for a deeper concentration in what I'm doing; I want to go with something for a long time, in music and in life experiences. That's why I like the beautiful, slow films, like those of Tarkovsky—things that unfold.

PS: You said that you're not into big moments. Does what you're seeking necessarily have to exclude them?

LCS: There's drama, and there's *drama*. The drama inherent in what I do is more of an interior sort. I'm interested in internal drama, where the changes that happen feel big within that context, but aren't, in the larger context of high drama, or high contrast. It's not about making important statements.

PS: Important statements in what sense?

LCS: In terms of a big sense of arrival, of having said something of major importance to the world. I don't think of art in that way. I think of it as an intimate engagement with material.

PS: How do you attain your aesthetic goals?

LCS: It's not a question I ask myself while writing; I'm not using those terms. I often think of LaMonte Young saying, "Draw a line and follow it." I'm kind of following the material, investigating it, seriously questioning it all the time, but never with a sense of a large solution that resolves everything. It's more experiential than that. I want to make something that keeps me involved or interested in it, and at the same time maintains its own sense of "necessariness," without losing focus. It's like being suspended in a certain place, for a while.

PS: Technically, how do you maintain that sense of suspension?

LCS: I have to listen so deeply while I'm working, questioning all the while. When I get to a point where I seem to make a rhetorical choice, I try to avoid it, because then it's talking *about* music, and is no longer the experience of the music.

PS: Lately, every time we talk, the word "melody" comes up.

LCS: Christian Wolff said that in the end, everything is melody. I've become more melodic, and part of the reason for that is pleasure. There is great pleasure in sound, and for me, part of it is melody, which might move in ways one wouldn't expect. The way I use melody is quite simple, only using a couple of different notes, which may be the reason I'm so attracted to Gregorian chant, with its intimate melodic meanderings.

PS: Do you make any pre-compositional decisions?

LCS: Not really. Sometimes the preparation might be through listening to music with the same instrumentation. I don't really have a bag of compositional techniques that I use. For each work, I develop the techniques that the music requires, in order to get at what is inspiring me. I seek a particular sound, or texture, and I try to get further involved in it, to render (to use Copland's word) the "sonorous" image. I might experiment with varied repetition, trying things backwards and forwards, upside down, but it's intuitive, speculative, and non-methodical, definitely not a pre-planned paint-by-numbers approach—it's about seeking the potential of the material.

I want the music to be a meditative experience, as opposed to a narrative, rhetorical experience. I want to allow the state of the piece to continue to radiate, and expand itself, to allow the substance to spread over the surface of time that we're in, in an evolutionary way. To that end, I've always been fascinated by slow movements in music of the previous century. Part of it is being able to hear everything, but I also love to expand time, to make it bigger than it normally is. It's not slow motion, but intimacy. I want to bring it up very close, so that it almost becomes your world. You could stand on a beach and look at millions of pebbles, or you could bring one up very close and it's bigger than the ocean, with all of its subtlety and nuances and gradations. I'm only in the beginning stages of getting at that.

PS: Is there a directly political view in your work? Are you reacting against something?

LCS: Not directly. It's more that I wanted to embrace the music that inspired me. Elaine Scarry (*On Beauty and Being Just*) quoted Wittgenstein as saying that when faced with something beautiful, one wants to replicate it. That happened to me, and that was what got me started as a composer. I heard something beautiful, and wanted to make it myself, to continue it, to surround myself with it. But yes, making work is political, and I am interested in artists who go their own way, and are experimental, turning something on its head. There are huge political stakes involved, because the choices you make in art have impact on so many different things.

Alexina Louie

ALEXINA LOUIE was born in Vancouver in 1949, the daughter of second-gener-ation Chinese Canadians. Following a decade in Southern California, she settled in Toronto, where she currently lives. For Louie, the few months before I interviewed her were full of pleasant summations. While finishing touches were being put on the video version of her six-minute tragic opera buffa Toothpaste *(www.tooth-pastetv.com), she received the honour of the Order of Ontario, in recognition of her career achievements. The overriding project that had consumed nearly all of her creative energies over the previous six years, however, was her opera* The Scarlet Princess. *Written to a libretto by David Henry Hwang (author of* M. Butterfly *and screenplays for Martin Scorsese, Francis Ford Coppola, and others) the score calls for a cast of three main characters, twenty-four-voice chorus and fifty-five-piece orchestra. The concert version was performed on April 23, 2002, at the George*

Weston Recital Hall, during the Opera America conference in Toronto. Nearing the end of orchestrating her 500-page score, she took time to reflect on the project, the process, and her operatic goals.

PS: Please provide a brief outline of the story.

AL: The story is taken from a seventeenth century Japanese puppet play that was later transformed into a kabuki play called *The Scarlet Princess of Edo*. The synopsis is as follows: the opera opens with a monk and his young lover who climb a mountain cliff to fulfill a suicide pact. As the lover plunges to his death, he realizes that the monk has not jumped and curses him. Years later, after the monk has become chief abbot of the temple, a beautiful young princess arrives at the monastery hoping to become a nun. The abbot immediately recognizes her as the reincarnation of his dead lover and his obsession with her begins. A supporting cast of nuns, monks, bandits, outcasts, ghosts and demons round out this tormented love story.

PS: Would you agree that the story is somewhat unconventional, in that the main character is a strong female lead, rather than a woman in a submissive role?

AL: Interestingly, when I selected the story, I didn't think specific-ally about that. It wasn't until I was well into writing the piece that I wondered if I made her such a strong character in part because it's already rare to have an opera *written* by a woman. Throughout the writing process, I continued to press my librettist not to make her into a demonic character. If she is to perform these horrible acts, the audience has to understand why. I guided him into making her a sympathetic character, shaping the psychology of her presentation. As an opera audience member, I am often put off by the fact that you don't get to know how the character got to be that way, why they are that way. I want the audience to buy into it, and I don't want there to be big holes in the characterization. With regard to the princess, I also guided David into focussing the language he used, to clarify her point of view. I often said, "That's absolutely fantastic, but a woman wouldn't think that way, a woman wouldn't say that. She wouldn't be so analytical; she would feel it this way." I don't generally spend a lot of time thinking about the gender situation of creators, but I did find it fascinating that I had to lead him to use words that a woman would use. Awareness and reflection of these gender issues wasn't something I was looking for—it's not at the forefront of my thinking, because you have to get on with making art—but there it was, a complete revelation!

PS: What possessed you to do an opera?

AL: I'd been reluctant to write one. Despite having been approached to write an opera for more than ten years, I never had any interest in the medium, because I thought it was overblown, and I like dealing with the subtleties of orchestral or chamber music. Secondly, I just couldn't bend my head around the form itself; that you had to go through so much recitative in order to stand at the mountaintop and hear a beautiful aria. I didn't get it. I didn't understand the form, and because I didn't understand, I didn't appreciate the form. It was only after I had done the Tapestry New Opera and the Canadian Opera Company-sponsored workshop that I came to understand that I could write dramatic music, and it was at this time that I wrote *Toothpaste*. By jumping in, I realized that I could do it, though I didn't foresee what I was getting into—this has been a huge job, bigger than anything I could ever imagine, and it's been a humbling experience. Even if you're aware of the specific demands of the genre, if you're aware of the problems, it's not until you actually go in and hear it that you grow and learn. You can intellectualize, but it's not until you wrestle with it that you know. It's not like writing a string quartet—if you make a mistake, the whole two-hour opera is in jeopardy, and that's a long, long time.

PS: When comparing your piece with nineteenth century opera, what elements have you preserved, and what have you discarded?

AL: I would say that mine is in the tradition of grand opera. It's in two acts, with a prologue. Because I have a brilliant playwright as librettist, the drama moves very well. The clarity and differentiation of characters is also part of operatic tradition, and I worked hard at that. I chose to maintain a recitative-aria structure, because the plot line is driven by dramatic events. I felt there had to be a very clear definition between recitative and song, so that when you arrived at a point where the character was in such a heightened emotional state, they would actually sing. Also, the piece is two hours long, and if I took the approach of many contemporary operas, of through-composed arioso, by the end of it, people would want to string me up by my toes. It becomes a matter of balance and weight, to control the musical architecture over a long period, which is completely daunting. Having workshops really helped me develop this, because I thought I had been pacing it well, but I realized that I wasn't, that it was becoming what I was trying to avoid. Part of that was because my libretto is so strong. It's a beautiful libretto, it's really fine, and there are funny things in it to offset the grand tragedy. Those humorous moments heighten the horrible ones. I really couldn't say enough words of praise for David.

PS: What is the relation between the text and the music? How do you set his text to convey the situation and psychology?

AL: I have to keep asking myself certain questions—what are the characters feeling, why are they singing this way? You have to assess the situation, to assess the dramatic location in the opera, and save things for later on. A composer does that anyway, say, in the architecture of a string quartet, but you don't want to blow your information all at one point, you have to hold back until the point comes that you feel it's time to release that amount of information. You have to weigh things, and that's hard to do over a period of six years. I had to make sure that the music of Act 1 matched the music of Act 2, which was written six years later. In this way, it's been a great learning experience. Over time, I would sometimes request more text, or another aria, where I could flesh out a character a bit more, to get behind the character. I also try to match the music with the personality of the character, and determined that I wouldn't set the text only syllabically, but also melismatically at particular locations, which assists in balancing the form.

PS: Has your previous work in film informed how you write an opera? Is there any overlap between the genres?

AL: I don't think so, although in both you're moving toward dramatic points, and you have to hold yourself back, to weigh the different dramatic moments. The difference is that in film, I don't control the structure—I serve the director's vision—whereas with opera, my take is that the composer is driving the bus. That's the other thing that I had to learn how to do, to take charge, because basically the responsibility was mine—shaping the work, asking for certain kinds of arias to allow the characters to reveal themselves more, to cut lines of libretto, and so on. It has required a great deal of commitment, to shape the work and take charge. The storyline, and the fact that it's an opera on a grand scale, required me to utilize all of the musical skills I have developed. It represents where I am at this point in my life. I haven't been shy about using my musical language; I haven't scaled back. It's a highly charged opera, very sensual. In some ways, it's an erotic opera. The opera represents the culmination of all my experience to date, both as a composer and as a human being.

Omar Daniel

OMAR DANIEL was born in 1960, and studied with John Beckwith at the University of Toronto. Since 2000 he has taught composition at the University of Western Ontario but continues to reside in Toronto. In the spring of 2002, several new works emerged from Daniel's composition desk, including a set of cabaret songs for the Queen of Puddings Music Theatre Company, and a new chamber piece for Ottawa flutist Robert Cram. As well, during the Opera America conference in Toronto, Tapestry New Opera premiered a fully staged version of his new twelve-minute horror opera Lisa, *written with librettist Alex Poch-Goldin. On May 7, 2002, Soundstreams presented two of Daniel's works,* The Man Who Told Lies, *and* The Flaying of Marsyas. *Written for narrator and ensemble (the Gryphon Trio),* The Man Who Told Lies *is a twenty-minute fable on a text written and narrated by Michael Redhill (known for his Giller Prize shortlisted* book Martin Sloane*). The second work,* The Flaying of Marsyas, *for violin and live electronics, featured the composer (who also plays the electronics) suspended upside-down on stage. For our interview, I chose to focus on this piece, and learn more about his creative process.*

PS: What was your inspiration for *The Flaying of Marsyas*?
OD: I wanted to work with live electronics, and create an interactive environment in which movement and bodily gestures are converted into digital information sent to sound processors that alter the sound of the violin. The second inspiration is Titian's painting *The Flaying of Marsyas* (1575-76), which depicts the final stages of a musical duel between the god Apollo and the satyr Marsyas. According to Greek mythology, Marsyas picked up the pan flute when Athena, daughter of Zeus, discarded it out of vanity—she thought that her face became bloated and ugly when she played the instrument. Becoming an expert player, Marsyas challenged Apollo, the patron of music, to a performing contest. Apollo agreed but stipulated that the winner could decide the punishment of the loser. The judging Muses awarded the victory to Apollo, who chose to hang Marsyas from a tree and flay him alive. His suffering and death were lamented by earthly beings such as animals, other satyrs, and nymphs, whose flowing tears formed a river named after him.

It's no coincidence that Apollo is depicted playing a stringed instrument, while Marsyas plays flute. In some circles, string instruments were considered more "divine" by virtue of the mathematical principles they could easily illustrate, and wind instruments were considered "pagan." The myth is not only a parable on the dangers of audacity and pride, but also the victory of Apollo's noble music over the rough and lascivious piping of his opponent. For my piece, I've distilled the Titian painting to its essential elements: Apollo playing a violin to the left, and Marsyas (in this case, the composer) hanging upside down in the centre. Fundamentally, throughout the piece, the god plays, and the satyr reacts, physically/electronically.

Another related source is Andreas Vesalius's 1543 collection of anatomical etchings entitled *De Humani Corporis Fabrica*. The woodcuts are attributed to Titian, and the poses of the flayed/dissected figures are employed structurally in the piece. Marsyas, while hanging, adopts the poses of Vesalius's characters to demarcate compact one-minute sections in the piece.

PS: Could you describe further the relation between the myth/painting and the composition?

OD: To a certain extent, the characters in the music are representations of the two main characters in the myth. When I went about composing it, the first thing I did was write a twelve-minute solo violin piece, which I thought about in relation to Apollo playing while Marsyas was being flayed. It starts with a virtuoso passage showing off Apollo's prowess on the instrument. After that first minute and a half, the piece moves through various compositional stages depicting first a type of seduction, with Apollo toying with Marsyas as he's hanging upside down, then a murder/death scene, followed by a concluding lament. By the time the death scene comes around, the electronic alterations to the violin sound produce something very aggressive and highly noise based, much less harmonious than at the beginning.

PS: What is the nature and function of the live electronics?

OD: There are two types—one is the altered sound of the acoustic violin, and the second is a collection of sampled sounds. Any time the violin is heard through the speakers, it's a digitally processed manipulation of the sound via the sensors attached to suspended musician, and triggered by body movement. The samples, which comprise about two minutes of the piece, reflect Marsyas's cries for help, and are based on vocal, metal, and flute sounds. The electronic movement sensors are as follows: I have a G-force controller that senses either gravity or acceleration—one is attached to the back of my neck, and the other to my right wrist. There are also touch controllers. These control things such as the volume of what comes out of the speakers. For example, when my thumb is straight, no sound comes from the speakers. When it is fully bent, the maximum processed violin sound comes out. There is also a flange patch, with one finger controlling delay time, another controlling reverberation, and another the spatial placement of the sound, and so on, effecting, in real time, the processed sound of the violin. Essentially, the hanging figure is reacting to the violin and sending it back, so what we're hearing is the emotional response to what is being done to Marsyas.

PS: Why did you choose to set the flaying, which takes place *after* the musical duel, as opposed to the duel itself?

OD: That's an interesting point. I think it worked out this way because my initial attraction was to Titian's painting, which I discovered first. As time went on and I delved into the myth a little bit, I was most attracted to representing the painting with a composition, but I could see the musical competition as a future avenue if I were to expand the piece.

PS: In the Renaissance, flaying symbolized the removal of the external self, and the peeling away of layers, perhaps emotional. Is this symbolism reflected in the music?

OD: I didn't include that in the concept, but... *(laughing)* I think the piece tends to wallow in the gratuitous more than the symbolic. As the piece unfolds, interestingly enough, the point could be made that in the very last section, the lament, the samples that are triggered, and the processing that is achieved by the hanging musician is the purest in the entire piece, so there may be something to that.

PS: How is the flaying reflected in the musical materials and techniques?

OD: In terms of the solo violin part, the music goes through phases, and becomes more aggressive toward the middle of the piece. Pitch-wise, it becomes more dissonant, the melodic contour becomes more angular, and overall, more violent. In the lament, the music hearkens back to material that is more consonant. From the point of view of the solo violin part, it's what one might consider standard and intuitive dramatic techniques for depicting a scenario that is becoming worse and worse. In terms of the electronics, the sonic quality of the voice, metal and flute samples have a sharpness and aggressiveness to them. Within the context of each sample, there is a metallic component, scraping or striking metal.

PS: The painter Georg Baselitz has often painted upside-down figures. Baselitz reportedly started painting them as such in an attempt to remove the person-to-person associations and give us some distance, some emotional detachment, which just may allow us to face the satyr, and to endure the sight of such a gruesome event. It seems the result will be quite the opposite in a live performance of your piece, and hanging upside-down will heighten the torturous nature of the story. I bring this up because in many Greek sculptures, Marsyas is tied upright. Why do you think Titian portrayed the figure hanging, and what is your intention in replicating this in performance?

OD: I understand your point about the Baselitz figures, but if you look at Marsyas in the Titian painting, and compare it with representations of him by other artists, Titian's is the most chilling, the most uncomfortable, and tortured. What struck me first about the painting were the tone and brutality, and the architecture of it; the layout and geometry. It's elegant in so many ways—the fact that Apollo is standing upright and to the left, a little higher, and Marsyas is hung in exact opposition. That is the crux of the concept to me in bringing it to the stage. It was the only thing necessary for the representation of the scene. All that is required is a violinist to the left and a simple suspension where I'm hung upside-down. It's about that relationship of the characters, which is the key geometry in the painting. It's very strange to see something like this, in part because it's very uncomfortable for me, especially as time passes. The blood rushes to your head for the first two minutes, and it's quite difficult, but after that, the body adjusts. You have to keep the body moving, for circulation, which conveniently relates to the poses and sensors of the electronics part.

PS: Apollo was seen as a prototype of Christ, the god of reason and intellect. His noble music is based on mathematical science and symbolized by the stringed instrument. Marsyas, the pagan, is seen as earthly and rough. Does the music reflect this, and if so, how?

OD: It's the kind of thinking I would approach in another reflection on this story. I have the idea to do a sequence of these pieces, maintaining and varying the relationship of an immobile electronic musician, immobilized either by hanging by the feet or wrists, or entirely strapped down, along with an acoustic performer or performers around them. One of the issues that have come up as a result is the relationship between composer and performer, and there's obviously another level of subtext there. People who experience this piece become concerned, because they sense the powerlessness of the hanging figure within the context of the piece. This tension interests me. It's no mistake that I've chosen myself as the composer to be the musician hanging on the stage, as it explores another level of the multi-dimensional relationship between composer and performer.

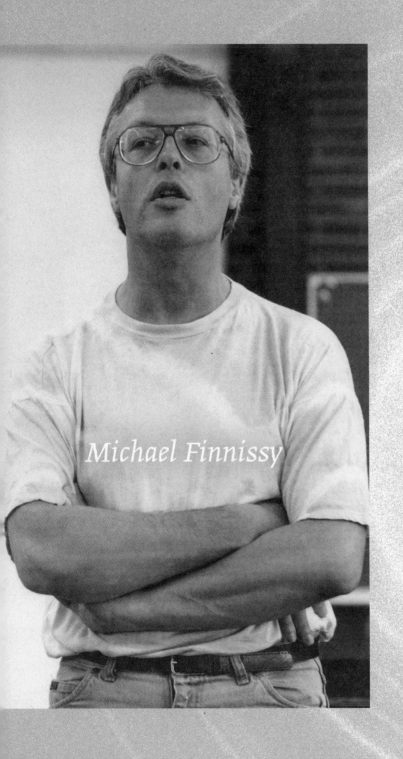

Michael Finnissy

BORN in Tulse Hill, London in 1946, Michael Finnissy now resides in Hove, East Sussex. He has long since established himself as one of the most prolific, challenging, and interesting living composers. His music ranges from brief miniatures to the encyclopaedic five-hour solo piano work The History of Photography in Sound, *and from light-hearted pieces for amateur music lovers to the extremely complex, playable by only the most committed virtuosi. On May 16, 2002, at the Glenn Gould Studio, pianist Eve Egoyan gave the world-premiere of Finnissy's twenty-minute piece* Erik Satie, like anyone else, *written especially for her, on a program featuring other music by Satie. Given this all-too-rare opportunity to hear Michael Finnissy's music in Canada, I jumped at the opportunity to interview him by phone at his home in Southern England.*

PS: What drew you to Satie's music?

MF: I probably started listening seriously to Satie's music around the same time I found Ives and Varese, when I was twelve or thirteen. I remember hearing a broadcast of *Parade*, and I found a piano-score of *Rélâche* in the library of the office where my father worked. I got hold of Rollo Myers's book too, for a school prize. Satie didn't seem so odd when you'd been fond of Edward Lear and Lewis Carroll. I don't think Satie was well thought of at the time (1958-60)—in fact, he was damned with the usual faint praise as a *miniaturist*, or an *eccentric*. I found him very *classical*—mathematically precise, Apollonian, concerned with balance and proportion. I suspected that there were darker sides to him, the *Rosicrucian* music, the late *Nocturnes*, even the *Gnosiennes*: a sort of perverse erotic charge. At that time, as a self-taught composer, I was interested in composers who had found *mysterious* and *personal* ways to write, without necessarily advertising their tool kit in book form. Satie seemed very *authentic* to me, unfavourable comparisons between him and Debussy, or Ravel, or Chabrier, or Stravinsky in terms of "technique" made no sense, and still don't.

PS: How is the piece about Satie?

MF: It's me thinking about Satie. Thinking in quite an orderly fashion, as befits the subject. Thinking about his music, re-inventing it. It's a fantasy. But it contains reasonably accurate information too, beginning with plainsong (the one for his birthday, near enough!). There then follows a longish section that quotes from Chabrier's opera *Gwendoline*. Chabrier's harmonic language—chromatic *chic*, with *sensational* (rather than functional) unresolved seventh and ninth chords—was obviously influenced by his trips to Bayreuth. I have emphasized the rootlessness and ambiguity of this material by erasing the bass line. Cage, who claimed Satie's influence generally, gets the singers in *Europeras 3 & 4* similarly to perform their arias without accompaniment: releasing, but effectively isolating and also alienating, them in bleakly *undefined* space. *Gwendoline* takes place in ancient Britain, in part because Satie was an anglophile. He also uses the term *Wagnerie* to describe *Le Fils des Étoiles*—although Mario Praz, in writing about *Peladan*, gives an indication that this term might be less purely musical than euphemistic for a sexually orgiastic

ceremonial, a sort of Black Mass. You see how my imagination demen-
tedly links things together! The beginning of the second part of the
piece has a two-step, a ragtime, the sort of popular music Satie used
to write for the café-concert. There are also distorted allusions to
Beethoven, though much more extended than those you find in Satie.

PS: Would you agree that yours is a musicological approach to the
composer?

MF: Perhaps in its *detective work* there are some crossovers into musicology or something similar. The piece maybe toys with notions of
analysis and commentary. But its sense of history is not linear. It's not
a re-construction of a piece by Satie. It's not composed as Satie would
compose, even if he were starting with the same material. I think
that all moments of history only exist at the present time. We can't
experience history chronologically, because at each moment in time,
our memory of the previous moment is already highly coloured and
distorted. There's an essay by Walter Benjamin, about exploding the
continuum of history. He's against this Hegelian idea of history, where
everything is organized linearly from primitive times to a sophisticated present.

PS: Your music confronts so many other artists' work, and your list of
compositions reads like a massive cultural inventory.

MF: I try to acknowledge influences openly. Why try to hide them? We
live in a sort of mausoleum-culture, so much music from the past
taking precedence over what we write, so few people giving us any
credit. I am making an inventory—or I'm cannibalizing the past,
eating and shitting. Trying to make some sense of it as "composition," not standing back and admiring passively. By devouring Satie,
I acquire some of Satie's power, his magic. Isn't this what people
who write symphonies think? "I'll have the residual power of the
symphony rub off on me!" It's just a choice. It helps me relate to the
larger *frame* of past musics.

PS: And usurp some of the momentum.

MF: I hope so. The reality that we, as living composers, are forced to
accept—as natural—that the music of the past is unquestionably so
much better than anything we might write and is going to be played
so much more than ours is, is just *bizarre*.

PS: Do you think it's something peculiar to this time?

MF: I think it began to happen in the nineteenth century, a facet of bourgeois culture, that the *good old days* are better than the *here and now*. The past is more secure, more comfortable, and you know less about it that's alarming or contradictory, you can tell more lies about it. I doubt that many authenticists mounting a performance of *Messiah* would, however, welcome the presence of Handel—it would undermine their authority! One has to invent the present as well, and I suppose we have to take something from the past, because our memories are necessarily of the past. The question then is what do we take? What principles do we adhere to? If we're going to become iconoclastic, what do we become iconoclastic about, or do we get on our knees in front of the past and just worship it?

PS: When you approach music of bygone days, there's a certain type of artist you're attracted to: Percy Grainger, Ives, Varèse, Obrecht, Gershwin, Satie, et cetera. What characteristics do they share?

MF: They're *mavericks*. They represent alternatives to the orthodoxies and canonically approved hierarchies. Outsiders, guests who weren't welcome at the party (read their reviews!).

PS: Despite the seemingly incongruous source materials, your music remains coherent. How are you able to maintain stylistic consistency? What remains constant?

MF: I (the one composing) remain constant. What makes Bach's music consistent, when it does the same thing? Bach draws on so many different, available Baroque styles.

PS: But with Bach, we can talk about codes, and mechanics.

MF: You can here too. There is a discourse, so naturally there are codes, rhetorics, all sorts of manipulation. In composition, the rhetoric has as much to do with how it will sound as any decision you make about big structures, indeed can you detach it from eventual sense of *structure*? From the sound of individual notes? Everyone is surely familiar with the old adage "It's not the material but what you *do* with it that matters"—well how do you characterize that *doing*?

PS: Given your transcultural approach to music making and art, how is it that you remain free of accusations of cultural imperialism?

MF: I haven't entirely. I had an unpleasant backlash to *Newcassel Sangs*—a work I'd written setting rhymes from Newcastle-on-Tyne, and there were those at the university there who thought I should not have appropriated sources from an area in which I had not been born, and where I had never lived!!! The criticisms are inevitably levelled by those who have never been to buy tea, spaghetti, or pineapples at the supermarket, who wouldn't eat Chinese or Indian takeout, and are free of all forms of ethnic bias or prejudice. In the main, however, I'm simply offering *alternatives* as source-materials. A piece like *Folklore* uses its material to try to evoke a pre-industrialized world, a world outside the contaminations of capitalism. I'm not trying to exploit anything *folkloristic*, I just like to try things, and listen to what happens. I'm exploring my *other* selves—the selves that are elsewhere and unshackled—and it's a part of a larger critique of the evolution of music. I make some very odd connections, but most people do that at one time or other. I find it shocking and disgraceful that Western European art/music could be held to be inevitably and unquestionably *the best*. The best for what, or for whom?

For me, these influences innocently come out of interests and soul bonding, sympathy and friendships with composers all across the world, and music I love all across the world. I don't see that there's anything morally sinister about referring to them. I don't take them wholesale, dress them up in English clothes, and pretend they're English, and I don't try to civilize them. I'm not even doing what Grieg was doing with the *Slåtter, Op. 72* (based on peasant fiddle-tunes) that he arranged very late in his life, very beautifully, but turning them into parlour piano pieces. I'm referring to fragments, as a way of saying that I think the idea of cultural purity is not one I'm very fond of.

PS: We're able to sense the sincerity of the approach, but it's shaky ground.

MF: I'm most at home on shaky ground! The kind of composition I do is essentially "improvisatory," so it has that in common with most folk musics. But it is also indebted to ideas taken from standard Western European *modernism*—the tradition of Brahms, Mahler, Schoenberg. I might try to establish a dialectic between the two, but it all happens in a very interior way, very subjective, not didactic in purpose. The permutational techniques, fragmentation, collage—that's not part of the folk-traditions I'm quoting, it's the world I'm living in, or my shared experience of that world.

PS: As both a composer and pianist, how do these two facets of yourself meet when it comes time to write for the piano? How does knowingly writing for another pianist inform this internal balance? Or does it?

MF: It does up to a point, particularly if I like what the other pianist does, and I do like what Eve does. I think it goes beyond questions of "Can I write 150 notes a second when this person is endowed with unusually speedy fingers?" For me it's more a question of whether I like what they find in music once they get "beyond" the notes. I had suggested to Eve that I wanted to write a piece about (or a "portrait of") Satie. She told me that she had wanted to programme his music too. Some people would have gone "Satie? YUK." I'd heard and seen Eve play; I'd listened and observed. You make the garment; hopefully it fits.

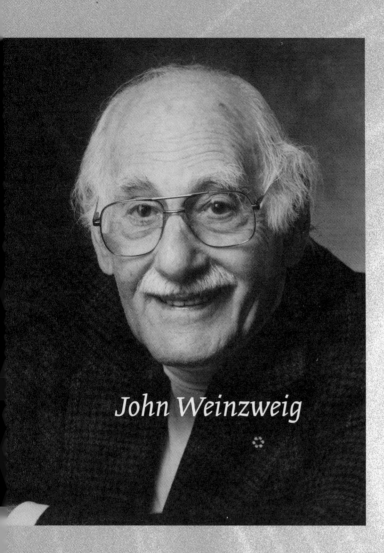

John Weinzweig

JOHN WEINZWEIG was born in Toronto in 1913. Following studies at the Eastman School of Music in Rochester, New York, he returned to Toronto and lived there until his passing in 2006. Weinzweig had a rich musical career and has often been called the Dean of Canadian composers. In 2002 the release of a three-CD set on the CMC's Centrediscs label—as part of the Canadian Composers Portraits series, which also includes disks of music by Jacques Hétu, Jean Coulthard, Harry Freedman, and Murray Adaskin—provided a welcome opportunity to interview him. Listening to the excellent CBC-produced documentary that is CD one of the set, and the subsequent two CDs of music, gave me a new appreciation of his work, groundbreaking career, dedication to teaching, and strongly-held beliefs on the status of composers in society. Divided into two parts, our interview covered many of the important musical and political issues that occupied him throughout

the eight decades of his career. While I usually take for granted the opportunities
I have to discuss music and ideas with my friends and colleagues, in this case I
couldn't help but recognize and respect that I was talking with a composer who was
in part responsible for the fertile creative landscape we currently inhabit.

PS: What is the significance of this recording?

JW: The portrait series came about when I wrote about and discussed the problem of the lack of Canadian music on CBC radio. To put it in perspective, think about the fact that each year CBC celebrates the anniversary of a European composer—not for one broadcast, not for one week, but for twelve months. The year, let's say, of Tchaikovsky, causes CBC to encourage performers to include a piece of Tchaikovsky in their program if they want to get a broadcast. Conversely, when a Canadian composer passed away, he or she received an obituary of a half-hour program and that was all.

After waging guerrilla activity on the CBC for about eight months, I had a meeting with the area head and vice-president of CBC Radio Music. I told them a story of my experience: 1970 was the two hundredth anniversary of Beethoven, and a number of Canadian composers and performers were in Bonn, celebrating Canadian culture. We were sent over there to have some works performed by the symphony in Beethoven Halle. There was a press conference when we arrived and I was spokesperson for the composers. I was asked why we were bringing Canadian music to Germany and I said that the reason is that in my country they're celebrating the anniversary of Beethoven. They were quite astounded, because there they have no problem celebrating their composers. I implied that we had a problem in Canada. I told this story at the meeting with CBC, and I think they understood my point. Not only European composers have a story to tell, but Canadian composers also.

They latched onto the idea of a documentary, and began work on it right away, which helped to turn the whole thing around. Another important event was that Elisabeth Bihl, the Executive Director of the Canadian Music Centre, was also present at the meeting. I felt that the CBC had been ignoring the Canadian Music Centre, and the CBC would not give enough airplay to recordings of Canadian music on the

Centrediscs label. This brought the CMC and the CBC into collaboration on the portrait series CDs.

PS: What do you think was the reason for the relative absence of Canadian music on radio?

JW: The CBC felt they were doing their bit for Canadian composers because they spent ninety thousand dollars a year on commissions. I wasn't satisfied, because those works were dumped on the Sunday night program *Two New Hours*. I felt their attitude was that Canadian music was unfit for daytime broadcast. They wouldn't admit that, but it was obvious that Canadian music had no presence in daytime. The only presence of importance was on *Two New Hours*, which runs on Sundays from ten until midnight.[1] They thought that they were doing their part to encourage Canadian composers, but I told them that they don't have to encourage a composer. A composer is going to be a composer. It's incorrect to think you're doing something for Canadian music because you're giving a premiere. The premiere is useful for the composer, but not for the listener. The *second* performance is useful for the listener. And the *third* performance, and so on. You will not have a Canadian culture unless you create the conditions for a repertoire, and you only get that with multiple broadcasts and performances— familiarity and knowledge. Imagine what would happen to Beethoven if he was a Canadian composer and you commissioned him to write the *Fifth Symphony*, gave the premiere, and that was it—he would be forgotten. That's what is done with our composers.

PS: Do you think this approach somehow reflects a more general societal attitude?

JW: Canadian music had a fairly strong presence in radio from the forties into the late seventies. The downturn stemmed from a 1983 CBC committee report that claimed CBC radio was not showing enough respect for popular music—that was the beginning of a putdown of our classical composers. By exploiting the weakness of the Canadian content regulations, many Canadian pieces were eliminated in favour of European music and Canadian performers. As a result, Mozart became the standard of radio sound. It was very obvious. Almost every program that you heard first had a piece by Mozart, to pacify the listeners. Canadian music, by Canadian composers, had ceased to be a threat, and we became strangers.

PS: Are the Canadian Composers Portraits an important step toward resolving that problem?

JW: The important thing that will come out of the portraits is if the classical music hosts include some of the composers' repertoire from those CDs on their programs. We have enough recorded material to offer a choice of programming. Canadian music is available and there's no reason why a piece by a Canadian composer shouldn't be included in a program with Mozart and Schubert. I simply want our national radio to include and to inform people of this country that there are composers who are writing interesting music. They've been highlighting writers, the poets, the novelists and the painters on special programs that have to do with the arts—but never on Canadian music. This could be the beginning of a whole new relationship between our national radio and the composers in Canada.

PS: What's the responsibility of the composers in this transition?

JW: Very simple. The role of the composer is to compose. That's all.

PS: But you are an excellent example of a composer who writes music but also teaches and does so much other work for the music.

JW: I tell you, I found out very early in my career that the music profession was also infected by what I call the politics of the podium. For example, I turned down a commission from the Montreal Symphony. They suggested that I might write a piece for two clarinets and symphony—who the hell is going to write a piece for two clarinets and symphony? Obviously, this was going to be an obstacle. I thought about it for a while and I wrote Dutoit and said, "Thank you for the commission but in light of the fact that the Montreal Symphony has virtually ignored my repertoire during my lifetime, I see no reason why I should spend eight or nine months writing a work for one single performance." But I wished him well. It wasn't personal.

PS: Don't you think that by accepting the commission and tailoring it to your interests that you're making a step towards counteracting the ignorance of your music?

JW: No. My name came up from a committee that was advising the Montreal Symphony. The selection wasn't made by Dutoit, it was made for him. Don't forget that I was not a young composer anymore. I had no reason to grab this commission. I didn't need them. It couldn't further my career—I either had a career or didn't. It reminds me of some years ago when the Victoria symphony had a grant to put on some concerts of contemporary music. They weren't doing very well at bringing in the audience. The next thing I see is a photo of a pair of singing dogs in the newspaper, hired for a contemporary music concert presented by the Victoria Symphony. Two singing dogs auditioned and hired from New York to put on their concert of contemporary music. I was very angry about this. I wrote a letter to the Canada Council and suggested, "Next time you get a request for funds from the Victoria Symphony I suggest you send them a box of dog food." That message was transmitted to the Victoria Symphony. As a result, I have not been performed by the Victoria Symphony.

If you speak your mind, then there's the risk that you're going to be left out in the cold, and I could accept that. I would speak my mind, and I would lose a performance here or there, but so what? That wasn't going to change my life. I could still write music and hope and dream that someday somebody will play it. If you're a composer, you hope and dream anyway. That's a big part of writing music.

PS: What's your ultimate goal for the presence of Canadian music, and what type of reception do you want for it?

JW: In Germany, when they program a piece by Stockhausen, they don't have to identify him as German. Here, when a Canadian work is performed, the announcer has to identify the composer as a "Canadian composer." That immediately tells you something: that we still have to identify the native composer as a member of our society. There's some-thing wrong with that picture. Until we get over that, we really haven't got a situation where the composer is accepted.

PS: So why should people listen to Canadian music?

JW: In the first place, they shouldn't be forced to listen to Canadian music, or any music. If you take Vienna, for example, they've had thousands and thousands of composers, and most of them have been forgotten. What remains and what survived is what we hear today. We have to go through that process in this country. We must be allowed to offer the music of our composers and let the listeners will decide over time what will last and will not last—we have to go through the process of time.

PS: Do you think that there's a noticeable quality to Canadian music? Is there a certain sound, a unique aesthetic?

JW: There is something in Canadian music that is easier for the foreigner to perceive than for the Canadian. For example, Darius Milhaud was in Toronto and I was asked to bring some composers together. I got them together in the concert hall of the old conservatory on College Street: Harry Somers, Harry Freedman, and so on. Milhaud was very interested. He had a special interest in my *Violin Sonata*, which had an unusual form in that its conclusion was a cadenza for the violin. He found many elements among us that provoked his interest. The conductor of the TSO at the time was doing my harp concerto and planned to take it to Europe on tour with the orchestra. He called me up to have a chat about the work and I went down to his office at Massey Hall—he asked me some questions and I knew that he knew my piece, he'd done his homework. We had a very interesting conversation, and in the course of it he said, "I don't understand Canadian music." That was the message that I got—that we have a Canadian music. He didn't understand it because it was different from what he usually did.

PS: How did growing up and living in Toronto affect you musically?

JW: I slowly realized that I should be responding to the sounds of my environment, and my environment included the sounds of North American jazz. It also included certain subjects that influenced my music as a composer for CBC drama during wartime. I wrote over a hundred scores that had to do with the war effort of course, but I also remember a series called *The White Empire*. I was in the air force for a couple of years and when I came home I had this commission, for a thirteen-week series about explorers who ventured into the Canadian North, and what happened to them. I had done some research into the music of the Inuit and found a collection that was made by the government. I was fascinated by that material and so I worked motifs from that research into my thirteen scores.

At the end of the series, the CBC director of drama was very interested in the music and suggested I make a concert piece out of some of the background music. They gave me about ten days to do it, and I did, calling it *Edge of the World*. It has a feeling of stillness, and coldness, and was a product of my experience in my environment that had to do with the history of this country. There was another series I did called *Our Canada*. The National Film Board was created in 1939 while we were at war, and they needed composers, artists, and writers. I was commissioned to do a number of film scores. The first arts project was the story of Tom Thomson called *West Wind*, and I wrote the music for it based on his famous painting. I had become involved in my country. I owe this to a number of factors—I owe it to the CBC. I owe it to the National Film Board. I owe it to the influence of our painters and writers.

However, when I was interested in Arnold Schoenberg's twelve-tone method, I felt after a while that his music was basically extending the culture of his own country. He was really connected to Beethoven and Brahms, and I realized that this was not my rhythm. I was influenced by the composers of that time, but Schoenberg's rhythm was not the rhythm of my environment at all. That's when I began to try to merge a new technique with the influence of my environment.

PS: And the influence was jazz?

JW: Yes. I loved the music of the thirties—swing. That never left me. If you look at my work for bassoon and strings, *Divertimento No. 3* (written in 1959), you'll notice the headings of the movements are called "Moderate Swing," "Slow Swing," then "Fast Swing." That's when the rhythm of North America or Canada took over my music.

PS: It must have been a difficult task to involve the European method of pitch and a North American feel for rhythm.

JW: Exactly, but I gradually came to it. Remember, I was brought up with European music, especially programme music, which was a strong influence on me: Liszt, Tchaikovsky, and Beethoven of course.

PS: Was it important for you when people such as Stravinsky came to Toronto?

JW: It was very important for me. Stravinsky permeated my thinking when I was a graduate student at Eastman. I did a paper on *The Rite of Spring* and that really turned me around. It was the sense of sonority and his powerful rhythm, but how would I reconcile them? The other music that I responded to was the music of Alban Berg. I listened to a recording of his *Lyric Suite* and was very moved by the emotion of it. How could I merge these two opposing sonorities, these opposing temperaments?

The thirties were still the period of the Neoclassic, but the Neoclassic was a combination of some new sounds poured into old bottles. We wrote sonatas and rondos, and we still wrote pieces called symphonies, but we hadn't found a new form for the new sounds. Then Copland came on the scene. Here was the music that seemed to be distinctively American. A lot of music coming out of the thirties at that time in the USA was based in American folk music, because they had discovered their own music. Collections were being published and I got hold of some. There was a great similarity between the western music or the folk music coming out of the small communities in the USA and the same kind of music in Canada. The thing about Copland was the clarity of his orchestration. His music was a filtering of the Stravinsky orchestration, simplified as well as clarified. And so Copland became a strong influence on me as well, eventually, and he became interested in jazz. When Duke Ellington first came to play Massey Hall, I was there. When George Gershwin turned up with his orchestra and was soloist in his *Concerto in F* and his *Rhapsody in Blue*, I was there.

Eventually all these things came together and I discovered the rhythm of my environment. You hear it in my music and you hear it in those choral works that I wrote, such as *Hockey Night in Canada*, and others in which I use common speech. When I became interested in music theatre, I would write my own text. I found my own way to choose words and phrases that articulate well.

PS: How did your career develop?

JW: I had a very slow development because composition was not taught at the University of Toronto. I was on my own. I had only had one year as a student of a composer and that was Bernard Rogers at Eastman. That was it. I'm almost a self-made composer. I simply learned from other composers. I would say that it was a slow career. I think it took me longer as a composer.

PS: Wasn't that the reality of the time?

JW: No, that was me. For example, Jean Coulthard was a contemporary. She travelled abroad and managed to get lessons with about eight or nine different composers like Darius Milhaud, Vaughan Williams, and Bartók. I had none of that. I couldn't afford to travel. I think the generation of composers after me developed much earlier than I did, and developed their craft much earlier than I did.

PS: So you've seen things flourish in the creative work?

JW: Yes. I tell you, generations of composers that grew up in this country—from the sixties, eighties and today—reveal a fine craft. And they've written many fine works that deserve more than just a premiere. There's also evidence of composers being influenced by other Canadian composers. I would say that Jean Papineau-Couture influenced a number of composers in Quebec. Certainly, Murray Schafer has had an influence on other composers, and Harry Somers as well. There's a tradition developing in the creative work and I want to see more of a performance tradition develop. I think Canadians have to realize that we do have a tradition. It's not very long, but we have it, and it's there for us.

NOTE

1. Based on their interpretation of the CBC-commissioned Arts and Culture Survey in 2005, the CBC has dismantled much of its art and classical music programming. *Two New Hours* was cancelled in March 2007 and, since that time, the CBC has demonstrated waning commitment to recording and broadcasting live performances of works by Canadian composers, basing its broadcast materials on commercial CD recordings. Despite national protests from CBC listeners, Canadian composers, and performers, the national public broadcaster has continued to move away from its mandate, as specified in the Broadcasting Act of 1991, and towards pop-oriented commercial music programming. Subsequent to the cancellation of *Two New Hours*, the CBC also disbanded the CBC Vancouver Radio Orchestra, which was the only radio orchestra remaining in North America.

Udo Kasemets

COMPOSER Udo Kasemets was born in Tallinn, Estonia, in 1919 and emigrated to Toronto, which he still calls home, in 1957. On September 5, 2002, Kasemets and friends presented a free concert at the Music Gallery entitled Cage 90: Memoryechoes of John Cage, *featuring Kasemets's ninety-minute Cage-inspired piece and recordings of Cage reading from his diaries. The following night, Cage's film* One11 *was shown. Additionally, late October brought a Music Gallery-hosted Cage mini-festival, with James Tenney playing the* Sonatas and Interludes *(October 24), Stephen Clarke playing Cage and Tenney (October 26), and Udo Kasemets and Malcolm Goldstein playing and discussing Cage on October 27. Given Kasemets's focus on Cage's work, it was necessary to learn more.*

UK: When Cage died (August 12, 1992), it was a real blow for me and many others. I made a promise that every year I would do something where I zero in on his music, perform it, and talk about it. In the fifties, when things came together in Cage's mind with *4'33"* and the *Music of Changes*, and his work with chance procedures and the *I Ching* came to fruition, it began to resonate with people quite a bit. In the sixties, there was an opening in people's thinking—scientifically and socially. The Beatles came around, drugs, the pill, feminism, everything came into being, and this was a wonderful, wonderful time for theatre, poetry, visual arts, dance, and art and technology. Even in academic circles, there was interest in all of these things. People were keen, and there was tremendous hope. The sad thing about it all is that in the eighties came a counter-movement that eliminated many of these dynamics, settling back into a very traditional way of doing and thinking. Society was moving in a marketplace direction, which affected everything. The whole marketplace and globalization situation suffocated the cultural situation, and creativity. What developed from the sixties and seventies was cut off. There were artificial links with the past, but not organic connections.

PS: So with these concerts you're trying to establish organic links?

UK: Yes. September 5 is the birthdate of Cage, so that would be his ninetieth birthday. We'll perform a piece using exclusively Cage's music as source material, and using different kinds of organizational systems, including the *I Ching* and other statistical systems to draw the material for a ninety-minute long piece. The backbone of the musical organization is that famous span of time *4'33"*, which has been from the beginning a very misunderstood work. People thought it was a hoax, but it really was a profound statement that introduces what always has been the basis of all music—that music happens only in the listener's ear and mind. The listener is always the actual music maker.

PS: How does someone who has never touched a piano...?

UK: That's exactly the point.

PS: It has to be heard to exist? If a tree falls in the forest?

UK: If there is no listener, there is no sound. Sound happens only as a collaboration between action/energy (natural or mechanical) and the ear. When I am talking, I'm setting vibrations of air molecules into action. There is no sound in my vocal chords, there are only vibrations started here, which move through the air. There is no sound in the air, only vibrations of all kinds. Our ear responds to a certain amount of these vibrations. The ear does a clear analysis of sound—the frequencies and characteristics—it's a wonderful, complex system. The brain then takes stock of all of this, and differentiates, and recognizes sounds it likes, and decides what is music. Cage felt that music is something indefinable. The response is always very personal and individual, as is the decision of what is and isn't music.

PS: Do you find the word "music" to be confining?

UK: Unfortunately, it has become a compartment. For people today, music is recordings, it's something to have and own—that's what they listen to and that is music. Art music isn't even mentioned in today's context, whereas one hundred years ago, *that* was the music. The definition of music shifts in the culture, yet ultimately there is no fixed definition for it. In this world, where there is so much information coming in, we have to make our own decisions, and become more concentrated on what is *really* what... on questioning.

At the beginning of the twentieth century, we were at the end of the development of tonal music. Like Schoenberg, Stravinsky, and Bartók, Cage questioned all of these materials/approaches, but later, and with different results. In 1967 he wrote in his *Diary: How to Improve the World (You Will Only Make Matters Worse)*, "In music it was hopeless to think in terms of the old structure (tonality), to do things following old methods (counterpoint, harmony), to use the old materials (orchestral instruments). We started from scratch: sound, silence, time, activity." He asked himself what is what, how do we begin again, and what can we do with whatever it is? He took very strong stock of one element in particular—time. After he studied with Schoenberg, he came to the conclusion that the primary element of music is time. Sounds and time. Pitches are secondary. The tonic-dominant relationship that had been central to Western musical thought for hundreds of years was only one possibility. The old context was gone, and something new had to be found. What do I do now, how do I think about it now? It was a tremendous mind opening, because everything was possible. But you have to find a disciplined way to deal with it, because there is so much of it, too much of it.

PS: Too much of what?

UK: Possibility. Everything is available, so you have to find ways to order things. That's ultimately how we deal with everything, to find some kind of centre. That is what Cage was establishing with the statement that was his piece 4'33"—all sounds are there, always, but the music is what you make out of these sounds. Now, in the twenty-first century, we would like people to be keen about hearing, and listening, to be still curious about sound. Due to technology, including the recording industry and radio, we have been taken into a sound environment that is totally different from the one in which all the other musics came into being in earlier times.

PS: So much is available to us, but if we listen closely to the world we live in at this point, in this place, we hear the hum of electricity, we hear airplanes, car horns, and telephones. How do we stay open to Cage's thoughts on sound when pollution is our primary sound material?

UK: Many years ago, I was sitting with him in a coffee shop near the airport. At this time, there was very much an awareness of sound pollution—Murray Schafer was writing books about these types of things, and I was very much tuned into this way of thinking...
(we pause as a garbage truck drives past, stops, and backs up, the reverse beeps and engine sounds drowning out our conversation)...naturally, the air traffic noise was also something being considered. A jet came in with a big roar, and Cage said, "Doesn't that sound beautiful?" I switched away from thinking that it was an airplane, that it was noise pollution, and listened to the sound complex created by the engines, which was indeed very beautiful.

PS: I have a hard time with that. I can hear sound objectively... but if we remove the association... the reality that too much of it is pollution, then we're passive, we're accepting its place.

UK: We are very much on the same wavelength, thinking about today's life, talking about the horrors of war today, the politics, atrocities, and corporate corruption, how some technology has taken things out of order. The beauty and the beast, they are always living together—this is what life is about, and we cannot put it into clear compartments. Unfortunately, you have to understand that it is all here, and ask yourself how you can live, how you can divorce yourself from all that is negative, threatening, and oppressive. What can I do to contribute to this chaos? That is where the act of creation and art comes in. It grows out of Cage's ideas, taking stock of what it is, who you are, and what you can do. I've always wanted to change the whole world, but at age eighty-two I've finally given up on that, understanding that I can't change the whole world. However, I can live up to the idea of what I think I can be as a human being, and what, as a human being, I can give other people to help them a little bit.

PS: Before the tape was running, you mentioned how Cage was a good example of a whole person, interested in the whole world.

UK: When he started keeping his diaries, he was very much inspired by Buckminster Fuller, whose ideas were very comprehensive, thinking about the totality and the individual parts, but always in the framework of the whole. Fuller's book *Spaceship Earth* was a new way of thinking. We started to see earth as a total planet only after the Sputnik went into space and pictures were taken from outside Earth's atmosphere. You are a young person, and you know the world as it is now, perceived as a total planet in the cosmos. We never thought of it this way—we were on this ground, here, and the change in viewing things outside of our small perspective was a tremendous culture shock. It was a completely new insight into the world. The visions change, and did so a great deal in the twentieth century. Einstein also gave a tremendous change in thinking about time and space, and people came out with ideas on quantum mechanics. Cage plugged into many of these ideas, particularly Fuller's ideas on how the world works and how humanity could make it workable in every sense. In his idealism, he was projecting all kinds of possibilities of human networks, using all available resources, making them re-workable so we wouldn't be exploiting things, but always "making more with less."

PS: So Cage's approach is not passive at all.

UK: No, no, no. It's not an acceptance of negativity; it's coming to understand what it *really* is, and how things work. Some of nature works in very aggressive ways that are not conducive to our everyday patterns, like the current floods in Europe, tornadoes, and so on. By understanding it, not trying to fight it, and learning how to live with these forces, we can use them to our advantage. It's very analytical, and this is what he wants. He wants us to think. When you stop questioning, then things go wrong. So, with music, it's not just something you buy at HMV—that is only a very small portion of it.

Pierre Boulez

BORN in Montbrison, Loire, France in 1925, Pierre Boulez currently lives in
Paris. Since bursting onto the international scene at the end of the Second World
War, Boulez has remained an influential and controversial figure in contemporary
music. Initially taking Schoenberg's dodecaphonic (twelve-tone) methods to the
extreme by systematizing all parameters of music composition, he became an icon
of technical severity. His additional concentration on conducting the music of
Berg, Schoenberg, and Webern did nothing to dispel this reputation—not that he
was trying to. While continuing to develop as a composer and conductor during
his self-imposed exile from France, Boulez authored volumes of polemical essays
and analyses, defining his time with both clarity and uncompromising personality. Since then, he has been music director of the New York Philharmonic, founder
of IRCAM (Centre Georges Pompidou, Paris), leader of the impeccable Ensemble

InterContemporain, and principal guest conductor of the Chicago Symphony. Having spent substantial time myself composing at IRCAM, I'm doubly aware of his achievements, legacy, and demand for the highest artistic level. As I prepared to speak with him prior to his arrival in Toronto to receive the prestigious Glenn Gould Prize (November 24, 2002), it became apparent that many of my questions concerned the dualities and dichotomies in his thoughts and activities, the interconnected and inspiring tensions that continue to make him an intriguing composer.

PS: Your analysis of music invariably informs your interpretations as a conductor. How does your work as a conductor influence your composing?

PB: In two ways. First, I learned the practicalities of instrumental playing directly. It gave me the opportunity to use instrumental possibilities much better than before because once you know something, you can dare more. As a result, I did not write any more "absurdities." I wrote difficult but possible music, with efficiency. Second, it was very influential in my way of conceiving the way music is perceived. Many things you *think* seem obvious are not obvious at all. Sometimes there is a very big difference between what you think and what you perceive. For me, conducting was very important in the way that I could study, especially when rehearsing. I could study the perception of not only my music, but also music of other composers. You get to know very quickly the differences between speculation and perception.

PS: Do you focus your conducting on works that open up new compositional terrain for you?

PB: I prefer to conduct things that are close to me, not only by the feeling, but also in their conception. There is no point in conducting pieces that don't interest me, either for the composer, or myself.

PS: I'm interested in your relation to the past. You've stated that you don't like explicit references to the past.

PB: I don't like to be *buried* in the past. I once made the comparison that the past should be as the *phoenix*. It should burn every day, and be reborn every day. If you are always only in *your* library, and think only of the things that are in your library, you are the example of a culture that is dying, because you do not dare to forget. One of the main privileges of being a composer is certainly to *have* knowledge, but also to *forget* this knowledge, and not to be totally squeezed by the past. The past is necessary, because it has been part of your education—you can't really just ignore it, but as I have said before, you should be auto-didactic by will, and not by chance.

PS: How does that reconcile with the fact that you expend a great deal of energy performing and maintaining selected repertoire from the past?

PB: Many of the works I played thirty or forty years ago were not performed in concerts at that time. I thought it was my duty and my privilege also, to make these pieces totally part of the repertoire. When I first conducted the *Variations* by Webern, or Berg's *Three Pieces, Opus 6*, they were practically unknown to most of the orchestras. Also, in 1945-46, when I was young, in Paris I had heard the music I liked, the music I loved, performed so badly and without any kind of profession-alism. People had no idea of the style, about how to communicate with these works, and there was a discrepancy between what you read and what you heard. I wanted to be satisfied with the performances, and to make the distance between reading and hearing as small as possible.

PS: More generally, do you think that the maintenance of past music is a hindrance to the development of music today?

PB: No. You can perform music of the past if you are not just a *specialist* of some period. You have specialists in Baroque music, specialists in Romantic music, specialists in opera, in Italian opera, and so on and so forth. I find specialism terribly distressing, because they are compart-ments in musical life. I like specialists only for surgery and medicine *(laughter)*, but not specialists in music.

PS: How do your influences resonate in your music?

PB: Well, I think I have absorbed quite a lot, but I go to the bottom of things, I'm not stylistically influenced at all. Maybe in my very first works, when I was twenty, twenty-one years old. At twenty-two, I developed a personal style, without really looking for that, but expressing *myself*, and finding the technical means for it.

PS: Would you say you've absorbed the *mechanism* rather than the *surface*?

PB: Not the mechanism exactly, but the *reason*. Why, for example, are the last Beethoven quartets conceived as they are? To go to the bottom, not only of the style, but the reasons *why* you are so fascinated by something. You can never explain it totally. There is always a kind of mystery, and *Gott seitdank* that it does exist.

PS: You identify the period between 1950 and 1954 as the one in which you took serial procedures to the extreme, followed by the development of a much more organic approach. How did the strictness of the method coincide with your imagination? Did you find it confining, or liberating?

PB: It was at the same time confining *and* liberating. Looking at Schoenberg's method, which was preoccupied only with pitches, I thought (especially given the influence of Messiaen and his rhythmic procedures) "Why not try to make everything under the same control and order?" At this moment, it was called *pointillistic*, because we were dealing with point after point after point, and the reunion of point. After a while, I was bored, because you can't only work with separated notes, you can't always only work with number *one*. It wasn't enough for me, and once I had taken the consequences of serialism as far as that, I was aware that anarchy produced practically the same results. It proved the absurdity of the extreme logic, which is equivalent to the absurdity of no logic at all. That was the turning point.

PS: What changed after that?

PB: With *Le marteau sans maître*, I began to work with musical objects that I could describe freely. I admired Webern for all his strict canonic writing, but also J. S. Bach. Bach also wrote very strictly, but not only—he had another dimension, a kind of free writing. For me, that became absolutely necessary, a type of contrast between *obligatto* writing and totally free writing, under a certain harmonic control. Also, Schoenberg's neoclassic serial music lacks the necessity of a harmonic language. There was no harmonic law.

PS: So you became interested in harmonic *progressions*, rather than just chords.

PB: Yes. I was interested in developing a harmonic language, and I must say this was the influence of Messiaen. He was very much preoccupied with harmonic language and consequence. I realized I had to focus on the harmonic. Conducting also helped me in this case, because I learned that counterpoint is not something you perceive quickly. On the contrary, the harmonic combinations you hear instantly, even if you can't analyze it. Even without analysis, you can perceive harmony very clearly.

PS: In a letter to John Cage, you wrote, "The entire drama of music is the conflict between the rational and the irrational." Could you elaborate on this?

PB: What I tried to find was a rational point of departure, because you cannot work by just improvising, you have to have a linguistic base, some laws, even if they are flexible. Once you have this, you must be open to what *happens*, so you're not constantly obliged to have a series of logical consequences. Sometimes there are *accidents*, you want to write something that comes to you independently—maybe you've read, or heard something. You have to accept that, and have the possibility of introducing the accidents into your logic. The logic will be partly and locally destroyed, but it will reconstitute itself. This is a kind of organic development that allows things to happen, in a different way than you have conceived them. For me, it's extremely important to have a language that is open at any moment, and not completely closed.

Going back to *Le marteau sans maître,* when I began to apply this approach, I worked with musical objects; for example, chords, which functioned vertically or horizontally. I would combine them in different orders according to the harmonic impression I sought to give. I was free to have any kind of order, any kind of rhythm, which gives you a totally different melodic line from the same *object*, which is *described* in different ways.

PS: How would you define intuition?

PB: Intuition is the door open to any accidents, to anything that comes to you at the last minute. In *Derives II,* for instance, which I've just finished, there are some moments where I decided I must have a sort of static development. I thought of that long ahead of time, when it would come in the structure of the piece, but I discovered at the last moment a satisfying way of dealing with it. I didn't foresee how to fill this section; it was conceived in the process of composing.

PS: Would you agree that you created the opportunity for that door to be opened by the rational procedures in advance of it?

PB: Yes. I'm looking at a very abstract process, and I find the geometrical solutions, which I progressively destroy, using these geometries to invent things that are not at all geometrical. In this way, I've learned a lot from Paul Klee. In his lessons at the Bauhaus (1921–31), he gave geometric *études*—do something with a circle and a line, for instance. He derives from that a theoretical point of view that he takes so far that finally it becomes poetry, after which the geometrical problem is totally forgotten. That process is very dear to my heart.

PS: I'd like to talk about the idea of a "work in progress." There is a trajectory for a composition, which for you is seldom singular, or has a clearly defined conclusion. In this sense, your works often have very complex genealogies. How would you describe these forms, and how do you develop a piece over a long period of time?

PB: We spoke already of an organic process, and it's really like that also, because sometimes I write something, and after a period of time realize there is more to do with it. It can take many years. I wrote *Le Visage nuptial* in 1946, for two ondes Martenots,[1] piano, percussion, and voice. In 1952-53, I thought that the work was not big enough for the René Char poem (*Fureur et mystère*), so I rewrote it for orchestra, women's choir, and two soloists. Having performed it in Cologne (1957), I wasn't satisfied at all. There were deficiencies—technical and musical problems from the orchestrational point of view—because it was my first big work for orchestra and choir. In some places, it wasn't *amplified* for orchestra, but simply transcribed. I knew I couldn't stand that forever, but I had no time to give to the piece then. Much later, in 1985-86, I began to work on it again, reconsidering the orchestration, and the way of *amplifying* the ideas of the original work. You find the trajectory of the first version, not *changed*, but *amplified*. It took forty years. It was underground for a while—I didn't think of it exclusively, but it was constantly in my mind, and now this work is finished. It's not always such a long process. *Dérives* was originally a short work written while I was teaching at the *College de France*. It was concerned with periodicity in music, but was too compact. Ten years later, I felt I needed to do more with it, and I finished it last winter. It was absolutely necessary to rethink this work, because the problem was there, and it was not completely resolved.

PS: You've given the visual analogy of spirals, and mazes, labyrinths to describe your process.

PB: Absolutely. It reminds me of a short novel by Kafka, called *The Burrow* (1923), which is a perfect image of what I think as a composer.

PS: Are there any other literary precedents for your way of working with open forms?

PB: Yes, there are two precedents, in French literature at least. The Montaigne *Essays*, because it was the only book he wrote and he added and he added all his life, and also *La Recherche du Temps Perdu*, by Proust.

I had a critical edition, which contained many sketches, and it's very interesting to see the initial intentions, even the length, and how it developed and developed. It was not only by extension, but how he placed some sections from the beginning at the end, and so on. Some anecdotes relating to a certain character are later attributed to a completely different character. It's interesting to see how he manipulates things, and amplifies those that are not in the initial project. At first, it's a novel in the usual sense, but ultimately, it becomes a reflection about art and how a novel is conceived, what a book is. He says a marvellous thing—that a book is made by the reader—and for me, the work is really finished by the person who listens to it.

PS: What attracts you to North American culture?

PB: Initially, New York was kind of a dream city. In France, during the war, we were between walls, and borders were impassable. We began to travel very slowly, in part because of the money, but also the visas required. The possibilities were difficult, and all were close by, like Switzerland, and Germany, but it took until I was twenty-seven. In 1952, I made my first trip to North America, with Jean-Louis Barrault's theatre company (Renaud-Barrault, Théâtre Marigny). We went to Montreal, Quebec City, and then New York. I already knew Cage, so I had a big thirst for knowing what they did there. Through Cage, I learned a lot, especially of the painters. I met de Kooning and Pollock, and saw how vital and lively the life in New York was. Since that moment, when I received this shock, I have always been eager to go back to the United States, where I also had connection with people in Los Angeles—with Stravinsky, Robert Craft, and Lawrence Morton. These were islands, where I was very well acquainted, and it was fresh air for someone coming from Europe.

PS: You've conducted and written for the world's best orchestras, and in doing so are no doubt intimately familiar with the problems some are having. It's a complicated situation. What do you think are the sources of the problem, and how do you think it can be resolved to create a more beneficial condition for the art form, composers, and listeners?

PB: One of the problems is that in the States, there are no subsidies, and everything depends on the money made at the box office, and sponsorship. As I told them a long time ago in New York, there is also a lack of flexibility. You have four rehearsals and four performances, eight sessions a week—it's totally codified. If you are under this kind of inflexible order, the life becomes fixed, and frozen. This type of frozen programming and attitude is detrimental to the orchestras. In New York, I split the orchestra into two groups, one of seventy, the other of thirty-five or forty. Then you have quite a different repertoire, and you can do quite a lot of things. In the non-subscription concerts, you could do interesting programs, confronting different periods and styles, older and new. We had quite a lot of success, with a very young audience that was enthusiastic about the music on these programs. You should be able to offer it to the audience that would like that, and more of the museum programs for different audiences. The problem is how to organize it, because you have the union system, the subscription system, and the composers and the performers. To adjust these requirements all together is extremely difficult—there is a basic conflict.

PS: Was the formation of the Ensemble InterContemporain a response to this dilemma?

PB: Yes, certainly, because we are, by definition, flexible. We have subscriptions, but it is varied. We also organize different sizes of concerts, some devoted to concerts of first performances by composers who are unknown. But we give a week of rehearsals to these concerts, as much as we give to known composers. Concerts of works we give by Berio, Ligeti, or Stockhausen can fill a thousand seat hall two times. It's a matter of confidence. Audiences know that our concerts are well prepared, and chosen with care. We want to give composers the best chance to be heard, and that we can do, because we organize our concerts *with* the calendar, and not to a kind of *guillotine* of dates. It's more difficult to organize, but that's a question of professionalism. We have thirty-one musicians, and all are familiar to us, so it's easier to organize. Everybody feels more personally responsible. They are also all on the same salary, and they are all considered soloists, so there is no hierarchy, which also makes it easier for us. That was my first wish when I was asked to organize the group, in 1975-76.

PS: We've dealt nicely with your thoughts on the past. What does the future hold for your composing? I read that you were considering writing an opera.

PB: Well… *(laughs),* you know, I've been considering that for fifteen years, so it's not a new idea at all, but in that time, two of the people I considered working with have died. I began to work with Jean Genet, but he was very slow to work with at that time, and he died shortly thereafter. The second time I tried, that was with Heiner Müller—Daniel Barenboim was interested in an opera for Chicago. I began to discuss it with Müller, and he began to work, but if you look at his posthumous records, there are some sketches and mentions of it, but nothing was done, and he died of the same illness as Genet. So… right now, I'm trying not to have a third person die *(laughter).*

PS: How do you think this point in time is unique for composers and artists?

PB: In my generation, we were a group of five composers: Nono and Ligeti were born in 1923, myself and Berio in 1925, and Stockhausen in 1928. We were a group who knew each other very early, and we had the same *ideal.* Progressively we dispersed, because that's normal and everyone has their own path, although we communicated. We were defined by the period, but at the same time, we defined the period we were living in. This group had two Italians, one Hungarian, one French, and one German, so we were very different from each other, yet we had the desire to meet and know each other, which explains the success of Darmstadt—it was a meeting place. I find there's a more difficult situation now than it was in our time. Now, I have the impression that although you can travel much easier and more quickly, there is a kind of fear of identity. For instance, when I am in the States the words "American Music" are important. For me, whether it is European or American doesn't matter at all, provided it is interesting. It's difficult for me to understand some points of view these days, this kind of protection of identity that we didn't have in our time. It's not an opening at all, for me at least, but I have this perspective because of my generation. Ultimately, I think it's unique any time you have a composer who has a personality.

NOTE

1. The ondes Martenot (translation: "waves Martenot") is an electronic musical instrument invented by Maurice Martenot.

Barbara Croall

ODAWA composer Barbara Croall was born in 1966 on Manitoulin Island, Ontario. She studied at the University of Toronto and spent a number of years living/studying in Munich. She now lives outside of Toronto in Milton, Ontario. While we were both resident composers with the TSO between 1998 and 2000, due to our various globetrottings and compositional work there was little time for Barbara Croall and me to talk and share thoughts on music. Since October 2002 was such a busy month for Croall—what with ERGO Projects' Finnish Exchange (she is Artistic Director of the group) and the performance of her violin concerto by the Esprit Orchestra—it was the ideal time to discuss her work more formally and to explore the impulses that shape and colour it.

PS: You're primarily a composer—what prompted you to form an ensemble of your own?

BC: There's a need for composers to work more closely with performers. While I was studying in Munich I worked closely with performers, and due to this contact, started to realize the importance of not just writing pieces for them to play, but trying things out, to be more process oriented. I wanted to make this possibility more available to composers. Some composers prefer to write the piece in isolation, but others really like the idea of being more engaged with the performers, and consulting with them, because it gives them ideas. Every composer is different, and with this type of ensemble, they have that freedom. It's important that they don't feel like they have to fit into any particular slot or box.

PS: What is the difference between your ensemble and other professional groups that you work with?

BC: I think that it's the individuals. There is a special kind of dynamic that comes about when people interact in this way. There are aesthetic differences also. For example, ERGO doesn't have a particular aesthetic approach or bias. We've commissioned and performed many different kinds of composers. Some groups, in order to be more focussed, tend to work with a specific genre or aesthetic—I can understand that too, but I want to promote an openness and acceptance of different viewpoints. You can still program concerts *thematically*, and have many different perspectives on an idea. I like the balance. ERGO focusses mainly on exchange projects, and that's how we began. In 1999, I was offered to put together a concert for the AdeVant Garde festival in Munich, so I asked some Canadian and German composers if they would like to write pieces. We then brought the German composers over to Canada and played their music. It's always a transatlantic relationship, where we present a program there and something similar to it here. I'm finding that more and more I would prefer to work on the international exchanges, because I feel that there still aren't enough opportunities like this for composers from Canada, to have their music played abroad, to have a different audience, a different reaction to their music, in another context. I also think being wayward teaches us things about ourselves, and we grow from that experience of going outside our own environs and peer groups.

PS: What led you to study in Germany?

BC: I identified more with some of the late nineteenth and early twentieth century composers there. I very much admired the music of Mahler and a lot of the Austro-Germanic orchestration, and wanted to learn more about it by going there, attending concerts and talking with musicians and composers who come from that lineage. I liked the way Berg, Mahler, Schoenberg and Webern had a sense of freedom to their music, to how they were using pitch. I know that sounds contradictory to how serialism came about from the twelve-tone method, but there was a very special twilight period in their music. Those transitional periods in musical and artistic history fascinate me, because that's where the germinating seeds of whole epochs emerge. There was also a freedom of expression. There weren't really any rules to what they were doing, and that was very exciting. As soon as the rules are laid down, it's already theorized. I know that Schoenberg and Boulez spoke of freedom through imposed rules, but there is an intuitive sense to the German expressionist period that I related to. The listener is inundated with a complexity of intertwined emotions. It's really music that comes from the gut.

PS: What's your balance of "gut" and technique?

BC: I ask myself that a lot. Technique is how we keep our bodies in shape. It's keeping your faculties in shape to do anything you want, so the potential is practically endless. I think in concepts of line, sonority, and timing. If one considers technique in broader terms, then you're not limited to Common Practice Period harmony and counterpoint.

PS: Your own education is slightly unconventional, isn't it?

BC: Yes, in that I did my graduate studies in Germany. Many of my colleagues had been thoroughly schooled in the three Bs (Bach, Beethoven, and Brahms), and felt a great deal of pressure to uphold those traditions. They had a very strong theoretical basis from that perspective.

PS: Do you feel that any related kinds of pressures exist for Canadian composers?

BC: The pressure for Canadian composers is sometimes the one to identify ourselves as composers of "Canadian" music. What is Canadian music? We come from so many different cultural backgrounds.

PS: How would you define that for yourself?

BC: My mother is Native (Odawa) and my father was Scottish. Having that as my first contact had a lot of bearing on my identity. I went to my first powwow when I was five, and since that age, I've spent many summers of my life on Manitoulin Island. It is another home for me, where I am around my relations, where I really come from. I identify with the land, going back many centuries. The ceremonies and social gatherings were also very important.

PS: One could argue that all people feel that way about where they are from. How does your ancestry specifically influence your music?

BC: It's mostly in the creative process. Even though I've had some degree of Western training, which I respect and have found enriching, I come from a very strongly intuitive way of thinking and creating. I don't think methodically about what I'm doing, I realize it after the piece is done. I don't try to think about pre-planning the music— maybe I'm already doing it without consciously realizing it, but if I feel something, I write it down. I don't think about theorizing or intel-lectualizing it, I go with the flow. For Aboriginal people, when you create something, it first comes from the heart, from your feelings and emotions. I'm not saying that artists from other cultures don't think that way, but many already have theoretical systems that create a see-sawing tension between intuition and theory. Songs that I learned and sang were not written down, it was all oral tradition; same with prayers and stories, it's all through listening. Writing things down came later, when there was a need to document these things, and the documentation was done by first contact Europeans.

PS: Is improvisation a large part of your compositional activity?

BC: It was initially, when I started composing. I would sit down with an instrument and work by ear, and that was my link to composing, because once I'd learned a piece by ear, I started making up my own. Now that I've learned a great deal about notation, I like to write things down, to be specific, but I'm currently getting closer to how I played music in my childhood, with more improvisation.

PS: What is intuition to you?

BC: Intuition is an immediacy of transferring your feelings into the outcome, whereas theory is thinking through all those stages and figuring out a method.

PS: Is there an aspect of Odawa music that intuitively comes through in yours?

BC: It comes from the relationship of singing to the drum. When I drum and sing myself, I listen closely, meditatively, to the sound of the drum, its resonance and spectrum. When I start from that, I pick up ideas and impulses. In the process of recording/writing down what nature is, you can learn a lot about what a sound is, what the rhythm is, the pitches. I listen to all of the sounds made by a singer or instrumentalist, which includes those that are sometimes thought of as imperfections—the grit, the dirt that is often camouflaged. It's all of those in-between sounds that I find most interesting, especially breath, the breath of a singer, the suggestion of breath that you hear when a bow lightly strikes a stringed instrument. These colourations, almost too complex to categorize as pitch-based, are more interesting than the pure sounds of tempered pitch. I find Messiaen to be particularly interesting, because he had complex theory in his music, yet his way of thinking was very intuitive, through his connection to birdsong. It's a contradiction, because he wrote them down, and when you write things down you change them, but there was an attempt to document and tabulate his experiences, as in the *Catalogue des Oiseaux*.

PS: What is the relation between your Odawa heritage and your Western art music studies?

BC: From my Western training, I'm able to write things down, and from listening to the drum and singing since an early age, I've learned to listen deeply, meditatively.

PS: But the influence of European music on you is deeper than simply notation.

BC: Possibly. When I studied with Art Levine, we studied Gregorian chant, and trace it back further. Chant is popularly known as the basis of Western music, but interesting enough, the lineage that it comes from is Asian and African cultures. You can hear bits and pieces of that in parts of the Roman Catholic liturgy. You hear traces of Byzantine chant, turns of melody, and so on.

PS: Do your influences coalesce, or are they juxtaposed?

BC: It's both. There are conflicts, but creative things can come about from conflict too, as we both know. I also see the similarities, interestingly enough. Western culture is such a complex intermingling of different things, going back thousands of years. So is Native North American culture, if you look at it closely through the history of trade between various nations. The histories are different though. European history wasn't interrupted in the way that indigenous cultures were.

James Rolfe

BORN in Ottawa in 1961, composer James Rolfe studied at the University of Toronto and at Princeton University. He now lives in Toronto with his wife, composer Juliet Palmer. Having completed the acclaimed opera Beatrice Chancy, Rolfe made the unusual decision of writing another one. Charlotte is based on the life story of Jewish-German painter Charlotte Salomon (born 1917), who painted her autobiography in an incredible sequence of eight hundred paintings prior to her death at Auschwitz. One of the main ideas of the opera is how and why she came to paint her life story at such a young age, and with such insight. Queen of Puddings Music Theatre presented a workshop performance on December 20, 2002, and the fully staged version began June 7, 2003, at Harbourfront Centre in Toronto. As we are prone to do, James Rolfe and I met and had a lengthy discussion on music, the difference being that this time a tape recorder was on, and his music was the focus.

PS: Over the past decade, you've written a great deal of vocal music. What is your attraction to the voice?

JR: I like challenges. Contemporary art and culture have gone in a direction that has left the voice behind. Composers of our generation were taught techniques and attitudes that don't really lend themselves to the voice—singers can't nail rhythms or pitches in the same way a pianist can. There are limitations and constraints, and I've always liked working within limitations. Of course, there is the timeworn cliché that the voice embodies human emotion and warmth. You can't really get around that, and it's something that modern ironic art and culture doesn't deal with very well. I want to deal with it. I want to surprise myself.

PS: Is your interest in singing also because of the narrative potential?

JR: Not just narrative, but the actual sound of the words, and their imagery. It turns abstraction on its ear, and becomes a very messy and complicated thing, with many layers of meaning: the sound of the words themselves, their meaning, and the narrative behind them. I've always been attracted to simple means that can be layered until they add up to something quite complex, almost chaotic.

PS: Is that what led you to write an opera?

JR: Yes. I'm still shocked sometimes to find myself writing opera, because it's not a medium I feel natural in, yet it's natural to tell stories, and to sing, and that's essentially what opera is.

PS: At the same time, it's nineteenth century television, and the genre most susceptible to the hangover of elitism in music-making.

JR: Sure. It takes a lot of money—you could see it that way. Along with that, there's a lot of weird institutional politics, and many fingers in the pie, but you could also say that about film. No one accuses film of being elitist.

PS: When you started writing your first opera, that wasn't part of your thinking. Having written one, what made you decide to do it again?

JR: (*Laughs*) Good question. What I like about it is writing blindly from the beginning to the end, and arriving at a place much different from where you thought you would end up. It keeps things interesting. I like compositional situations where I start at the beginning and go moment by moment by moment, following primarily the logic of the moment, and seeing where I end up.

PS: But don't you know where the opera is going because of the story you're telling?

JR: To some extent, but there are many ways of telling the same story. The process forces you to deal with problems you might otherwise avoid—things that have baggage. For example, in the case of *Charlotte*, one point the story forced me to work with Beethoven's *Ode to Joy*, which has been much used and abused. Opera forces you to confront and be accountable for the actions of the characters, to portray them vividly and not shy away from their blemishes. You can't cop out, you have to be the advocate of the characters, with compassion and accuracy, and say what has happened. I admire Mozart in this way, because he's able to portray different characters so truthfully. He subtly colours each character through technical means such as range, harmonic language, and ornamentation. It still sounds unquestionably like Mozart, but he is generous enough to allow his characters flesh and blood, and individuality.

PS: While you like it that opera takes you outside of yourself and into new musical problems, I'm not certain that breaking new ground is at the forefront of your thinking.

JR: Ultimately, there's nothing new under the sun. A lot of pieces that sounded stylistically old have been put down, and I find that ridiculous. I'm currently very interested in the music of Kurt Weill, who suffered because of this. He wrote a lot of music that was accessible, and it was *very* well done. It's one thing to look at the newness of *style*, and another to look at the newness of what it's actually *doing*. Stravinsky is a good example of this—he changed suits many times in his career. *Beatrice Chancy* superficially sounds like a step backwards stylistically, compared to what I've written before, but it's new for me.

PS: There are two perspectives—new to you, and new with reference to the body of music that exists. The former may be a way into the latter.

JR: It's a circular thing, not linear, especially now, because we have access to almost every period of music at once. It's difficult to define conservative and radical now, because they're less meaningful terms than they used to be. It used to be a clear-cut polemical divide—you're either with us or against us, *à la* George W. Bush, but that thinking isn't applicable when there are so many simultaneous perspectives.

PS: What is convention in music?

JR: It's always been said that music is more conservative than other arts, and that change comes more slowly in music, but I think the word convention is *key* when thinking about that. Music is an art form that operates with conventions passed down through oral history. Playing an instrument is taught verbally, with physical examples. The mechanism of teaching is by word of mouth, and there is a conservatism about that kind of tradition. Things will evolve more slowly as a result, or there may be more resistance to change, by the nature of the means of transmission. Ultimately, music comes from other music. There is also a stronger weight of convention because you're dealing with performers as well as composers. Getting back to opera, singers have the largest set of constraints. You want to write things that will make them sound good, not like idiots. The attitude of the radicals would be, "We'll let the singers catch up with us," which is the same as Beethoven saying, "What do I care about your lousy fiddle when the spirit takes me?" That is the modern attitude in music. The question is how you deal with the physical constraints of the performance medium, which forces you to deal with convention.

PS: On the surface, your music is... I'll say more *conservative* than a decade ago, but underneath, it's actually much more subversive.

JR: I think the best example for me is Schubert. He was an incredibly revolutionary composer in the way that you're describing. On the surface he's conservative, because it's a clear form, very classically balanced, and with beautiful melodies, but he stretches his tonal structures over such a long period of time, and subtly does such weird things to the harmony that he actually undermines tonality earlier than he is given credit for. In a way, he's the predecessor to both Wagner and Morton Feldman. He's an example of a composer that is "acceptable," because everyone loves Schubert, there is always an attractive surface that is palatable to conservative listeners. It's beautiful music, but underneath that, there's a formal strangeness and alienation about the material that is quite modern, quite beyond how it appears. Another composer who comes to mind is Bernstein. He's by no means my favourite composer, but I respect the fact that he wrote pieces that were appropriate to the occasion. *West Side Story* is a great musical, appropriate to its venue. Kurt Weill also wrote music appropriate to Berlin in the thirties, and then changed his style to adapt to New York in the forties. He was really lambasted for that. Virgil Thomson thought it was a criminal waste of talent, but I think Weill was a hero to do that. He doesn't care about the surface, the style in which it appears. He's secure enough as a composer and not afraid to adapt his language at the risk of seeming lower class. I think that behind all this there's an unspoken issue of *class*, one that we "high-brow, high-class" composers often pretend doesn't exist. It's simply a snob versus slob issue, and I didn't become a composer to conform to other people's expectations of what I should write.

PS: So why don't you call your operas "musicals"?

JR: I don't care if they're called musicals or operas. It's largely funding agencies, marketers, and producers who have the problem. In my mind, these distinctions are crippling for a creative artist. If they think they have to behave, and not do certain things, it's depressing.

PS: An extension of this thinking is that you're as likely to quote Grandmaster Flash, Jimi Hendrix, or the Day-Glo Abortions as you are Bach or Beethoven.

JR: I tend to write music that comes from whatever's in my head. Currently, there are lots of nursery rhymes and kid's songs in my head. It's great having a little child around, because she brings in all sorts of unlikely music and books. Just as certain types of minimalism can be very complex, it's also the case with some of these "simple" songs.

PS: How did this broad spectrum of music come to be absorbed into your music?

JR: It's taken me a long time to realize this, but I think being a composer is not about being consistent. In Western culture, there is the expectation of consistent behaviour, probably stemming from our religious roots. Christianity evolved through central control. There is no pope of music—Boulez probably wanted to be, but he failed, and a good thing, too. You really have to be stubborn to continue on as a composer. If it weren't a totally free field, to do what you see fit, I don't think I'd bother. But freedom is also a very difficult thing to deal with. I said that I like to work within constraints, but I like to choose those constraints, and not work within other people's constraints. In that sense, I'm a New World composer, as opposed to a European composer.

PS: Much of what we've been talking about is in relation to other music, and how it's something with which you confront yourself compositionally. Where are *you* in that? We've defined the sources you absorb, but not the core.

JR: I guess what's coming across is that I'm a relativist. That can be a bit of a euphemism—moral relativism is something a lot of right-wing American commentators go nuts about, but yes, I think everything is relative, and I'm relative to my environment. I don't just mean Canadian music now, I mean the whole past and present, of music and music across the world. There's an evolving web, and I'm situated somewhere in it. I might hear a new piece of music that will really alter my environment, or I might write a piece that does the same. I don't have a strong sense of *needing* a core, or *needing* a polemical viewpoint and firm aesthetic grounding. I don't have a fixed point of view, and I don't want one.

John Beckwith

COMPOSER *John Beckwith was born in Victoria in 1927 and has lived in Toronto since 1945, except for a number of years in Paris, where he studied with Nadia Boulanger. He taught at the University of Toronto between 1952 and 1990, serving a term as dean between 1970 and 1977. Beckwith is one of Canada's great musical resources. Through his vast knowledge of the repertoire, dedication to teaching, and ongoing activity as a composer and researcher, he has been an important influence on many Canadian composers. On March 7, 8, 14, and 15, 2003, the University of Toronto Opera Division performed his fourth opera Taptoo! at the MacMillan Theatre in Toronto. In addition, discussions of the work took place in Walter Hall and at the Munk Centre. Taptoo (from tattoo), is a signal sounded on a drum or bugle to summon soldiers or sailors to their quarters at night, and a display of military exercises offered as an evening's entertainment. The term is also derived from the Middle Dutch* tappe *(a spigot or tap), and* toe *(to shut), or shutting the tap after last call. I caught up with him just days before he left on a short trip to do research on his former teacher, Alberto Guerrero, and talked about the opera and musical life in Canada.*

PS: What prompted you to begin your critical writing on music?

JB: I think it's just the way I am. I was always somewhat interested in writing and composing too. In my youth, I did a lot of journalistic work—sometimes it was just for fun, while in university you're obliged to keep up with knowledge being produced. You feel the urge to share some of the things you find out and I think that led to doing critical and research writing. It's a counterpart to my work in composition.

PS: You've also said though that it's in part because no one else is doing it.

JB: I recently read an interview in which the composer Denys Bouliane said, *"Où sont les musicologues?"* I've often felt the same way, not only with musicologists but also with music theorists. They are very happy to produce an elaborate analysis of a piece by Elliott Carter or to write some musicological investigation about music in Finland, but the number of well-trained, professional people in those disciplines who have applied themselves to our music in Canada is very few.

PS: Why do think that is?

JB: I think we've got a certain pride in literature and in visual art and film, but, gosh, in music, the creative music—when I think of it, the repertoire just comes and goes. People don't seem to think of it naturally. Your question is a wonderful question—I don't know why... certainly in the United States now it's become an important thing to do for performers, opera companies, orchestras and so on, to keep doing not just new works, but works from the American repertoire. That habit just hasn't impinged on Canadians to any very great extent, though one can think of exceptions. I have always preached that there is a Canadian repertoire and it goes back further than most people are aware. One of the things I dislike is when people call this a young country. It's not a young country! In hardly any sense is it a young country, but certainly not in terms of our culture. I set some words by Marc Lescarbot (*Les Premiers hivernements*) that were written in Canada, in what is now Canada, even before Shakespeare wrote *The Tempest*.

PS: What drew you to make so many arrangements of Canadian folk music?

JB: In the eighties, I worked with Lawrence Cherney in a summer series called "Music at Sharon." One of the things we liked to feature there was earlier Canadian music. First of all, because the Sharon temple itself is a spectacular example of early Canadian architecture— a unique example—it seemed interesting to try to associate that venue with things that had been earlier in the Canadian repertoire. We did a lot. I count up what I did and think it comes to about two hundred, mostly short pieces.

PS: Would you call this an example of nationalism in your work?

JB: Oh, yes. I guess that's the simplest way to refer to it. Some people feel it's not the politically correct way to look at today's world—now, we're thinking more of globalization, and sharing between different national communities. Some years ago, Professor Robin Mathews, from the University of Ottawa, made the comment that in Canada to think internationally is to ignore Canada. I think that's true. Canada isn't part of that international community in many people's eyes. That's one of the reasons why we don't have a sense of our repertoire that other countries have. So I don't mind for my generation and for younger generations to think nationally instead of internationally. Maybe we can focus more on our own production in music—make it better known.

PS: What was your intention in focussing on Canadian subjects in narrative and text-based works?

JB: It seemed to me a more natural way to handle a project, to think about how it relates to me and my environment, and my upbringing in this part of the world. On several occasions, I've been offered a commission for a vocal work and I've gone to a Canadian writer and said "Will you write me something?" Then I can maybe influence the writer, and the writer can influence me directly.

PS: I used the term nationalism, but we really haven't defined it. In Canada, theoretically it's also eclecticism and multiculturalism.

JB: That's true. Thirty or thirty-five years ago, the CBC asked me to do some arrangements of Canadian songs, some for Donald Bill and some for Maureen Forester. I think they thought I was going to do songs in French and English—I did songs for Maureen Forester in five languages and they were all Canadian, they were all songs originating on Canadian soil. I think that's a part of our national point of view and it's going to come out in our music, if we're honest. But nationalism can turn into bigotry and you don't want that, of course. Referring to culture, nationalism is the openness to what is peculiar, what habits, and what experiences are peculiar to this country, peculiar to us. There's a rich field of possibility to draw upon.

PS: Canadian culture and subjects are an important part of *Taptoo!*, aren't they?

JB: All the operas that I've done with James Reaney have had a close connection with Canadian life because in his writing in general, that's his theme. Not just Canadian life, but Southwestern Ontario life. In the case of *Taptoo!*, we're dealing with the founding of Toronto in 1793, the events leading up to that, and those that followed. It covers maybe a thirty-year span in short scenes, moving not just realistically, but rather fantastically sometimes, trying to pick up on what motivated people at that time, how Canadians established themselves as distinct from Americans.

Canadians found that the American form of democracy was too broad. To say that you must have freedom in everything was a little bit too sweeping. They wanted democracy, but in defined terms. Another example is Simcoe, who is a central character in the opera. He was very anti-slavery—that didn't hit the Americans until fifty years after. Canadians also established much more of a connection to British parliamentary forms, which made the people continue to call them-selves colonists for the whole of the nineteenth century. We've gotten past that now. I think that except for those who are monarchists, it's not operative for most of us, not the way it was even in my youth, but certainly throughout the nineteenth century.

PS: How would you describe your musical approach to setting this histor-ical story?

JB: When I was contacted to see if I would like to write *Taptoo!*, I hadn't thought of writing another opera. When I read it, first of all I thought it was an awfully good piece, and secondly I recognized that, when he writes a libretto, Reaney always thinks about what role music is going to play—he doesn't just write a play and say "Here, set this to music." He had already researched a lot of the musical component for *Taptoo!*, the military music of the fort, the drum and bugle music, the dances, the church music such as it was, books of hymns they sang from, the patriotic music, and so on. I had the option either to look at those pieces, at those elements in his script and use contemporaneous tunes, or to think up tunes of my own in the same vein. I decided to use quotations, in fact about twenty different tunes from the late eighteenth and early nineteenth centuries, some of them very well known, like "Hail Columbia!" I chose music that had its own character and would lend flavour to the story. I call it a documentary ballad opera because that's the way ballad operas worked in the eighteenth century. They consisted of current popular tunes that were laced together with a story, and with contemporary musical emphasis. It's a combination of eighteenth and nineteenth century popular and sacred tunes, treated in a late-twentieth century way.

PS: How do you treat the tunes? Is the material layered in the work?

JB: Yes. Sometimes you draw from that a kind of *leitmotif* that signifies a certain mood or a certain character and then it comes up some time later in the opera in the same situation. I think you just deke in and out of those quotations thinking that since it's a sung piece you don't want to have it so farfetched that these characters would sing in this way. I've always felt that about opera, that I don't want it to be so artificial, by having a very complicated *a capella*, twelve-tone music for people who are supposed to be farmers. I hope it makes it believable that these people would sing their thoughts in this way. You have to accept the artificial feature that people do sing their thoughts, but I like to feel, yes, that these people would sing their thoughts in this way. Partly it is to distinguish things like that class, but also to distinguish where they are in history.

PS: Has this always been your approach, or is it something that developed through each of your four operas?

JB: Around the time that I either was working on or had just finished my first opera, I wrote a little article for what is now called *Opera Canada Magazine*. It was a slightly different title then. I made the point that if you're going to see Canadian opera (there weren't that many at that time), if you're going to see Canadian operas, they're not going to be the same as European operas. I guess I had that sense always that coming from here you're going to use some of the conventions, some of the forms of operas, but that it's going to come out differently.

PS: *Taptoo!* also relates to another Canadian historical opera, doesn't it?

JB: It's the prequel to Harry Somer's opera *Serenette* for which Reaney also wrote the libretto. The initial thought was that *Serenette*, *Taptoo!*, and then a third opera would be like a Canadian historical operatic trilogy. It's looks unlikely that the third opera is going to happen because in the nineties funding changed so drastically, and the timing for my piece was wrong, so, we waited.

PS: Ironically, it was first performed in the US, wasn't it?

JB: Actually, they did three evenings of it, and the first evening was an invited performance at Potsdam, New York. For an opera that many people will think is very anti-American, it was interesting that the first actual stage performance took place there. I don't think it's all that anti-American, but it does show that the Canadian point of view is different from the American point of view.

PS: It seems to me that there was suddenly a great deal more interest in opera across the board from so many composers.

JB: It's an exciting medium. In my own case, I was an opera buff from about the age of ten or eleven. I used to listen every Saturday to the Met radio broadcasts and I learned all the standard operas at that time and loved it. I heard some great singers. It seemed to me naturally something that I was ambitious to do. But I think now it's more of a sense, particularly in North America, that there's a repertoire of work that one can respect. And the opera companies that were very diffident to do new operas—like the Metropolitan in New York—they did a new American opera about once a decade. Now they're doing new American operas practically every season, and that affects the whole scene. You get the idea that composers are turning their attention that way, then other composers want to do the same. I think it's exciting, and some of the new pieces coming along are interesting.

PS: You once said that you felt "encouraged that young people want to go into this career even if it seems hopeless." Do you still feel that way, and what did you mean?

JB: Your music doesn't get played very much if you're Canadian. If you want it to be played, you have to do the marketing yourself, and who has the time or the money? I looked at the front page of the *Globe and Mail* this morning and I thought "Wouldn't it be lovely to have *Harry Potter*'s agent"? The book isn't even out yet, and six months before it's on the front page, three columns wide. That isn't quality; it's agentry. I've nothing against a Harry Potter book, but it's not quality that does that, it's buzz, it's the machine. Canadian composition: you can't do that. You don't have the resources. And then, there's a thing that in general music gets listened to less and less. If it gets performed it's a great thing, but it gets listened to less and less. There's less sense of taking music as an entity that you can give yourself to for a period of time, having a beginning and a middle and an end.

PS: A real experience of it...

JB: An experience you give yourself to. It was a question on one of the opera quiz broadcasts some time ago: "What do you like to do while you're listening to the opera broadcast"? You were supposed to answer, "I like to open my mail, I like to iron my shirt, I like to dig in the garden," whatever, but my answer is that I like to listen to the opera. That's what I was thinking of when I was saying it's hopeless—but hopeless is overstating it, because I'm not without hope.

Yannick Plamondon
& Marc Couroux

YANNICK PLAMONDON was born in 1970 in St-Gabriel-de-Valcartier, Quebec. He spent a brief time in Toronto, and currently lives in Quebec City. He was the 2003 recipient of the Jules Leger Prize. Marc Couroux was born in 1970, raised in Montreal, and teaches at York University in Toronto. On March 30, 2003, The Esprit Orchestra premiered Plamondon's thirty-minute piano concerto, Stark, Utter, Forego played by piano soloist Marc Couroux. Couroux is known for his improvisations, brilliant technique, distinctive piano sound, and strong views on the concert "ritual." Stark, Utter, Forego is a three-part work with substantial live instrumental amplification, as well as an unusual formal approach—in the third section, the soloist plays overtop a previously recorded, computer-fragmented, ordered, and transformed rendition of the solo parts. The "sampled" materials *function as both recapitulation and cadenza. The special collaborative nature of the piece spawned the idea of speaking with these friends together.*

PS: Yannick, I think of you as a composer of question marks, and Marc as a philosopher and multi-tasker. Why on earth did you write a piano concerto, and Marc, what on earth are you doing playing one?

YP: It's always important for me to start with something people know. Having an orchestra, a soloist, a concert hall, a premiere. Everybody's sitting in the hall, knowing in advance what is going to happen— known quantities. From this point, I'm working *with* and *against* expectations.

PS: What's the role of pianist?

YP: He's the focal point, the hero. Everything comes from the piano part. It's the relation of the individual and society, me and Marc, music and society, me and the music—a network. The concerto is one of the only forms that permits this type of exploration.

MC: The premise is very simple. If you're going to write a concerto, it's going to be heard in a concert hall, in the usual context we associate with orchestral music. You have to do something about it as a composer. You can't just receive this tradition and write a piece that's already consigned to the dustbin of history. You have two choices— either say, "Screw that, I'm not going to write music for concert musicians anymore," and start a garage band, or you can use the tools you have as a composer, your training, and the background you've grown up in. But it's stuck with the ritual that comes with it, so you have to try and slip something in there. Yannick is perfectly suited to this task of destabilizing the tradition because he works with materials that *come* from the tradition. He plays with these materials. The listener will be receiving these romantic paradigms—the hero versus the mass—but they'll be screwed around with, they'll be in different orders, formally altered, stretched out, or compressed. As a listener, you're taking this material in, but you're taking it in a kind of strange way.

YP: I agree. My problem is that I like the resources, the instruments of concert music, so I have to go where they are. Society tells me that these resources are in concert halls. My point is to work with these resources where they are now, expecting that one day the intentions of my music will lead these resources and these institutions to change the context. For me, the change of context comes with the creation of events. I hope the audience will say this music forces them to think about going further with the idea of concerts and people sitting in the audience in the classical way. My perspective is to work progressively. I want to push them, where the impetus for changing the space is coming from the work, and not from political pressures.

PS: What do you want to change it to?

YP: For me it's very difficult to say precisely what it should be. But it's clear that it's not stimulating enough the way it is right now.

MC: There's always been a kind of dissonance between what I feel is the sort of the energy centre of music today and the fact that the music we make today is stuck in a concert hall, stuck in a museum. It doesn't really live any more. I totally agree with Glenn Gould—this idea of having a pianist climb Mount Everest at every show is kind of a dumb thing because people are just spectators, watching, waiting for you to fail. It's a very bad dialectic, where people aren't really listening, they're there because they feel this is the cultural thing to do. The notion of a cultural alibi is a potent one. Too often, people go to hear Brahms symphonies because they want to *appear* cultured.

PS: Seems like people aren't going to hear Brahms symphonies anymore though.

MC: In Montreal they are. My attitude hasn't been to ditch the process entirely because I think there is still some valuable work we can do. I could say I'm not going to do concerts anymore and stay in the recording studio, or I could do concerts in different venues, with technology, and interact differently with the audience. I'm increasingly moving in that direction myself, but the other option you can adopt is to change it from inside. What Yannick is saying is true—you have to work with the code that you have, with the audience that you have. You're stuck in a museum. What do you do? Well, what are the codes of this museum? They are nineteenth century codes, and the gestures are as well. So, you have to know them, and to know your audience. You have to know who's going there, what music they're used to hearing, and play with those as a composer. Yannick does that. Someone else who does that is Jean Lesage. He knows the code.

PS: Yannick has said that the social-political field of the concert is still caught in the seventeenth century solution, sustained by nineteenth century artists, for a twenty-first century public.

YP: People still have in their minds a very clear idea of what they're going to hear at a concert. There's no imagination. You go to it, you know where it is, it happens, it's finished, you're out—the same thing you experienced many times before. I don't feel comfortable with that, probably from my own cultural background. I'm not coming from a classical music background, but I like these sounds, in themselves and for themselves. My problem is that these resources are institutionally captured by some very old, defined institutions. I don't want to just fight with them by saying they're bullshit.

MC: You'll never win. That's the point.

YP: As a composer, if you really want your message to come across and you want the formal recombinations of your music to strike the listener in a particular way—in a way that will make them see another world—you have to take into consideration what their references are. Each time, I want the piece to force them to go further.

PS: And yourself too...

YP: Yes, it's the same thing. It's a voyage, an exploration. That's what I really like about Marc. He was a very huge inspiration for me from the beginning. I remember he inspired me with this idea of creating a kind of experimental tradition here in Canada, which is not very well known. For me experimentation is not something that happens at the level of syntax; it happens with the form or constraint of the work.

MC: You have resources—musicians, and the public with their very specific relationship to the concert music codes. That's material that you can work with as a composer. Will it really have a huge impact? I don't know. But you have to try. I'm not saying let's burn the concert halls, but let's find a way to reinvent them from the inside.

YP: To burn the concert hall and put everything in the trash—that's a very sixties way of doing things. When I heard Esprit Orchestra before, I thought, "Man, there's not enough strings in that band." With this commission, I wanted a full investigation of the orchestra, to redesign the sound of the orchestra. I don't want to take these economical constraints—basically, Esprit Orchestra doesn't have all these strings because they don't have the money to pay them. So, I decided not to ask for sixteen more string players, but said, "Give me a sound engineer, good microphones, and some time to redesign by amplifying." From that point, I'm starting to change the situation. I don't want to write a piece for six violins with all these woodwinds and try to imagine a sound design according to these economical constraints. It's total nonsense for me.

PS: I think you're using the economic constraint as part of your idea, but turning it back on itself.

YP: To my advantage, yes. That's my job. I need to choose the constraints and when I cannot control them, try and turn them. But I don't want them to be a limitation for my sound imagination.

MC: With technology as mediator as well. That's an important idea in our time.

PS: The meeting point for you two is one of critical exchange. It's not possible in the conventional sense to say "Marc, you're the pianist and Yannick is the composer." It's problematic, but it's also refreshing.

MC: It's not the traditional hierarchy where the composer writes a piece in his little room in an ivory tower and gives it to the performer who learns it assiduously, plays it, and throws it away. It's an exchange; it always is and always has been.

PS: You also improvise a great deal and lean towards composition more and more, so you're exceptional in that regard.

MC: Unfortunately. I wish I wasn't. But, Yannick is one of those people who have always been open to the notion that this ritual we're involved in is something that needs to change. When we met many, many years ago, there was already a sensation of dissatisfaction from both of us, that there's something wrong.

YP: The discussions that Marc and I have together have changed my vision of music. He's not just the interpreter, or just the performer in the piece. He's more than that.

PS: A collaborator?

YP: Yes, it's a team play. What I like in Marc is that you have to create the piano sound and to embody it into the score. He's going to read it and recreate these colours according to the syntax and the deep nature of the matter you're dealing with.

MC: From the outset, as a performer you have to question your relationship with sound, purely the act of producing music on the piano. You can't play this piece if you don't do that. It's kind of the same way you approach Xenakis. You can't play it with a Chopin attitude. You can't possibly do that. You have to ask, "Where does the next sound happen? How do these things go together?"

PS: At the same time, your knowledge of Marc's very distinct sound must have influenced you.

YP: Yes.

MC: So, in a way, it *is* kind of something I'm imposing on him.

PS: But in an inspirational way.

YP: Exactly. There are some other important aesthetic elements too. I talk a lot about Robert Smithson and the idea of entropy. From the renaissance, most of the metaphors art critics used were related to biology. You have the cell that grows, you have development. Smithson chose another kind of metaphor for art critique—geological or mineralogical metaphors, starting with the idea of entropy. If you look at some of my recent pieces, you will see that most of the time, the material is revealed in its final stage of evolution. All of the things that come afterward are losses of energy, deconstruction, and entropy, flattening out. It works that way in this piano concerto—I'm bringing elements that are at the peak of their growth. Nobody's going to see the progressive growth from the cell to adult object. Most of the time you have sudden transitions leading you to other, mature elements, until we get out of breath somewhere. At the end, we have these static (not circular) non-linear time designs.

MC: One thing that's always interested me about Yannick's music is that he uses material that's very tonal, very consonant, sometimes based on pop songs or other popular cultural references, and how the formal restructuring of these elements makes the music interesting. I think we often have this kind of black and white duality of modernist and postmodernist. You know, modern music is dissonant and all over the place and chaotic and incomprehensible. And postmodern music tries to play these very obtuse musically meaningful games, following a literary model. John Rea is good example of that. Yannick is taking material that is basically rock-bottom tonal material and playing with form in a way that reconceptualizes or reformats it in an interesting way. As a listener, you're perfectly capable of following this material. But at the same time, the way it progresses makes it very interesting.

He isn't calling on your knowledge of the musical literature or otherwise to try and get the meaning.

YP: They're not structural flags/landmarks. I don't expect any recognition of it. It's a recombination.

MC: It's not about creating local "Ahas!"; it's about creating one generalized question mark. The way you started off the interview, mentioning question mark, was a perfect metaphor for what Yannick does. He's leading you, taking what you know, the most basic, tonal classical music things, symbols—and combining them. You're able to follow the discourse and that takes you to interesting places that aren't the simple, usual postmodern thing. You're constantly drawn into the narrative by the nature of the material.

PS: Tell me about the amplification of the orchestra—its function and reason.

YP: I would like to have the largest amplification possible, so the volume is pushed as loud as possible, into the limits of feedback. It forces the performers to adjust the way that they're playing—if they play too loud, for example, it's going to sound so huge that they have to pull back. Everyone will be more sensitive. At the same time, the piano starts to be larger. It's hyper-sensitivity. You have crescendos written on all the parts, but no dynamics, so everybody has to adjust, and the conductor has to control all the sound.

PS: Why?

YP: It generates another space, a totally different scale.

PS: You're rearranging the hierarchy as well.

MC: It's an acoustic reconfiguration too, and a ritual reconfiguration, I guess. When you're making musicians hyper-aware of every gesture they're making and you're rethinking the relationship between the soloist and the orchestra and by definition the audience is getting amplified sound suddenly, you're shuffling around quite a few social elements.

YP: I would say perception.

MC: As a listener, you're not going to listen in the same way. Not only in terms of acoustically, because you're hearing amplified sounds— which is quite a different thing from acoustic sound—suddenly you're faced with the notion that there's this incredibly unbalanced thing going on onstage. There's a strange relationship and transfiguration, the energy that is coming out is quite different. Interaction on stage is quite a specific thing and when you start playing around with technology to change sound levels, to change the response pattern from a musician, you're changing the interactions between musicians, creating a hyper-awareness of your environment.

YP: Yes, yes, sure. There was a bet on this idea. We're going to see if it happens. We'll try it.

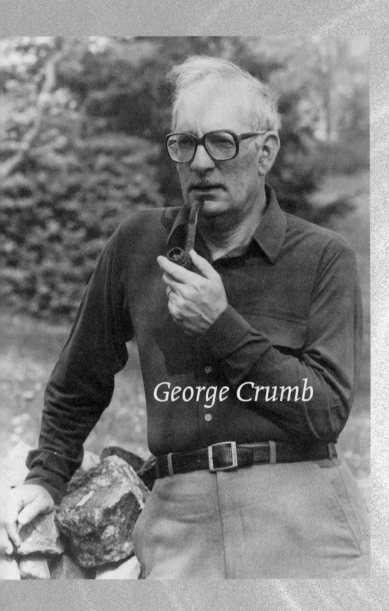

George Crumb

MARCH 2003

GEORGE CRUMB was born in Charleston, West Virginia, on October 24, 1929, the Black Thursday of the great stock market crash. Throughout his career, he has composed numerous mysterious, introverted, and distinctively orchestrated works that are part of the post-1950 musical canon, including his Ancient Voices of Children, Black Angels, Night of the Four Moons, and Vox Balaenae (Voice of the Whale), among others. On Sunday, April 13, 2003, New Music Concerts brought him to the Glenn Gould Studio in Toronto for a concert entitled "The Unknown Crumb." In an affiliated event, students of the Glenn Gould Professional School performed others of his works on Friday, April 11 at the Royal Conservatory. Since first learning about his concert, I looked forward to talking with this renegade American composer.

107

PS: You've written that "the truly magical and spiritual powers of music arise from deeper levels of our psyche, and that every composer, from his or her formative years, has acquired 'a natural acoustic' that remains in their ear for life." How did your sense of time and place, and your environment in the Appalachian river valley influence you as a composer?

GC: I was influenced by the particular acoustic of the Kanawha river valley in West Virginia. You would hear echoing effects from sounds that were across the river, and it had a kind of ricochet effect, because sound travels very well over water. I think this just became part of my hearing. My music is involved with echoing effects and this is precisely the acoustic of such a place. I love instruments that appear not to ever want to die out, like tam-tams and gongs—the sounds just keep reverberating. When I write for piano, usually the damper pedal is depressed, so the strings keep ringing almost to infinity. Of course, I was also influenced by composers like Debussy, whose music seems to reflect that same obsession with the slow decay of sounds and reverberation.

PS: Did your early musical experience and geography affect your unique sense of instrumental timbre as well?

GC: Well, I'm not sure really. I had a classical background because my parents were primarily classical musicians. To fill out the family budget, they would play occasional light music and the pop music of the day. My father would play in combos and he conducted a theatre orchestra in the days of silent film. Later, he also conducted a Masonic band, and a concert band—these were all the sounds I heard then— orchestral sounds, sounds of the band. I also heard a lot of chamber music in the house, played by our family. The radio was blanketed with a layer of the country music of that time, and I heard some folk music early on, as well as gospel music.

PS: I've always imagined you tinkering away in a laboratory, as a sound inventor, an instrument builder, although building with conventional instruments.

GC: I've known a lot of musicians, and I've gotten a lot from them. I've never really owned many percussion instruments—just a few that I happened to inherit. But I learn a lot from being around players. When I was writing *Black Angels* I worked out a good many of those very special extended string techniques myself. I play a minimal amount of viola, but enough to play around with the sound. I don't think I actually invented any instruments in the sense of Harry Partch, but I tend to dabble with instruments and to borrow instruments from non-Western cultures, in the tradition of people like John Cage. I've continued that, and maybe gone beyond Cage in a way, at least with regard to African instruments.

PS: Your pieces often carry with them reflections of other music or quotations or veiled references. Why do you quote other music?

GC: Philosophically, I think of all music as being one thing. I wrote that I was haunted by the thought that all the many musics of the world are coming together as one. Well, I think that's happened. The earliest music that I know is quite as contemporaneous as any very recent thing in my thinking. That also extends geographically—through time and through space—so that the instruments or the music of other cultures is a possible source for me as a composer, and the sources can be almost anything at all. Composers would find their own use for them, in just the way the contemporary Japanese composer would adapt Western instruments to their own thought.

PS: How has music from other cultures influenced your work?

GC: Certainly in the borrowing of instruments. I've used things like the sitar in my *Lux Aeterna*. I've used any number of African instruments, and so many oriental instruments. That's one level. Another way is maybe more aesthetic. The suspension of time that came into my music, probably its purest form is in certain Asian musics, where there is almost no sense of harmonic movement—it's so suspended.

PS: Given that your work references music from other cultures, and the late romantic, early twentieth century period, as well as containing material written exclusively by you, how do you maintain stylistic consistency? Is that important to you?

GC: The intention is to create an organic style in which all the elements are assimilated, so that the music projects not as a mishmash, but as a direct artistic statement. I think examples of similar things might be in Mahler's music, or in Debussy. Charles Ives combines things sometimes incredibly, like the jazz elements in *Central Park in the Dark*. You have opposite musics there. A composer like Béla Bartók uses all the technical systems, plus folk music, *and* the whole tradition of Western music. So, it's up to the composer to take all those elements and create a unified style. If the music doesn't project that way, then the composer fails. All the different things in the music are subservient to the expressive intent of the music.

PS: The composers you mentioned like Debussy, Mahler, Ives, and Bartók—you've referred to them as *anti-purist*, or composers with an anti-purist *approach*. What did you mean by that?

GC: I meant that they didn't reduce their technique, their system, or their aesthetic to one very narrow way of looking at things, like Anton Webern. Their music is open to diverse influences, almost contradictory things. The way Mahler uses klezmer in the *First Symphony*, or how he refers to Beethoven or Bach in the *Kindertotenlieder*. He uses Chinese poetry as a source of inspiration, and band sounds that aren't really converted into orchestral brass sounds. All those things become structural elements in his piece.

PS: How do you grapple with the contradictions of these materials?

GC: It intrigues me that those were the composers who were all grouped at the last turn of the century, and now again I think they've become more and more relevant because our age is typically like that, that influence is coming from everywhere. All the popular musics, the ethnic musics, the whole tradition of Western music, there are collisions all over the place. I really can't see any kind of a purist way of approaching music given the staggering array of various influences.

PS: When you're referring to other music, you're tapping into larger frameworks, of societies, belief systems, et cetera. Is this associativeness important to you?

GC: I think one has to reinvent it. I must say that there are two ways of dealing with other music—let's say in this case with respect to traditional folk music. One of the ways that just about everybody does is by making arrangements of it, as Aaron Copland did, decorating it somewhat. The other way interests me much more, and that's the way Charles Ives did it. He completely absorbed—the way Béla Bartók did—the *ethos* of the folk idiom into his musical bloodstream. The spirit, the genuine spirit of folk music, rather than just pitting it as some sort of genre/style that is easy to treat.

In this way, I'm looking forward to seeing how people in Toronto might react to the folk song settings *Unto the Hills*, because I'm doing another one of those. I've almost finished one that is involved with spirituals, and may even do a third set—(*laughing*) I've become a composer of American songbooks

PS: How did you work with the folk songs?

GC: These are treatments of tunes; it's not so literal-minded. People tell me that they came away from it knowing that it was still my own music, although I'm starting with materials that are borrowed. With this one, I really had in mind not a trained voice, but that particular genre of voice that one associates with folk music. It will be sung by my daughter, and she does that really well.

PS: Do you wish that the listener would tap into the context surrounding the music? That he/she would recognize the disparate origins?

GC: Yes, that's nice when it happens. Of course, I'm thinking of Stravinsky now and those early ballets, most of the thematic materials are Russian folk tunes. We don't recognize those particularly as folk music. Nor do we in the ones Tchaikovsky uses: themes of the *B-flat minor Piano Concerto* are folk tunes from the Ukraine. But nobody knows that, and we respond to them as interesting thematic ideas. Either one way or another, the music will have its effect, even if one doesn't realize the other connection that has existed in another life, so to speak, before it was incorporated.

PS: Do you remain aware of when quoted material stops and your own invented material begins?

GC: When I think of it consciously, I'm aware of when I'm quoting. But I usually cut in and out, like a film technique I could cut right at any point or I could cut out of it before a cadence or something. I feel completely free to distort a quotation in a hundred different ways. It's never a literal quotation in my music. Something is always changing. The timbre is different, or the instrumentation, or there is an overlay of some kind that has nothing to do with the original music. All kinds of things can happen. Much of all music is borrowed, whether subconsciously or consciously. There's probably only five to ten per cent of original thought in most composers' music.

PS: If we deconstruct our intuition and take it apart according to influence and its effect on us as composers.

GC: I believe that's true.

PS: Psychologically, your music has a duality that is always present, a polarity of light and dark, of life-affirming and deathly forces.

GC: There are opposites like that, yes. I've always liked music that had the quality of presenting opposites. Not only music, but also poetry, like Lorca's—so dark at times, and yet it can be joyous. I feel Mahler's music can be the same. It has qualities of irony that are reflected from this duality. It has an ironical cast too. To me, Mozart is one of the most ironical of all composers. His music is just loaded with undercurrents, the most innocuous little beginning of a piano sonata seems to run very deep psychologically. A lot of my music is vocal, and the text itself shows opposition of a kind. I'm trying to treat that musically, also with opposite types of things—to have the loudest and softest music side-by-side. I love contrasts of extreme register, contrasts of timbre, et cetera.

PS: Despite this polarity and plethora of sources informing your work, at the same time it's not contrapuntal music.

GC: I don't use counterpoint. I wrote my hundred Bach fugues when I was a student. I followed Schumann's advice and play a little *Well-Tempered Klavier* each day, and that's almost my favourite music, but I find no need for counterpoint. I guess I'm influenced by composers who never used it much—Debussy's almost has no counterpoint whatsoever. Asian music doesn't have counterpoint. They get along without it. How much counterpoint is there in Mussorgsky, or Chopin? It seems like the fringe people that were tremendously inventive in certain directions excluded counterpoint—they found other ways.

I think my music is so highly infused with timbral nuance that to lay that over contrapuntal lines would be overkill. Besides, I like open space and utter simplicity. I can never get my music simple enough. To me, even a two-part counterpoint defeats a sense of openness. I love it in other composers' styles, but I don't hear it myself.

PS: I noticed that the score to *Black Angels* was finished on Friday, March 13, 1970. This was the height of conflict in Vietnam, almost precisely thirty-three years ago. The piece was conceived as a parable on our troubled contemporary world. And, here we are, on March 18, about twenty-four hours away from...[1] Given the range of international influence in your music, I feel the need to consult with you in some way about this, to know what you think.

GC: This is a frightening moment in history. I don't like the way things have developed.

PS: What is the relation or *can* be the relation between music and politics?

GC: Normally, it's not such a close relation. I don't think it ever was. The modern thing called political music is really a very small item on the part of composers. If you think of the past, is Beethoven's *Eroica Symphony* a political work? It had Napoleon's name on it to start with, but it became much more universal. It's almost absurd to think of Napoleon in connection with *Eroica*, because it's a testament that goes way beyond politics. It applies to all ages. I guess *Survivor from Warsaw* of Schoenberg would be a modern example of a kind of political music. It's effective on a certain level I guess, but it diverges. It's just on the very edge of what music can accomplish. Music is more comfortable with very generalized themes. You make your reference in a program note or something, but the actual music can't become so terribly topical. It loses something.

PS: Yet at the same time, psychically it seems to be part of the repertoire of influences that you're working with.

GC: Oh yes, I agree that music will pick up resonances. In the contemporary world that is almost unavoidable—the tensions of a time, the aspirations of a time. Music maybe reflects the new astronomy in a sense. As for all the tension in the world right now, things go in cycles. Here we go again with what's really an unnecessary military adventure.

NOTE

1. On March 19, 2003, U.S. President George W. Bush declared war on Iraq.

Peter Hatch

MAY 2003

COMPOSER, *teacher, and festival organizer Peter Hatch was born in Toronto*
in 1957. He has lived in Waterloo, Ontario, and teaches composition at Wilfrid
Laurier University. I tend to meet up with other composers at their busiest, on the
cusp of large projects, and at the delicate point where their work makes the leap
from imagination to realization. These moments are special, and rich with poten-
tial. Such was the case with Hatch. When I talked to him, he was just gearing up
for a portrait concert with Montreal's Ensemble Kore, and preparing for the May
2003 release of his CD, Gathered Evidence, *on the Artifact label. As well, he was*
about to present one of Canada's most multifarious new music festivals, Open
Ears, of which he is artistic director (May 7–12, 2003, in Kitchener, Ontario, the
festival takes place every two years—www.openears.ca). Fortunately, we were able
to co-ordinate for an interview in between rehearsals.

PS: If I were... If I were to ask you about time... If I were to ask you about time in music...

PH: The psychological aspect of time—our experience of time—is endlessly fascinating. Our sense of personal experience in time, and then what's going on in clock time... it's quite amazing. Dealing with musical time, I don't think we know a lot about it. Any time you're working with duration and rhythm, in all the ways you can define rhythm, you're automatically working with time, but it gets complicated very quickly. There's the immediate moment, but then there's also anticipation, which is an experience of time, but not a present moment experience of time. It is, but it's concerning something that's about to happen. And then there's memory.

PS: If I were to repeat the same question, what would it be the second time?

PH: There's no such thing as exact repetition. It depends on how you look at it. If you look at it in terms of the fact of the question itself, then it is the exact same question, but in terms of the answer it would provoke, it's not. There's going to be a different nuance. It's then about memory, elaboration, and ornamentation. You could ask the same question exactly the same way, but in terms of the responses it will provoke, it's going to be different. Gertrude Stein was a master at understanding these kinds of things. In her writings, she provokes responses to those kinds of questions in a very immediate way. You can read operas of hers where she'll have Scene 3 preceding Scene 2. It puts out the question of sequence, and about the way you're experiencing things through time. It's not just repetition—she goes beyond that.

PS: What about rhyming and music?

PH: You can have a sense of varied nuance and repetition. Stein uses rhymes and puns and things like that to bring up different connotations of what she's saying, sometimes in very abrupt ways. This thing sounds like another, but it brings in a completely different sound world, and a completely different meaning. The Stein influence on my writing certainly is very real, but rhyming in music is a little more difficult to talk about.

PS: More generally, how do you approach the relationship between text and music, and the possible worlds of relation between them?

PH: I haven't done a lot with text setting in terms of the sung word.

Listeners divide into two types: those who are very aware of texts when they're being sung, and those who aren't. I'm in the latter category, for the most part. It's a way of listening, a way of attending to the music. On the other hand, the spoken word really thrusts the text into your face in a more direct way. It's a different kind of relationship.

PS: As a composer, do sentence structure and speech rhythm also interest you?

PH: Absolutely. If you're reading Stein—and she's the author whose texts I've set more than any other—for the most part the meaning that comes from her texts is not through the content so much as the form—the syntactical structure. She'll even do things that don't make sense in the normal manner of reading it, in a formal way. Those things carry huge amounts of meaning, whereas often the subject matter, the semantic meaning (which is also sometimes quite interesting) is often not the point.

PS: How do these ideas apply to your music?

PH: Sometimes it is kind of the opposite of theatre—I have a text interlude in the middle of a musical piece, instead of vice versa. The earliest example is a solo percussion piece I did called *When do they is not the same as why do they*. It was sort of an epiphany for me, in which I made a direct connection between Gertrude Stein's short story called "As a Wife has a Cow—A Love Story," and this percussion piece. The connection is between the rhythm of her text and the rhythm in the music—it's not a direct transcription, but a matter of transferring the formal syntactical structure into what I was working on.

PS: What about your interest in text as it applies to rap music?

PH: You know, I was doing/studying this kind of thing before rap really appeared, although I was aware of rap at the very earliest stages. There was a group in New York called the Last Poets that I discovered— they'd released an influential recording in 1970. They were basically street poets following up on the old bebop, and beat poets like Allen Ginsberg and Lawrence Ferlinghetti. But they were doing it out on the street with African percussion. A lot of their texts were very political. It's really early, early, rap.

PS: What do you like about it, and does it connect to your other, early twentieth century literary interests and their application to your music?

PH: I can't say that I've really investigated rap in a thorough way, but I've enjoyed it, and my students keep me up on what's interesting. I think my use of spoken text came more from the percussion piece I was talking about. At one point in the piece, I thought it would be neat for the percussionist to speak the text instead of playing. That was the first time that I employed text that way. It's also tied to my interest in instrumental theatre and expanding what performers do. With instrumental theatre, you have to be very careful about what you can ask of people and what their capabilities might be, but speaking is something that everybody does, and can relate to.

PS: Speaking in an instrumental piece is a tremendous disruption of the concert drama, isn't it?

PH: It can be. I love that kind of shock. That's the kind of thing I pursue in my music. That's the "Oh, wait a minute, where are we? What's going on here? I thought we were in a classical music concert."

PS: So you would do that to dislocate?

PH: It's really more to locate—to bring awareness to the moment. At that point in the piece, the audience's relationship to the player—and I suspect the player's relationship to the audience—changes dramatically, all of a sudden. It's gone from this known quantity of a solo percussionist doing his/her thing to this person who is speaking to you, and maybe conjuring up words from the world of theatre and so on. Hopefully it's shocking in a really nice way.

PS: What other elements of theatricality or unconventional musical practice have you incorporated?

PH: My opera *Ask Alice* is fully staged, but the score is two minutes long and is in two acts. Each act is about a minute long, but there's also an instruction in the score to repeat the opera five to eight times exactly. There are a lot of layers to this. The text is sung in a very traditional operatic setting. The words are attributed to Stein on her deathbed, said to her partner of many years, Alice Toklas. She said, "Alice, what is the answer?" There was a pause, and then she said, "In that case, what is the question?" The first act is the first line, and the second act is the second line. The first act is frenetic, and very, very intense, and the second act is a rebound off that. The exact repetition does a few things. First, it obviously is an homage to Stein and her love of repetition: "A rose is a rose is a rose." Second, it was intended to conjure up the idea of recurring nightmares. I think everyone has had the experience of a recurring nightmare, and it always seems to come back exactly the same way—at least it hits you the same way, but of course, the experience of it is differently nuanced. I've been quite amazed when the opera has been performed how it wasn't until the second or third repetition that some people even knew it was being repeated, that they figured it out... It is interesting what that says about our attendance to things and assumptions we make.

PS: Jung wrote that nightmares repeat until one recognizes their reason.

PH: There's also a cubist influence. I love the idea of multiple perceptions of the same object. People have said that about my music—it's as if you hold this thing up and slowly turn it. It was actually the English composer Christopher Fox who said, "It's like the twisting and turning of gathered evidence." The only time maybe I consciously tried to do that was years ago in a piece called *Blunt Music*. There were these units—six or seven of them—that simply get repeated over and over again, but each one is just in a slight variation. And sometimes, it goes back to the original one. So you get the idea of basic cells, but exactly what that cell is, is hard to define because it's a combination of all the variations. All of them together produce what that thing is. I also don't think it's any coincidence that cubism arose at the same time psychology was being more or less being invented. Freud was absolutely at the forefront, with the idea of looking at more subconscious perceptions as being valid or very real. Picasso wasn't necessarily out studying Freud, but it was definitely in the air.

PS: You once quoted from Stein's *Lectures in America* saying, "The business of art is to live in the actual present, and to completely express that actual present." How would you define the concept of actual present?

PH: That's very hard. When I discovered Stein years ago, it came at the same time I had an incredible epiphany, something that is still working its way through me. One of the things I was discovering was Joyce's concept of the epiphany, but also tied into it was an interest in Eastern philosophy and the idea of the present moment and the eternal now. I had just studied the first part of Heidegger's *Being and Time*, and the concept of *Dasein* (being there). I can almost picture the camping trip where they all came together at one point and hit me like a thunderbolt, in the way that Hollywood likes to depict the way these things hit us. Suddenly everything clicked and made sense. They all went together. The actual present to me is reflected in all of those kinds of things—a definite sense of the immediate and the present moment. Of course, Stein was after, more than anything, what she called the continuous now. That's something that I, both in my music and my life, am trying to pursue, that sense of always being in the moment, being there.

PS: What is the present tense of contemporary music today?

PH: We're in a very interesting time, where things are shooting off in all directions at once. I think there's a sense of openness right now. Multi-directionality and pluralism is really fascinating. I get the feeling that we're kind of between things right now, and I think it's a wonderful thing. There's nothing really settled about what's going on—there are things that are settled, but I'm not sure that they are the most interesting things going on. I align myself with the classical music tradition, as many of us do, and think the whole position of the composer within the classical music tradition is really at a turning point right now—for the better. Right now living composers are more or less invisible to the general public and the classical music world. There is an increasing visibility going on, which is pretty interesting, because at the same time what's going on is affected by many influences outside that tradition.

PS: Is that a specifically Canadian situation issue, or North American?

PH: Obviously, all of this stuff is at some level, international, but there are differences. We feel the American influences obviously very strongly, but at the same time, there is more of a tie to European traditions, especially in Quebec, but also across the rest of Canada. I think it really does make a difference that our general approach is multi-cultural as opposed to melting pot. We're a particularly interesting place in this whole spectrum.

PS: You've got your ear to the ground. You're aware of the street-level music making, as well as the conventionally considered classical music. How does this broad knowledge base affect you as artistic director of a major Canadian new music festival?

PH: Hopefully it's good. With the Open Ears festival, the basic idea is that anyone with open ears, with an openness, from any kind of background, can appreciate what's going on. As long as you're open, you can come and appreciate it. We can all say that, but I think Open Ears actually tries to push that idea to the forefront. We have pretty eclectic mixes of things, and aren't pigeonholed. There's quite a bit of cross-over, but always in the sense of considered listening. It's not about making a connection to a bigger audience, it's about looking at a wide spectrum of what's going, and playing what's interesting to listen to. I think the connecting thing is that they are considered listening. There are people coming from the background of rock and electronica and so on, who are listening well and coming up with quite interesting and sophisticated ideas, if you really sit down and listen to them. It's trying to break past preconceptions and say, "Look, this is interesting to listen to. Listen."

PS: Give me an example of the breadth of programming.

PH: My favourite is the Saturday night of the festival. At eight o'clock we're presenting the Kitchener-Waterloo Symphony, with Hans Zender's reworking of Schubert's *Die Winterreise*. What Zender has done is taken the Winterreise song cycle and orchestrated it, but it's more than orchestrated: there are large parts that just have the sung line in a normal sense; there are other parts where the singer is using "Sprechstimme," or spoken word. There are extended techniques in the ensemble, there's theatre involved. In a sense, you could call it a remix of Schubert. And immediately following that, we're presenting Paul Miller, or DJ Spooky, That Subliminal Kid, which is how he's best known. He's doing a remix of Pierre Boulez's *Pli selon pli*. Spooky is known mainly to the hip-hop or electronica crowd, yet he's investigated Xenakis and Boulez, and just had an installation based on the work of Marcel Duchamp. Those two concerts, in all aspects, from who these people are, what backgrounds they are, the spaces they're in, I think is an interesting juxtaposition. And then you get this connecting point in the idea of remix.

PS: We can identify the influence of popular culture on a lot of recent art music. Do you think there's any reciprocity to that influence?

PH: Yes, I think you can get people like Spooky, the electronica people, who are acknowledging the important things that were going on in the fifties, sixties, and seventies. There are remixes out of Pierre Henry, Steve Reich, and Verve label jazz musicians. You get Spooky doing installations based on Marcel Duchamp, or remixing Boulez. They grew up in this tradition of a more commercial approach, but there are people who are doing things that are not commercially driven. Also, these divisions are breaking down, and it's all getting harder to define in some ways. The whole *musique actuelle* scene in Montreal is a mix of jazz, rock, electroacoustics, classical... People like David Mott, François Houle, and the Montreal band Kappa all come from jazz-influenced backgrounds but it is often a stretch to call what they do jazz. Then there is electroacoustics versus electronica/DJ culture. Both sides are looking at each other very closely. Sometimes it's skepticism, sometimes with good results. It's all up in the air right now

PS: When you're spinning records, you're dealing with the past. When you're remixing Schubert, you're dealing with the past. What happens when every record has been scratched and spun, when everything has been referred to? Is there a finite point?

PH: I don't think so. It gets back to what we talked about earlier, where you hold that object up one more time, and it looks different. It will never be the same because the perceivers are always changing. Even if that sonic or visual object is the same, the perception of it never will be. If it does look the same, then the problem is with the perceiver.

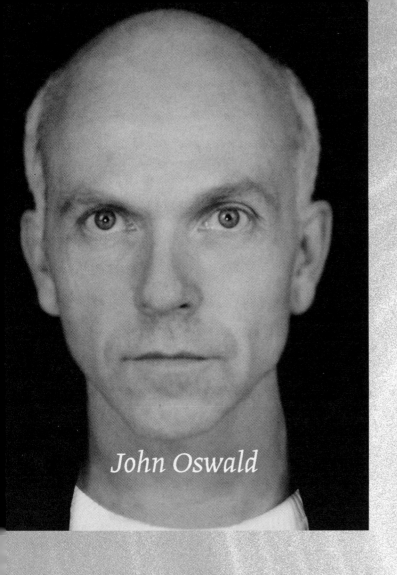

John Oswald

JOHN OSWALD was born in Kitchener, Ontario, in 1953 and now lives in

Toronto. He is active as a composer, saxophonist, media artist, and dancer. It may

seem obvious that music by a composer whose primary work is with recorded media

will be found on CD. *In the case of John Oswald, however, actually obtaining that*

CD *is another story, riddled with dull corporate legal wrangling and artless propri-*

etary issues. When his own label, Fony, wasn't able to obtain all the necessary

*copyright permissions to release the two-*CD *retrospective boxed set 69* plunder-

phonics 96, *it was "hijacked" by the American label Seeland, and can be found in*

what Oswald calls "braver" record stores. As well, in 2003, Empreintes Digitales

released the CD *of his one-note piece* Aparanthesi, *and sound art publisher*

Avatar released their first DVD, *entitled* Moving Stills (Census Q), *Oswald's almost entirely visual composition. Rather than simply review these disks, I found it most interesting to listen to them, and then talk directly with him.*

PS: To a large degree, your work implements technology, and therefore electricity. Salvador Dali once said that if you put him in a jail
cell in the dark, he'd create by closing his eyes and making colours by
pressing his finger onto his eyeball. Without electricity, how would
you create?

JO: I have this interesting conundrum in that everything I'm doing
professionally these days gets routed through computers—to create
sound, visual, and audio media, and to create scores for other musicians to play. I balance this in my life by having what would normally
be called "hobbies," doing improvised music in which I play an
acoustic instrument, the saxophone, and a similar activity in dance
called Contact improvisation. I've been doing these two things for
well over a quarter of a century now. If all the computers broke down,
I'd probably spend some more time playing the saxophone, and some
more time dancing. But I think I'd find great appeal—as I do sometimes—in pressing my fingers on my eyeballs when they're closed.
Stan Brakhage got me going on that though—not Salvador Dali.

PS: How did you get into free improvisation, and what do you like about it?

JO: I think improvising comes naturally out of an interest in communication between people, particularly conversation. What's intriguing
about the dance and music improvisation I do is that it's more polyphonic than your average verbal conversation, which is usually taking
turns—call and response. If you really start contemplating the ideas
that are both part of and behind most conversations, it can seem
much more polyphonic than it is in *actuality*. In both the improvised
dance and music that I do, they don't have an initial score to incite or
control some sort of activity. Usually, it requires more than one person
to be simultaneously involved in making noise or movement; or by my
analogy, making conversation. That complex kind of interaction and
simultaneous activity is the thing that really fascinates me.

PS: What sort of thought process is going on when you're playing?

JO: I think in the best of times, thought processes that are by and large
if not exclusively based on language are shut down to a large extent.

There are visceral responses using other sensory intake, and other internal response mechanisms.

PS: Is it a type of deep listening and immediate response, without obfuscation? Being "in the moment"?

JO: A moment for me is approximately a thirtieth of a second. Conveniently, it's also what they use as a frame rate in video. When you make things faster than that, depending on whether it's coming in your eyes or ears, things blend together in funny ways. When you're dealing with articulation in music, it can break down to a hundredth of a second. So, let's say that a moment is between a thirtieth of a second and a hundredth of a second. Anything beyond that has to do with prediction and retrospection, things that are definitely involved in improvising too. I have a poor memory, so I perhaps toil more in moments than I would choose to if I had a different set of intellectual equipment.

PS: In what context do you play your free improvisations?

JO: I play with the Canadian Creative Music Collective (CCMC) on a weekly basis in Toronto. Michael Snow is the remaining member from the founding of this group back in the early seventies. The most recent thing I've played was last weekend in John Zorn's game piece *Cobra*. That was a bit of an unusual case for me, accepting something other than a free playing situation. There are generally all sorts of rules amongst improvisers, but they never seemed to be agreed upon by the participants, either before or after the event. The CCMC will sometimes sit around before playing and say, "We should do this. We should do that." Inevitably, we never do those things. I think it's Mike in particular who tends to make these suggestions, but his personality being what it is, he likes to set up rules in order to break them. So, quite likely, if he suggests something, it's the opposite of what's going to happen.

PS: What's the relation between your improvisations and your other composition work?

JO: The sense of dynamics. I mean both temporal and spectral dynamics in improvisatory performance and the sense of the dynamics of momentum in improvisatory dance. Contact has a lot to do with people leaning on each other and wrestling, and I've to some extent internalized that dynamic that influences the more sedentary activity of composing. When I'm working on music, it's hardly ever in real time, it's usually the equivalent of drawing or painting. I spend a long time making something that can then be apparent in a short time. I don't, as a rule, use any of the kinds of gestures that I use in real time improvised music in creating a composed piece of music. I do, however, recognize those dynamics again in listening to them, which is an important part of my composing: the direct empirical reflection of what I'm doing. So, I recognize those dynamics and tend to encourage those things, the complex give and take of various elements. It's a bit like responding to your dreams. The same way a dream you've had the night before can flavour your whole day, even if you can't put your finger on the details of it. Keeping my foot in this improvised activity ongoing flavours everything else I do. It also gives me the opportunity just to play, which I find an invaluable part of composing.

PS: Man Ray said, "To create is divine, and to reproduce is human." Where are you situated in that, artistically?

JO: *(Laughing) Eye Magazine* said I was "a god-like being." What comes to mind from the Man Ray quote is that one of my prevalent activities, the whole category of "plunderphonic" endeavours, comes out of reproduction—it's completely dependent upon recorded music. The image activity I'm also doing now, which entirely involves photographing people, again is a reproducing activity. The photographs are taken under fairly strict parameters and most of the creative activity happens after the photographs are taken, in post production. In a way it seems like it's parallel to the plunderphonic activity, where I'm taking familiar music. Now I'm taking familiar images of people I know, and working with those. Hopefully, I can be seen as being human, as opposed to, let's say, inhuman, in this activity. I don't have to make any claims for divinity.

PS: What's your definition of "plunderphonics"?

JO: I should find the one I just wrote *(shuffles through papers)*...
"'Plunderphonics' is a term I've coined to cover the counter-covert world of converted sound and retrofitted music where collective melodic memories of the familiar are minced and rehabilitated to a new life."

PS: In the last few years, there's been an avalanche of change. Plunderphonics is by no means unusual now.

JO: Oh yes, I agree with that, independent of whether some people think it's okay or it's not okay. In fact, my next interview this afternoon is about a particular category of popular music that seemed to have gained a couple of different monikers in England. The one that seems to have stuck is mash-up. People keep asking me about mash-ups, since several of the pieces I did over the last thirty years seem to flow directly into that category. I guess I'm a mash-up pioneer, although as far as I know, none of the mash-up people has heard of me.

PS: What do you view as the precedents for your plunderphonics?

JO: There were very definitely distinct pieces by Luciano Berio and Karlheinz Stockhausen that first come to mind. Berio's *Omaggio a Joyce*, which was a fantasy elaborated from a reading of a text from James Joyce's *Ulysses*—the bar scene, which is also the sound scene. Also, Stockhausen's pieces, particularly the *Hymnen*, but also *Telemusik*. Those two pieces in particular, used direct audio musical quotes, as opposed to writing out musical quotations to be replayed—an approach that has been around since music has been written down.

PS: There's also Louis Andriessen's *In Memoriam*, made just after Stravinsky's death in 1971, where he took a Mozart symphony and *The Rite of Spring*, and spliced silence from one into the other.

JO: More recently, I've found other pieces from that period, like Luke Ferrari's take on Beethoven, but I keep going back to those Berio and Stockhausen pieces. Also, Xenakis's *Concret pH*.

PS: How so with Xenakis?

JO: There's a larger category of my "electroacousmatic" activities that has the plunderphonics angle—the idea of taking familiar sounds from the environment and exerting the same processes on them—which goes right back to *musique concrète*. There's something about the simple materials in the Xenakis piece, which are just the embers of a fire, and made into things that, for instance, sound like bells. It's done in a very concentrated and bold way, as is almost always the case with Xenakis.

PS: To what degree do you feel that your plunderphonics work is dependent on the listener's knowledge of the recorded source material?

JO: Someone can have a very successful listening experience without ever having heard the source material before—if, for instance, one managed to get through life without having heard Bing Crosby's *White Christmas*—but I have no sense of what that experience would be. My experience of these things has to do with familiarity with the sources. It becomes more familiar as I work on it, of course, just through repeated listening and sometimes analysis. I retain the conceit that I'm still hearing it as someone else would hear it, because we have this common initial response to a material under the same circumstances. Popular music sources get inside one, even if you don't like them. They are involuntarily accepted.

PS: Do you find that these reference sources imprint themselves on you?

JO: I do have this very odd feeling of—it's usually not of a sense of collaboration. I don't feel like I've collaborated, even where there was an explicit agreement. I don't feel like I've collaborated with the Grateful Dead, because the way we set it up, we never went into the studio together. I didn't allow an opportunity to discuss what I was doing to them. My critical approach to creating these things has the advantage of it never quite seeming like my music. It seems like I'm producing someone else's music, and I have that third eye, or third ear kind of advantage to appreciating the material.

PS: More than most pieces, yours are like tattoos, in that we recognize the materials, but some of the source material fades or decays from our collective memory over time. New "hits" take their place.

JO: I thought tattoos were forever. That's encouraging news.

PS: Because of this, do you agree that in some ways your pieces have a more pronounced expiry date?

JO: Ten years ago, I would have totally disagreed. I would've expected that most of the pieces I was referring to had some sort of permanence, and that given some degree of ebb and flow of popularity, people would always be listening to these things. Look at the history of listening to J.S. Bach, for instance. It's had that ebb and flow to some great extremes since his time to the present. I have a feeling that with recording the ebb would be ever so slight. Ten years ago, I would have disagreed completely, but I've noticed more recently that historical perspective extends only to a couple of years. This is from speaking to people who are a generation or two younger than I am, and have what seems to me a very narrow sense of history. A lot of people have absolutely no sense of anything that's happened outside their lifetime, and sometimes within the range of their lifetime. I mentioned before Bing Crosby's *White Christmas*. I use that one specifically because for close to fifty years it was the most popular recording, in terms of sales and airplay, but there's a whole generation of people who seem not to recognize it now. That requirement we talked about before, of recognizing the source in the transformation, in some cases just isn't there. I didn't expect it would disappear so quickly from generation to generation. Perhaps there is a lifespan in these pieces, although I think the appeal might be with a narrower portion of the population than I've always thought was possible. I've always thought that these are potentially popular pieces in themselves, partly because of their close proximity to pieces that have proven to be popular.

PS: As the source material fades, is it, in fact, your technique that emerges, or what you do with materials?

JO: It might be possible because I think there's lots of interesting things that go on, not independent of the source, but as a result of the source material, that end up probably being interesting on their own.

PS: Ultimately, we're highlighting the fact that they're layered. Over time, I think it's inevitable with any music, but in some ways it's more pronounced with yours, how some layers subside and others emerge more clearly.

JO: I think with my plunderphonics oeuvre in particular, it's less likely to be identified with an era. There's something less timely about most of the pieces I've made. They definitely have some degree of the era of the source because more often than not we can place a lot of these very popular examples whether Beethoven or the Beatles to a given period down to the decade. But since I don't think I've been directly influential to any particular musical styles, and given that in some cases you can't tell it's manipulated recordings, some of them exist out of time. I think particularly with this other category of mine, which are just performable plunderphonics pieces that have been notated and in all cases to some extent derived from the classical repertoire, particularly the very popular classical repertoire, there's even less of a sense of when they were composed. Some would definitely be accused of being part of the postmodern era.

PS: Why do you use Beethoven and the Beatles as sound sources so often?

JO: I don't know. The facetious answer is that I start going through the alphabet and get them...

PS: Why not Boulez then? Or Berio? Don't enough people know their music?

JO: Well, there is that. I was very conscious of it when I was working with Webern's music. It hadn't risen to the level of any sort of familiarity with the public. I know that having grown up with this isolation of the twentieth century composer from any sort of popularity in classical musical circles, in order to make music that I thought was... let's say, useful... it was necessary to create bridges. One of the most obvious was Beethoven because he's probably the most pervasive composer in this society. If I made pieces that sounded like Beethoven, by the advantage that I am using Beethoven's music, I end up sounding like Beethoven. Perhaps then I wouldn't immediately be branded a twentieth century composer and wouldn't experience those kinds of things that happen where people leave the hall before the piece begins. Having said that, I have no particular great attachment to Beethoven, and I rarely, if ever, sit down to listen to Beethoven when I don't have to. It just pops up all over the place. He's obviously on the same level as the Beatles by the fact that some of his music is so easily recognizable by the broad populace. Tchaikovsky is up there too. It's easy to say you like Beethoven, a bit harder to say you like Tchaikovsky.

PS: Listening to the plunderphonics pieces, your technique is often to contort the expected beat, but also, rather than processing or cross-synthesis, to vary the speed, transpositions of pitch, duration—effectively, the scale of the sound. What's your goal with these types of transfigurations?

JO: People point out the odd rhythmic aspects of these things quite often, and I think that's where that dream sense of improvised music comes in. The unpredictable, dare I say organic aspects of rhythm in freely improvised music having a great influence on rhythms that more often than not were originally a straight-ahead four-four.

PS: But it seems the transposition—elongating, or transposing up or down the original source material—conceptually, that's very important.

JO: Yes, although it's almost exclusively transpositions in octaves. I've never really been a sampler player, and never liked anything you do easily on samplers—having a sound source that goes up and down the chromatic scale, getting shorter as you go higher, and longer as you go lower. Those kinds of effects I've used very rarely. It's something that overly emphasizes the artificial nature of the original recording. More often, I tend to revel in illusion.

PS: You seem to take the original idea as though it's a balloon, and you blow it up. With helium.

JO: Yes, which is when Dolly Parton sounds like a chipmunk. Doing things in registers extreme from the original, like taking the opening of *Lohengrin* and speeding it up sixteen times—I think I got the original impulse from the science fiction writer J. G. Ballard, who envisioned a future where people ingested Wagner's operas in seconds, at ultrasonic frequencies, and discussed the varying aural ambrosia of different performances. So, I tried that out. Even earlier than that, I'd been listening to other things, particularly Stravinsky—and some of them have to do with these octave transpositions. It goes back to when I was a kid and had a four-speed record player and tended to listen to LPS at 78-RPM. It's not exactly an octave increase in speed, but you do have an approximate doubling of speed and the sense of things going by twice as quick, which in some cases I thought was very exciting. When I got around to doing this on tape recorders, it was definitely octave transpositions.

PS: Why?

JO: Out of curiosity in part. That's the initial impetus for all these things, wondering what they sound like under different conditions. Quite surprisingly, given the way the record industry tries to legislate listener activity, there've never been commandments printed on records that say "Do not play this at the other speeds on your record player." Back in the old days, when you did have those choices, to change the speed, I did.

PS: We listen a very specific way to the plunderphonics pieces. Listening to them can be very concrete, very comparative, and mnemonic. Is there an element of the abstraction in your other music that you wish were in the digital?

JO: Very definitely, the primary intent of listening, say, in my improvised music activity, is to engender conversation. I have never really cared too much about how listeners may hear an improvisatory performance, and I don't really care if there are listeners or not—maybe I've got some kind of allegiance with Milton Babbitt here. But I do care in the extreme what the person I might be playing with hears. And how they're responding, and their sense of what's going on can only be read in the way they're playing. So, it's a direct feedback circuit that gives me some sort of impression of a listening activity.

PS: In the midst of all the samples, transpositions, transformations, progressions through scale and frequency, the recognized materials (borrowed or stolen), where are you?

JO: I'm on the other side of loudspeakers along with everybody else.

PS: Where is *your* imprint?

JO: It's something I never really found appealing in talented people— that they have a distinct personality and can only play one way, although some people do that one thing quite wonderfully. I think I've been able to be quite amorphous in this production role. If you think of me in the traditional record producer's role—the person who cultivates and brings along the personality in the recording, whether it's a particular character or conglomerate of characters or style—in that respect I think I manage to be somewhat transparent. At first, I was dismayed when people would say, "Your music always has quirky rhythms." I've got so many different rhythmic characters I've incorporated into these pieces that I'm disappointed to be categorized that way. So, the short answer to the question of where am I in these things is—I'm invisible. I don't think people picture me while they're listening to my music in the same way that they'd be picturing Glenn Gould slouched over the piano while listening to the *Goldberg Variations* or even a scowling Boulez hovering over his score. I don't know if I'm inaudible, but at least I'm appreciably invisible.

Francis Dhomont

FRANCIS DHOMONT *was born in Paris in 1926 and recently returned to live in the south of France. At the time of our interview, however, he was living in Montreal. The name Francis Dhomont is synonymous with excellence in electro-acoustic music. Active since the early days of the art form, he has forged his own impressive path, supported by a wealth of paradigmatic works, the majority of which are available on* CD *from the Empreintes Digitales label. Those interested in further study of his work will want to find French publisher Licences's large format bilingual art book,* Sonopsys, *and Uli Aumüller's film/*DVD, My Cinema for the Ears. *As for experiencing his work in public, Toronto was privileged to hear some of it at the New Adventures in Sound Art "Sound Travels" event on August 9, 2003. Among the numerous Centre Island concerts was an octaphonic concert presentation of his acousmatic[1] piece* Here and There.

PS: When you began your first experiments with electronic technology in 1947, what were your tools, and what were your results?

FD: The means were extremely limited. All I had were low-quality amateur tape recorders. There were many problems with these machines, so I had to build my own tools and modify the tape recorders in order to make them do the electroacoustic music I wanted. Because I was living in the countryside in the south of France (Provence), there were practically no professional shops where I could get them fixed, so I also had to learn how to do that myself.

PS: What were your early goals as a composer working with the tape recorders?

FD: It must be said that I encountered recording technology well before I started to compose electroacoustic music, well before encountering Pierre Schaeffer and the phenomenon of *musique concrète*. I was composing instrumental music at that time, and I came to electroacoustic music much later, in the 1960s. My goal at that time, which is always the same goal, was to make music. Technology doesn't interest me—it's what one can do with the electroacoustic technology that interests me.

PS: Having had traditional music studies in counterpoint, theory, harmony, and composition... what influence did that have on you?

FD: My traditional studies have left a trace. On form—the structure of the composition—and also the polyphony.

PS: Today a composer in electroacoustics has approximately sixty-five years of inherited precedents, a growing body of work as reference. Do you feel that it's still important for acousmatic artists to have similar traditional studies in music theory, harmony?

FD: In my opinion, it's not necessary. It's not necessary to study traditional solfège,[2] but what is needed is to educate the ear. It's absolutely indispensable to learn how to listen, because in acousmatic music, we work with the perception of sound.

PS: In 1963, why did you make the decision to work exclusively with recorded media?

FD: I was a bit tired of instrumental music—my own and that of my contemporaries. With instrumental music, I couldn't find the answers to the questions I had as a composer. I was searching for something else. With the experiments I had done using magnetic tape in the late forties, I felt there was a new mode of composition available with these tools. Encountering the work of Pierre Schaeffer and Pierre Henry reconfirmed that interest, and inspired me to change from instrumental to electroacoustic music.

PS: What did you mean when you said you couldn't find the answers to your questions working with acoustic music. What were those questions? What were you seeking?

FD: It was a long time ago, but... I was listening to a lot of music, and I had the impression that it was always the same thing. Not that the music was always the same thing, but I had that impression. The thing that was completely new and different was the sound of electroacoustic music, and it provided some answers. The sound was completely different, and I had enormous interest in this.

PS: You've made the change from calling your work acousmatic "music" to acousmatic "art"? Why do you leave out the word "music"?

FD: That's an important question. One of the reasons is that in the past twenty-five years the public, the people who listen to our art, don't believe that what we do is music. They ask, "Why don't you make real music?" It's because of this that I asked myself the question, and I think it's better to say that we make art. It's more "sound art" than it is "music." People perceive it this way also, because it involves noise and other sounds, not articulating a musical language. Therefore, removing the word "music" and replacing it with "art" made the statement much clearer. Art can be something new. I consider that what I do is music, but I always find it boring to answer the question of why we don't do real music. In people's minds, music has a lot of tradition and historical background, a lot of dimension, such as people on stage, a manuscript, melody, harmony, a beat, and instruments. None of those things is present in electroacoustic music. The word "art" can always be redefined, and is much broader—it leaves the door open. *(Laughing)* Many of my colleagues don't agree with me on this, maybe because they think that the word "music" is more noble, and also because there might be performing rights concerns. The performing rights societies might not decide to represent that art form.

PS: At the same time, you haven't really left acoustic music behind. You make substantial reference to other music as source material in your pieces. What is the function of these materials?

FD: That's a complex question, but very interesting. Effectively, I am always close to the universe of music, and music that is instrumental and/or vocal. I've always been very involved with it. I don't want to cut off from traditional music, but electroacoustic music has other dimensions of interest. One of the biggest changes in the evolution of music is that in acousmatic art there is no longer the articulation of the note, but the articulation of the sound, of the morphology of the sound. So there is a break there, but it is within the continuity of evolution of music. That is why we can hear references to instrumental music in my pieces. In *musique concrète* and its successor, acousmatic music, nothing is forbidden. Instruments may be used in *musique concrète* or acousmatic art, but not in the conventional fashion. We take the sounds, record them, and treat them, processing and changing them.

PS: By extension, with your sound materials, you make reference to so much else—literature, the natural world, images, scenes and places. Are all sounds equal? Are they treated as found objects?

FD: There is an old saying in *musique concrète* that anything that makes a sound is good, and thus may be used. All sounds are treated equally, be they figurative or abstract. There is no hierarchical system, but it depends on the work. Some pieces may use elements that refer to reality, or are narrative, and referential to things that we know and experience. Therefore, there is a hierarchy of material in those pieces. For example, in a piece that would be very abstract, if I include in that abstract piece the sound of a word, or the sound of a singing bird, then those are very strong images that create a link with reality, a special climate. There is a change in perception between the abstract world and these things that pop in as reference to the realities from which they derive meaning. This is not something that occurs by accident, but rather, it is voluntary on my part. Be it painting or music or literature, I think one important aspect in art in general is the poetic climate or atmosphere. A feeling of poetry is needed in a work of art.

PS: You've mentioned your interest in the spectral morphology of sound. Could you define this and give some examples of how it's applied in your work?

FD: The term "spectral morphology" was invented by Dennis Smalley, who has written pages and pages about this phenomenon. But in a few words, it establishes the difference between instrumental music, which is the articulation of conventions of codes—notes, harmony, rhythm—and spectral morphology, which in music is more the articulation of colour and timbre. Spectral morphology is the study of everything that happens within the sound as it resonates. Pierre Scheaffer's terminology for describing the same phenomenon is matter, which (in very broad terms) is the spectrum of sound, and its form, which is the amplitude of sound, and how it evolves in time. Schaeffer creates a link between matter and form, just as in spectral morphology.

PS: Could you also talk a little bit about sound as metaphor?

FD: Yes, but sound is not only metaphorical, it's physical. But it is true that in some or many of my pieces, sounds I use have a metaphoric value, and metamorphosis is important. In *Espace/Escape*, which is a piece about voyage, escape, displacement, and notions of space, there are many sounds that make allusions. Some sounds are realistic in terms that they evoke notions of speed, displacement, or travel, and are also figurative in terms of the sound qualities they evoke. They can be either literal (for example, a train passing by), or abstract in terms of a sound that has a lot of internal movement. Just like an abstract sound that moves from left to right—the movement is there, but it doesn't make reference to a train or a plane, or anything. But the feeling of movement is evoked by its morphology.

PS: In addition to the technical and sonic richness, your work also has vast psychological breadth, exploring the complexities of the subconscious. Is this territory something that has always attracted you to electroacoustics?

FD: My interest in psychology has always been present, but electroacoustic music has allowed me to understand psychology and the subconscious better. When I was writing instrumental music, I had so many rules to obey and follow at the conservatoire or in music school that I couldn't attain the liberty that electroacoustic music offered in terms of exploring the subconscious. Electroacoustic music offers a lot of freedom, total liberty of expression, but at the same time, it creates the danger that one can just do anything, without care. With electroacoustic music, I learned how to become freer than I felt with instrumental music, but I also had to find or invent my own rules, in order not to create an insignificant sound, or meaningless noise.

PS: The freedom is a curse and a pleasure.

FD: Exactly.

PS: While the materials of acousmatic art may be fixed on tape, in performance they are by no mean static or fixed in space. How is the live concert experience of acousmatics important to the true experience of it?

FD: Listening to the music on CD at home can be a good representation, and a good image of the work. In the concert hall, where there are multiple speakers and the person is centred—that spatializes the sound—a new dimension is added to the music, an amplification. However, all music fixed on tape isn't necessarily stereo, because there are also multi-track pieces, conceived for presentation in the concert hall, even though it's fixed on tape or hard disk. Both listening modes are valid—privately, or in the concert hall. It's a big subject—we could talk for hours about this.

PS: If we define acousmatic art as the hiding of the sound source and its dissociation from the listener, isn't almost everything we hear acousmatic? The radio, CDs, television? What separates these from acousmatic art?

FD: We cannot say that because when Mozart composed a symphony, he didn't conceive it this way, without the musicians onstage playing their instruments live. When we listen to music on the radio, what we listen to is a recorded art. We may say the listening experience is acousmatic when you listen to a piece of instrumental music on the radio, television, the telephone, et cetera, but the music itself—the art form—is not acousmatic in its form, just in its reproduction. We have to make a distinction between the acousmatic listening mode and the acousmatic composition mode, which is a different way of thinking about the art. For example, I can compose a piece for piano, it isn't an acousmatic piece, though it could be listened to in an acousmatic mode on the radio. The acousmatic is a specific, original way of thinking.

PS: You once wrote, "the road least accessible is always the one to choose." Why?

FD: I believe we can obtain something of interest with work, with effort and research. If we don't do that, then we repeat what we've already done. I believe that we always have to search, to try harder to give ourselves difficulties in order to reinvent all the time. For example, when one buys a synthesizer or some software, these things come with "presets." We saw very much with the DX-7 that many composers just used the machine as it was delivered by the manufacturer. But there are composers who go farther. What was interesting were the people who went into the machine or the software and explored and tried to get new things out of it. That is the hardest path, but it's also the most interesting. But I'm not quite content with this formula. I want to add something that's contradictory, because the truth lies in the contradiction and the dialectic. Sometimes we have a musical idea that comes very easily by itself and it could be the best one.

PS: Where is acousmatic art going? Does the increased relation between electroacoustics and technomusic concern you? Do you worry that electroacoustics will suffer from commercialism, or a lack of thought?

FD: Yes. There's a problem. That is certain. Many of the technomusicians use the same means as electroacoustic composers, and transform the sounds we've invented. Those aspects are good, but the risk is that in the near future there will be only techno left. There is good techno, but there is also some that is very temporary in content. With anything that is becoming commercialized, there is a tendency to have less content. Nonetheless, it's still necessary to continue to have composers that still search, that look inside music for new things, continuing to research.

I'd like to make a comparison between poetry and bestselling novels. Bestsellers are well known and popular, but that doesn't mean there should be a reduction of research in other literary form, because it is within the research aspect, where things are discovered and that in the near future will nourish the art form. Because bestselling novels exist that doesn't mean we shouldn't have poets who keep exploring the writing form. Similarly, we should allow composers who search for new sounds, new ways of expressing themselves because that is very important for the development of the art form. Not all electroacoustic composers do techno or know how to do techno. I hope that both techno and electroacoustics will continue to evolve, in parallel with each other. We shouldn't take the model of the pop music concert, or let popular music become the only mode of musical expression. There are composers who want to have a large audience and make a lot of money, and that's fine, and there are composers/artists that want to be more in the expressive arts and reach a smaller audience, not necessarily to make money out of it. But those people who select concert music should not complain that they don't have an audience, because that is the nature of the form. I am very happy when a hundred people come to my concert and have interest in it. I find that wonderful.

NOTES

1. Originating with Pythagoras's unique oral teaching style (delivered from behind a curtain to prevent his physical presence from distracting his disciples and allowing them to better concentrate exclusively on the content of his message) the term acousmatic is closely associated with Dhomont's work. Applied to sound, "acousmatic" is loosely defined as "a sound that we can hear without knowing its cause."

2. Singing using *solfa* syllables to denote the notes of the scale, with Do being the first note. The system is generally accredited to Guido d'Arezzo, who created this method of allocating shapes to notes on the scale in an effort to help his monks learn chants and melodies for the mass.

Martin Arnold

NOMADIC composer Martin Arnold was born in 1959 and raised in Edmonton, Alberta. He studied at the University of Victoria and The Royal Conservatory of Music (The Hague, Netherlands) before settling in Toronto. Amidst his life as composer/listener, writer/reader, performer, and sometime gardener, Martin Arnold remains in close touch with the fascination that brought so many of us into music. The wide range of music and art he's enamoured by and the openness with which he studies it were recurring themes throughout our conversation, and contribute to the combination of sharp intelligence and pleasant charm he exudes.

PS: What is simplicity in music?

MA: It's an interesting question because I think you almost have to limit the idea of simplicity to an appreciation of material, in which case it doesn't actually become very interesting in terms of musical experience. I think that even the simplest materials can become incredibly complicated in one person's listening based on what experience they bring to it, and all those things that you can't control within what's sounding. Basically, I don't think music is simple. Listening to a pop song is actually incredibly complicated; when music is actually attended to in a way that it can somehow alter your mind—which is practically the goal—that is never simple.

PS: Gertrude Stein said, "I like a simple thing, but it must be simple through complication."

MA: It's funny how, depending on what kind of rhetorical path you reach through, you end up describing similar states but naming them oppositely. My only qualm with Stein's statement is there's something that seems implied about some kind of essential simplicity as being a cherished spiritual state that I don't feel very close to, conceptually— you know simplicity as a transcendental state of arrival. On the other hand, simplicity can be used as a metaphor for lacks of control—lack of hierarchy, lack of superstructure, and lack of narrative appendage— all those lacks that I celebrate. However, one can think in terms of complicating the reception of, let's say, a piece of music to facilitate those same lacks.

PS: Do you strive for a kind of simplicity?

MA: What I strive for is a sense of openness, more than complexity or simplicity. It's sort-of a state where I don't want there to be sense of strict order and intent, or hierarchy, things like that. I get to that by imagining myself listening to it. While composing I'm already wondering about where the piece might take me—as a listener. I don't mean that I can do this in any concrete, definitive way, but it's that kind of loose imagining that backgrounds my material choices. In regard to a specific composition, this might result in me writing a string of similar gestures going on forever—simple diatonic melodies, things that, materially, might be called simple; but I don't actually think of them that way. I try very hard to make a piece not seem like it's about its strategies or its material and methodological attributes—where a piece might be named "minimal," or part of a "new simplicity," or "new complexity" for example. I try to make it not clear what those generative motivations might be as a way of opening up the listening experience.

Having said that, I think that there are a lot of things I do that the word "simplicity" goes with in a nice way. I listen to so much pop and folk; musics that get called simple. Yet it seems so unbelievably complicated to me how many ways one song can be comprehended versus another one, versus this person's hearing of each, et cetera. It's those sorts of experiences that make me balk at naming what I do from a methodological standpoint. I may think, "Yes, just leave it alone, don't add something else"—those are material concerns around simplicity. But as a core way of working, it's not really where I start, or how I'm used to naming what I do.

PS: At the same time, some of your materials and gestures are definable by their limitation, their refinement, or their exclusion.

MA: Yes, although I guess I try to not to be exemplary that way. I keep trying to find wrinkles. It's not like that post-Louis Andriessen Dutch thing, where a lot of that kind of *(sings)* Chunk chunk chunk chunk hard, in-your-face, simple rhythm was actually exemplary; a general-ized political-aesthetic statement: "No, we can hit you this hard, we can hit you this ugly." There was this whole meta-narrative around what they were choosing to do, that had its own political agenda to it. I try to muddy the waters in terms of how I present material or what I might end up including within a piece—how long it goes on for, whether it has a hum-ability. I try to offer meanders that will maybe take you away from thinking what the piece is in a taxonomical way, and lose yourself in it as you might in a pop song. Just little things to make it not exemplary. It's really important to me that people aren't fundamentally thinking about how I'm positioning myself as a compositional strategist. I still want to be able to lose myself in my music when I hear it. That's what is foremost in my mind. Anything that can be theorised after that, I'm not oblivious to, but it's not gener-ative to what I do.

It reminds me of a story—I studied with a visual artist named Mowry Baden in Victoria, and I remember him saying to me one time that "taste doesn't matter." At the time, I thought that was nuts, because saying "taste doesn't matter" is taste—I heard him implying a preference, stating a distinguishing, discerning judgement. He sort of nodded and smiled and left me there. I think what he meant was that yes, if taste matters, it matters. If you want to keep reaching out to taste, you'll always find it. But you can remove taste from a place where you're always thinking about it; remove it as a sensibility that informs what you do; be in a place instead where you wonder about what something is instead of whether you like it or not. It doesn't mean that taste isn't present, but it isn't something that you have to reach out to anymore.

PS: What do you mean by "getting lost" in a piece?

MA: I'm going to return to popular music again; but not because I think it's any more conducive to getting lost in or a more quintessential experience in which to get lost than, say, sitting down for an hour and three-quarters and listening to all of Olivier Messiaen's *Vingt Regards...*—which is something I do pretty regularly. It's just that with music of that expanse and material density and innovation it's easy to think of getting lost as an issue of not grasping or understanding what's going on. You're lost in the sense that you can't follow and make sense of all the shifting machinations of the composition. That's not the kind of "getting lost' that interests me. With pop music, everything can obviously be utterly familiar in terms of the operation of musical materials and yet precipitate a receptive state that doesn't adhere to the logistics of other waking activities.

It amazes me how you can listen to a pop tune over and over again, either on a day or through your whole life, and it always seems amazing; it can continuously fill you with wonder and, in a sense, turn you into a subject you don't really recognize. That is, it's not just that the material I'm receiving when I'm listening to music is radically different than when I'm reading a shopping list, the music can radically alter my position, presence, self-awareness, and even self-consciousness as a receiver. "I," as a familiar receiving subject, get lost. That's the kind of getting lost I'm interested in whether I'm encountering Messiaen or Neil Young. The current song that's consistently setting this altered me adrift somewhere out in the unordinary is a song written by the British traditional singers Lal and Mike Waterson called "The Scarecrow"—the version sung by Mike. It's permanently in my CD player right now, and I can put it on anytime and be absolutely altered by it. It's also the one I use when I'm working and the dumbest songs I haven't heard in thirty years come into my head and are beleaguering me. I can sing "The Scarecrow" to myself and it will usually get rid of them. Magic.

PS: Is that not temporary, or an impermanent situation?

MA: The actual experience is transient but I think music can create a kind of permanent location, a place you can return to; to discover new things and have more experiences. I think a lot about musical experience as an altered state. I think it's a state that's available with art in general or, in a sense, what art is doing within human activity. It really is this kind-of dreamlike sniff of another version of your mind, or another version of you as an organism, that there are other versions of human nested within us. That's also a political thing too, because in general it can become a place to rethink.

PS: Agreed. At some point, your concerns about openness and a type of sought-after experience become a technical issue. What does it mean as a composer?

MA: Yes, there has to be a practical, productive side to it. A lot of what I've been talking about here, and certainly my approach to composition, is indebted to my teacher Rudolf Komorous; his aesthetic of the wonderful. However, technically—that is, compositionally—his execution of his aesthetics is so different from what mine has turned out to be. I think his margin of the wonderful is a strange, interpretive margin around standard repertoire—post-aristocratic, bourgeois European music, which he loves and knows so well. He's able to use the whole narrative structures of those musics and unravel the threads of them—but really lovingly, it never involves satire. He's able to make that multi-layered play of difference that standard repertoire embraces, so unknowably strange. What follows what and when, the juxtapositions and baffling but uncannily elegant transitions, how tension and resolution operate, are so dream-like in Rudolf's music— but utterly substantial, like those dreams you wake from and have to work a bit to believe they're not your real world; well, not the world you go to work in. Anyway, I could never do that stuff. I just didn't really have the core relationship to standard repertoire to handle that, and the subtleties of its narrative history.

ps: That's an issue of your time and place, isn't it?

MA: Yes, well also cultural—I guess that's big picture time and place. The repertoire I discovered in undergrad that continues to inform so much of what I do is early music, particularly late medieval polyphony and early English consort music. I listen to Christopher Tye's consort music a lot. The treatment of all five voices is very even. You don't get a sense of a clear lead melody being harmonized. And texturally, anything can happen anywhere—sustained pedal points ringing out in the highest voice, anything. Also, I've listened to the recording of his "In Nomines" hundreds of times and I still couldn't tell you which one I'm listening to if you just started one anywhere—and that includes the beginning. I mean, I haven't really tried; I haven't felt inclined to—but there is a lot of music that insists that you learn to recognize it; this meandering modal counterpoint doesn't. And along with this, I don't really listen to these pieces as individual pieces— any number of them can meld together into a sustained experience. Anyway, the point is I'm inspired by music that doesn't assert its identity, that doesn't try to perform its workings in the sense of bringing itself over to an audience that's imagined to be receiving it in a latent way. My feeling with Tye's music, for example, is that its counterpoint is weaving away regardless of whether anyone is listening—it's not trying to impress in any sense of the word. This allows my imagination to actively enter into its activities and inhabit it in my own way.

The other experience in undergrad that I think of together with finding early music was discovering the sixties Peter Maxwell Davies stuff that was based on Medieval and Renaissance models. What amazed me with that body of work was that, even more than with the consort music, you were aware of a lot of activity going on and a sense of really imaginative textures shifting around, but it was as if you couldn't really focus on anything; there was nothing to direct you how to listen. Yet it wasn't estranging, you were welcome to have your attention flow along with all that texture—and the textures could be really attractive. You just weren't sure exactly what it was you were attending to. Davies could come up with really incredible sounds—something that was really important to me at the time (well, I guess orchestration is still a big part of what I do). But I compare him to another big influence from that time, George Crumb. I still feel

I learned a lot from the imagination of Crumb's music, not just all those incredible sounds but also his sense of what could co-exist in a piece. However it's music I find harder to get lost in now. It's exemplary. I feel like I not only hear an amazing sound but the composition frames it in such a way as to say "isn't that an amazing sound?!" The Davies work I was into (his music has changed a lot since then) would offer all these wonderful inventions but, as with the consort music, they would seem to be solely a part of the movement of the piece—they didn't seem to be there to impress me and I could attend to them or not. It's interesting thinking about influences and their history in these terms.

John Cage's music is very important to me and has been for a long time. His ideas background a lot of how I think about music—trying not to incorporate conventions that assert meaningfulness within a composition; finding ways of letting the listener to feel permission to find their own way through a piece; using systems that can generate music that can surprise me even though I wrote it. However, none of Cage's thought made much impact on me until I discovered his music. People who want to keep Cage as a philosopher and not as a composer will always cite 4'33". That can be an amazing piece to listen to but it's also exemplary—it's a clear example of an aesthetic agenda. Most of Cage's music is not like that. I get utterly lost in the *String Quartet in Four Parts*, the *Concerto for Prepared Piano*, *Cheap Imitation*, *Chorales*, *Atlas Eclipticalis*, *Ryoanji*, the *Roaratorio*, any of the late processed-hymn compositions, and on and on. These are not mere object lessons in methodology or philosophy.

When I first started to think about what I could do as a composer, the real core thing for me became a sense of continuity. I realized that I had to find a way to make things just continue—where all kinds of details could drift past your ears, but without being presented in a way that would make them easily graspable. A lot of how I dealt with that in terms of trying to keep things "wonderful"—in the sense Rudolf talked about, where you don't know how to prioritize things, where you don't know what's important—was to just to try and make things continue to flow. The special moments should never seem rarefied or elevated. For huge stretches, you might be listening to something relatively pleasant, but you wouldn't really have a clue why it was still going. It wouldn't have a narrative coherence that way either. Things could seem to go on too long or too short, but the music wouldn't give any clues why this should be the case. These are experiential conditions my music aspires to. I think unlike Rudolf, where I feel like he's radically altering narrative conventions—dreamlike alterations, I'm working at having narrative fall away in a sense; hopefully things are just going along in a way that doesn't seem to be about telling something. I guess I think I write a kind of consort music. That happened fairly late. It didn't happen until '91 or so where, I kind of got enough things in place methodologically that I felt like I finally knew how to make a piece continue. There was definitely a concrete material epiphany I had that I've basically been working on since...

PS: In the film *L.A. Story*, Steve Martin said, "We always know when something's begun, but we never know when it's ended."

MA: When did he say that? I mean, that's pretty good. What's the context of that?

PS: Love. It was about love.

MA: I think I kind of agree. I do feel like every time a piece starts you really feel like there's a beginning, something is going that wasn't. But there doesn't have to be a firm ending. What we call a piece of music is something we compile in our memories, anyway—one never hears a piece of music all at once. So a piece can continue to resonate, spill around, and reorganize its identity in a listener's memory long after it has stopped sounding. I like the idea that people would, rather than trying to make something coherently unified out of what I do, have some stretch of counterpoint still running around in their head in a half-remembered way. I certainly don't think of my pieces as unified or coherent.

PS: If you don't think of them as unified or coherent, how is it that we can differentiate between them?

MA: A composition with a title starts sounding then stops sounding and sounds different from other compositions. But coherence has to do with intelligibility and how clearly statements hold together; unity implies a singular identity being ascribed to a cohesion of elements. Coherence is out the window anyway, though, just because... I guess it depends on what you mean by coherence... I guess what I'm getting at is related to asking the question, "Was driving from Toronto to

Edmonton a unified or coherent experience?" In a way it was because you can name the roads you were on and it definitely had a start and a finish. But there was maybe nothing to say that you couldn't keep going to Prince George, or that you couldn't stop someplace for a long time. Or when you're recounting it, I doubt if you'll be recounting every part of it evenly. Depending on who you talk to about it, what that trip was as an experience could be wildly different too. That trip could all be about some insane night in Portage La Prairie. That actually becomes the story of that trip. The fact that you can say it started here and ended here doesn't really define its order.

PS: Eco talked about the flow of random thoughts, et cetera, but when we recount them, we describe and tell the story in an organized, linear fashion, with a beginning, middle, and end.

MA: We've hit on this a few times—how you decide to talk about things will create a frame. I think there are people who try to make coherent outright versions of their compositions where their fantasy would be that everyone would agree on what a given piece is. For me, it's completely other to that. I would like there to be as many imagined versions as possible. How many little possible wrinkles or prolifera-tions of ways of thinking and experiencing can come from a piece of art? For me experiencing art is co-creative with the maker. I guess that's the other thing for me—I write music from being blown away by other people's stuff—not just music, but other people's art—to me it's just thinking, "Is there some way I can take part in that?" If I wasn't able to do that listening to my own music—a listening that keeps a piece changing my mind—I think I would stop composing.

PS: Isn't what you're talking about, more about the receiver? Couldn't it happen with anything, even music that is compositionally closed?

MA: Yes. And I think it has for most people. I still remember the first time I went to hear a symphony orchestra. It was the most unbeliev-able thing I'd ever heard. I remember this incredible situation of watching all of these things moving, and my ear couldn't make anything that I was experiencing match what someone was doing. There was too much going on and I had limited experience. So it was just this magic thing that was happening around this amazing activity in front of my eyes, but which I couldn't add up. It made it all the more magic in the sense that I could see everything, and hear everything, but I couldn't break it up phenomenally in my brain enough to enclose and grasp the experience. It was unbelievable, but then I got to know more of it, and I started to study it. Now I can't usually hear a symphony like that anymore.

But you're right, it can happen with any music, and I think that was one of the things that was great about studying with Rudolf—all of a sudden, you do start finding exactly these things in Smetana and Corelli and Fux and Hauer and even late Beethoven. There's a whole way that you can enter listening to music that is freed of certain conventions. A lot of the other thing we're talking about has to do with conventions around listening, and how our culture brings us into that experience—whether it's popular music or classical music, or even the fact that they get named popular or classical. What does that bring to your idea of what you're supposed to be listening for? It is still a really radically culturalized experience? But artists can be aware of these conventions. And if they're trying not to be exemplary, if they're trying not to be great, trying not to be geniuses—or lucky enough in my mind to not be able to succeed at that even if that is what they wanted—they can compose and offer sounding creations that are more conducive to facilitating breaking through listening conventions. I think a lot about what those conventions might be and how those might be entering what I'm doing. It's not about repudiating them. It's not about polemics, it's about recognizing those conventions as obligatory and trying to find loose ends that they might have, to alter how comfortable they might be in terms of the person's experience of what you're offering (and actually, "conventions" seems like far too limited a word to embrace the cultural phenomena we're talking about...).

PS: So many of the conventions of listening are really learned responses. We often learn a singular way of listening, a sort of categorization/ commodification of pieces of work, which excludes a great many of their elements.

MA: Yes, absolutely.

PS: Let's talk about "alternative." "New music" is considered an alternative, and if you want to consider yourself part of that, you're an alternative to the alternative. But interestingly, your alternative to the alternative closely allies you more with other things, like pop music, and garage bands.

MA: The thing about the version of alternative that you just described is that it focusses on the artifact, the piece of music. So, new music is alternative in the sense that peoples' habits around perceiving music aren't used to accepting those materials, let's say. It's always looking at the thing and saying, "How's it materially different than this other thing?"

PS: At the same time, I can't let it go at that, because I'm sure that you're aware of links that you don't want to cultivate, with what could be considered mainstream new music in Canada. It's not just a result, it's studied...

MA: That's true. That has to do with certain observations around social milieus as much as anything. There are ways that experimental musicians I know from non-classical backgrounds interact with music making (their own and others') that I find very inspiring. I guess the kind of "alternative" that rankles me is one based on elitism. A problem with the way classical music—whether it be standard repertoire or new composition—is presented in this culture is that its value is ascribed to the specialized knowledge and perceptual skills it is implied the listener must acquire before they can "correctly" grasp its apparent greatness (somehow this is circling back on the simplicity discussion). And this greatness is presented as being transcendental, outside of and beyond nationality, culture, and history. Of course, there are material differences that have evolved in this tradition—around issues of duration, form, treatment of harmony, et cetera—that will give up different riches as a listener becomes more familiar with dealing with them. However, this is not a hierarchical issue: there are a lot of people who can sit through late Mahler who wouldn't have a clue what to do with the P-Funk All Stars jamming for three hours straight without ever stopping the music.

The kind of alternative that interests me is not based on style and materials. It's alternative because, whatever musical history it engages, something about the way it moves makes the listener wonder about what's going on—destabilizes how they thought music— any music—should be appreciated and judged. People who listen to experimental music that runs its experiments on punk, pop, or jazz don't think they have to acquire specialized knowledge. They just know that they are encountering something challenging (in every sense of the word). It's interesting that you used the term "mainstream new music" because, in the only way that matters to me, it is mainstream—as mainstream as Shania Twain. It aspires to enter the pantheon of timeless greats and wants to reassure the listener that it's just like listening to Brahms if only they would try a little harder. Having said all that, I think there's no question that I'm a classically trained composer no matter what setting I'm working in—and I'm happy with that; it's important to me to bring issues I wonder about around extended forms into different settings. But it's wonderfully problematic that way. Your review of the Marmots CD (my group that incorporates non-Classical musicians) was really canny that way. On the one hand, there's this weird turning away from a high-art surface to the pieces. On the other, it's obviously self-conscious in this turning away. You can still hear someone thinking about that. I wish it was less like that, but I recognize that it is. Maybe I'll get better at covering the tracks somehow—I don't know how right now.

PS: You can't mask awareness... plus, there's a difference between awareness and cunning.

MA: Right, the tone around the awareness. I think you can hear in a composition if the composer is positioning her/himself above her/his material. Maybe that's what I was getting at with Rudolf and his relationship with standard repertoire. You never felt like he was taking the piss out of it on the one hand, or lionising it on the other. For all of this massive skill that he was presenting, there was still this strange open-heartedness about it where you didn't feel like you were being told something. I don't like cynicism.

Helmut Lachenmann

HELMUT LACHENMANN was born in 1935 into a family of Evangelical ministers in Stuttgart, Germany. Following conservatory studies and time at Darmstadt, he worked with Luigi Nono in Venice. Since then, he has consistently written some of the most interesting, challenging, and perplexing music imaginable. On November 3, 2003, Toronto's New Music Concerts presented a portrait concert of his work. The concert, on which both Lachenmann and his wife (pianist Yukiko Sugawara) performed, provided me the special opportunity to talk with this fascinating artist.

PS: You've gone to great effort to find new types of sounds in your music. What was your intention?

HL: It's true that I'm trying to search for new sounds, but this is not my aesthetic aim or credo as an artist. With conventional or unconventional sounds, the question is how to create a new, authentic musical situation. The problem isn't to search for new sounds, but for a new way of listening, of perception. I don't know if there are still new sounds, but what we need is new contexts. One attempt was dodecaphonic music, which was an incredibly courageous step by Schoenberg. It wasn't perfectly received in society, because occidental society kept being administrated by the tonal conventions, until today. In our everyday life, we are surrounded by an art and entertainment service that is dominated by the tonal music tradition.

I was raised with the Second Viennese School of Schoenberg, and of serialism, for those of us in Europe, as well as with the aleatory techniques of John Cage, which seemed to be a sort of redemption of our serialistic attempt. I felt that I needed to find my own concept of music. When I searched for it in the late sixties, I called it *musique concrète instrumentale*. The original *musique concrète*, as developed by Pierre Schaeffer and Pierre Henry, uses life's everyday noises or sounds, recorded and put together by collage. I tried to apply this way of thinking, not with the sounds of daily life, but with our instrumental potentialities. Thinking that way, the conventional beautiful philharmonic sound is the special result of a type of sound production, not of consonance or dissonance within a tonal system. In that context, I had to search for other sound sources, to bring out this new aspect of musical signification.

PS: At the same time, you don't make electronic music. You don't make *musique concrète*.

HL: I am working with the energetic aspect of sounds. The pizzicato note C is not only a consonant event in C major or a dissonant event in C flat major. It might be a string with a certain tension being lifted and struck against the fingerboard. I hear this as an energetic process. This way of perception is normal in everyday life. If I hear two cars crashing—each against the other—I hear maybe some rhythms or some frequencies, but I don't say, "Oh, what interesting sounds!" I say, "What happened?" The aspect of observing an acoustic event from the perspective of "What happened?" This is what I call *musique concrète instrumentale.*

Thirty-five years ago, electronic music was for me uninteresting because what you hear is voltage all through the same membrane of a loudspeaker. A loudspeaker is a totally sterile instrument. Even the most exciting sounds are no longer exciting when projected through a loudspeaker. There's no danger in it anymore. When I was thirty years old I worked in the electronic music studio in Ghent, and today all my students have to work in the studio because it helps to open their minds to all dimensions of sound and time. But what I'm talking about is the experience of sound in the here and now.

PS: You've said that with electronic music, the sound is imprisoned in the speakers. Don't you think that the sound of the violin is trapped within its tradition?

HL: Yes. That's true, but this is a wonderful prison that invites us to separate its walls. If I bring together the pizzicato violin string with a plucked string on a piano and a harp, at that moment, it's no longer just a traditional violin—it's part of another family of sound. I have the ambivalence of a sound, which may be familiar to me, but I hear it in a new way. With electronics, there is no ambivalence. There is no history there. I went to IRCAM several times, listening to and seeing all the great inventions of electronic music, but I left it, saying to myself it's not for me. The problem of new sounds is a dialectical problem. Everything that's alive is new. A C major chord in Palestrina's music isn't the same as a C major chord in Wagner's *Der Meistersinger.*

Every tremolo, or interval, or tam-tam noise is as intensive and new as the context you stimulate for it. To liberate it, for a moment at least, from the historic implications loaded into it, this is the real challenge. It's about breaking the old context, by whatever means, to break the sounds, looking into their anatomy. Doing that is an incredible experience, full of this ambivalence I mentioned. You can still see that you knew that sound before, but now it has changed. The creative spirit did something with it. This is the only reason for me to make music—to hear, in a new way, what you knew before. To remember the human mind, and what we could call spirit, or creative intensity. It's the transcendental and humanistic aspect. All that other stuff—to participate in the service of culture, to write another symphony or another avant-garde work, or to organize one more minimal music piece, to exploit the great supermarket of fascism and add another nice piece to it—such music would be replaceable.

PS: So it's a rejection of habit?

HL: You could say it like that. Refusing, maybe. Balls breaking it, and opening it. It's not a destructive process, but rather a deconstructive process. When we come to Toronto, my wife will play a thirty-minute piano piece of mine. At the premiere, people expected I would use the piano strings, or "prepare" the piano, but I didn't. I worked directly with intervals, and resonance.

PS: Is this *Ein Kinderspiel*?

HL: *Ein Kinderspiel* is another, older piano piece, and I'll play that one myself when I'm there. It uses a lot of pre-established patterns. But it's not really about the pitches. The music is not the pitches.

PS: What is it then?

HL: Exactly! This is the best thing you could say. Maurice Ravel said, "Maybe *Bolero* is my best piece, but unfortunately it doesn't contain any music." You see, this is the wonderful question—"What is it then?"

If someone says to me that what I do isn't music, I say, "Wonderful."

Finally, we have not music. The whole world is full of so-called music. You can't find any place where you can be away from it. A train station, an airport, everywhere. Finally, you make a situation in which you have to reflect again, to ask again, "What is music?" With *Ein Kinderspiel*, you hear the chromatic notes from top to bottom, but you hear the piano in a different way. It's a different instrument now, you hear each key anew. Each of the seven pieces uses a different pattern, and the patterns are totally unmusical—banal or primitive to such a degree that you're able to hear what actually happens in the background of that sound. And then you hear resonance in a different way. The last piece gives, through resonance, hallucinations, or imagined melodies, that the pianist can't even control, because it comes through the resonances, which give you many other lower frequencies. If it's not music, I'd say it's a situation of perception, which provokes you to wonder "What is music?"

For me, this is the deepest experience. When people first heard Schoenberg's *Kammersymphonie*, they said it wasn't music, and they were right, because they saw that it was a completely different way of moving on, with the old means. When Johann Sebastian Bach wrote harmonizations of the good old Lutheran chorales, people said he should be fired from his post at the church, because he destroyed their beautiful music, which they habitually used to pray to God. They were angry, yet today, we are fascinated by the intensity of these pieces. These composers changed the idea of music, and this is our occidental musical tradition—that music is changed by the authentic creative invention of composers. Look what Beethoven did with the same sounds used in the more aristocratic music of Mozart or Haydn. He used it in another way, maybe because it was a time of revolution, maybe because he was a little bit crazy. The whole change of styles and means in European music, from the first monodic music until today, follows the idea of destroying the conventional idea of music.

PS: Do you find that performing your music in a different geographical context changes the perception of your work?

HL: I think so, yes. It's clear. I had some experience with this in Japan. I am totally a European musician *(laughs)*. I can't help it. And why should I? It's okay. But in looking for other ways of thinking about time, for instance, or of sound, my music resonated in a certain sense with the traditional Japanese music. Many Japanese people felt a connection with their own music that has large time-spans, and some raw elements, like in Noh theatre, or Gagaku. I had my opera performed there three years ago, in Tokyo. And it was incredible, even for me. It was like a different piece, because of the situation. It wasn't the same as in my home. They are open to long time dimensions, which the Europeans, like many, may have problems with. They can breathe with that. The idea of something being totally simple is in Zen a very deep idea. I always ask my students to make the sounds empty. Every sound is full of expression before the composer even touches it. Each tam-tam, each harp, has an idyllic view and aura before the composer does anything. Making the sounds empty of all the connotations that fill them is a very deep idea.

PS: How will the elements of social critique transfer when you have your music performed in North America?

HL: We shouldn't talk too much about social critique. If a piece is authentic, it's automatically a critique of our standardized culture, without even the intention of being. Our culture is full of standardized elements. A composer is not a missionary. A composer is not a prophet. A composer is not John the Baptist, who made critiques to the people, saying, "You are all sinners." This political aspect is an illusion. If I thought music was a higher message, then I think I must give some sort of political message, of freedom, of liberty. My teacher was Luigi Nono, a communist. He always had the hope of touching people, and changing their consciousness. I think art does such things, but the composer who wants to manipulate the spirit, or conscience of another will always fail. It's not possible. In Toronto once, I listened to the Sunday morning TV evangelists. That is entertainment. An artist should not be that.

If he's sensitive about his musical, structural, material purity, then whatever he does shall have such an effect of touching people. But through the other side, which he doesn't control. Each fugue or invention of Johann Sebastian Bach was not done to make the world better, but it did make the world better, by switching in a certain way, because it was one of the documents of totally concentrated, totally free human spirit. Not more, not less.

I made an opera that has a social critique story (Hans Christian Andersen's *The Little Match Girl*). Its subject is the coldness of society, and ignorance toward the poor, or the outsider. But at the same time, it's the perfect fairy tale. Because at the same time it's such a sad and serene story, it's much more touching than any pathetic message told directly. Thirty years ago, in a programme note at Donaueschingen, I wrote that I hate messiahs. I hate harlequins. One is a deformed varia- tion of the other, and they're both part of our entertainment service. For every vulnerable person, for anyone who is unprotected, serenity is much more touching than a harlequin or a messiah. I love *Don Quixote*, and I believe in the little girl with the matches. The story of this little girl, just trying to live, to find her own way, who sees a vision in the light of the matches and then dies, is much more provocative than a story that starts out to make a better world. That you can leave to the pop artists. People can pay them for that, and think it is wonderful, or whatever, but that in the end, that is commercial music.

PS: You've written and lectured extensively on your music, while at the same time, admit that your trust in language is receding.

HL: I can talk with a student, and when they want to know something, then I'm using intellectual means to describe the music. But we know exactly that the intellect is only one part of our mind, and one very limited part. I try to make a precise definition of that which can be defined by language, to keep the mind free for what cannot be expressed by language.

PS: The irrational?

HL: Exactly. The irrational, the transcendental, all the things we can't define. It's impossible. I speak about the means I use in composition, why I use them, I try to analyze the cultural situation in which we're living and are formed by. I try to make a diagnosis of all those things, then I try to explain structure, and the construction, because composing is about describing time, with the help of sounds, or vice versa. These are totally practical problems, like an architect has, or an engineer, but we speak about it not to make a design or a construction for itself, because the elements we're working with are full of significations. I try to link the attention to what is behind it. So if you want to explain the secret of Mozart's music—how can you? You can describe the formulas that he didn't even invent, because he was a child of his time. But you can analyze it whatever way you want. Then you listen, and you realize that you didn't speak about what really happened as you were listening to it. It's the best way not to mystify the irrational. When you talk about magic, again you're at the problem of entertainment. We should be rational, the rational is helping us, but we shouldn't forget the transcendental, which is the crucial point of art. Without it, it doesn't deserve the word art.

PS: It has been said that your music is "negative." Do you agree?

HL: I often see myself described as a composer who is against, who is destructive, refusing. But to view things more clearly, you have to remove what is preventing you from seeing. Therefore, each decision also has a negative component.

PS: That's part of everything.

HL: Yes. Tonality was something that wasn't rejected, but had to be overcome. We have to find new antennae in ourselves, to listen more, and this is a wonderful adventure of discovery. For me, my music has as much beauty as any conventional music, maybe more. Beauty is a precious idea. I want to liberate this term from the standardized categories. I'll give you a little example. I used to teach children, and I presented them the music of Stockhausen, et cetera. They said that it wasn't beautiful, they didn't like it. I asked them what they liked, what they thought was beautiful, and they first hesitantly named some pop music. The next week, I went there and brought two pictures with me. One was an attractive photograph of the movie star Sophia Loren. The other was a drawing by Albrecht Dürer, who had drawn a picture of his mother: very old, with a long nose, and bitter looking face. She had a hard life, and her face was full of wrinkles. I showed the two pictures and asked, "Who is more beautiful?" They were totally confused, and then came the wonderful answer I'll never forget—it was the highlight of my life. A girl said, "I think the ugly one is more beautiful." This is the dialectical way. Looking at this picture, one feels the precise observation of her son. Not to make it more beautiful, not idealized, just showing it. It was full of intensity. To me, as important as beauty is the word intensity. I search for this in music.

But rejection? I'm allergic to the idea that my music is rejection. Did Schoenberg reject tonality because he made atonal music? No. He was going with what he had learned from tradition. The whole direction of occidental music is going on from tradition by provocation. Provoking humankind to new experiences. This is human, this is beautiful, this is serene, and it requires the participation of the listener in this adventure. Provocation in this sense is not a negative thing. Society's laziness creates these polemical situations. I've had such scandals because of these thoughts, where people were angry because, on the one hand, they love music, and this was a music they couldn't follow, they were lost, and on the other hand, they preferred a comfortable way of thinking about music. Maybe they need such comfort, because they are full of fear in everyday life, there are so many catastrophes. Going to an opera or concert hall, they don't want to be confused. But I think in that situation, you shouldn't have fear of being confused. You should be glad to be confused. It's the most active way to live. Confusion is to discover oneself in a new way. This is my dialectic of provocation and beauty, and music as a great and wonderful adventure. I like to speak of music in positive terms. I was so happy when you asked me, "If it's not music, what is it then?" This is a question we should cultivate. I wait for pieces that bring me to this existential question.

Juliet Palmer

COMPOSER and sound artist Juliet Kiri Palmer was born in New Zealand, and moved, to Princeton, New Jersey, in 1990, where she met her future husband, James Rolfe. They currently reside in Toronto. On many occasions, I have had the opportunity to spend time talking and breaking bread with them in the creative household they share. Having previously seen Palmer's interdisciplinary performance Flotsam & Jetsam (2001) at Kitchener's Open Ears festival, and having already interviewed James, it was clearly time to have a slightly more formal discussion, and to learn more about her work and diverse creative goals.

PS: In your dissertation, you write that it's "a defence and celebration of the playful in music and art." You mention a number visual artists (Jeff Koons and Marcel Duchamp, for example), but I'd like you to talk about examples of the playful in music.

JP: At the time that I wrote that, I had just gotten very excited about C. P. E. Bach's music that I heard as being extremely playful in terms of rapid jumping between ideas and a kind of over-the-top rate of change that borders on the comic. He was one person whose music I wanted to look at more closely and understand how it works. I looked at Franco Donatoni's music as well, partly because his outward stance was so playful, but I think there's a deep silliness going on as well. When you look at how he talks about his music—perhaps I just have trouble being extremely serious, so even if someone else is, I hear it as being silly. I was looking at how his music itself might manifest that playfulness. His piece *Refrain* has a kind of hint of jazziness, but not quite, so it teases you into listening in a way where you're actually going to be frustrated, or disappointed, or surprised, and that approach intrigues me. I'm interested in music that isn't what it seems to be. For me there's no appeal in writing a piece that's a convincing example of any particular style. I'd rather write a piece that seems like it's something and then it's not. It fools you. Then your whole understanding of the genre or style is altered. It's that alternation between different states and different ways of thinking that interests me.

PS: It's expectation?

JP: Yes, frustrating expectation. I started thinking about it in terms of an oscillation between different states. In that oscillation there's an energy released. You have a basic example of that in a kid's game like peekaboo. What is so funny about that? I mean it's just... someone's there, and then they're not. It's hilarious. So, alternation between two extremely different states can bring humour, but humour is extraordinarily perplexing to comprehend or to plan.

PS: What's an example of humour in contemporary music?

JP: I find a lot of my own music funny.

PS: Humour is pretty subjective though.

JP: It is, and highly contextual. A lot of it has to do with timing, but obviously, humour relies on a language that people understand. If you're using a gesture, which to that particular audience has become

hackneyed or has become a signifier of some particular situation
or language or style, then the way you use it can have a humorous
effect. But if you're audience isn't party to that, then it's lost. How is
Beethoven funny? Or the Haydn symphonies that are hilarious the
whole way they end, which is so silly because there's a convention of
cadencing and he does it the nth degree that it becomes ridiculous. So,
it's funny.

PS: I've never thought of Beethoven as funny.

JP: *(Laughing.)*

PS: What would you consider to be unplayful in music?

JP: Music that takes itself so seriously. Rather, composers take themselves so seriously that they lose sight of the connections between
their own art form and the outside world, or other art forms. There is
no sense of a play between ideas—it's just a presentation of technique,
or a manipulation of musical materials.

PS: How did this become an issue for you? Did you feel there was an
absence of playfulness in contemporary music?

JP: Yes, that's why I was talking about a defence of playfulness, because
I felt there was this pressure to be serious, to embody somehow a
particular set of ideals that made your work authentic contemporary
music. That was very interesting to me.

PS: Were you reacting to your own choice to go to Princeton, one of the
more serious places?

JP: It is and it isn't. Steve Mackey, who I studied with, has an incredible amount of humour in his pieces. Ideas that are just off the deep
end. He has an orchestra piece where at one point there's just this
recording, quite a hokey recording, from a boom box, of his dog
barking, which sounds like a gimmick, but it's very well integrated.
I guess that's what I'm talking about by playfulness—allowing your
imagination take flight beyond convention.

PS: What's the line between that and entertainment?

JP: There's still an element of seriousness involved in the endeavour.
What we're playing with is our ideas. I had heard all about Cirque du
Soleil as this incredible postmodern circus, and when I saw them, I
was so disappointed because I realized that it's entertainment. There
was no intellectual rigour to what they're doing.

PS: How are these ideas evident in your own work?

JP: There are some pieces that are obviously playful. For instance, back in 1999, I went to Voix Nouvelles at Royaumont. Les Percussions de Strasbourg were there that year, and somehow or other, I ended up having to write a music theatre piece and I immediately thought the European theatre music piece is Mauricio Kagel. And from everything I'd seen, I really dislike them because I didn't find them at all funny, but I felt they were meant to be funny. So I took upon myself the challenge of exploring that language for these two performances. The audience viewed it as pretty funny, and at same time, the material they were dealing with was quite bleak. That's another that quite interests me. I find that humour is a good way of approaching material that otherwise you couldn't face head on. So, in this case it was the futurist manifesto by Marinetti, which has some horrific images glorifying violence. It tells everyone that you should take a shower of blood. It's a very high macho position that he's taking, and I wanted to subvert that with the piece.

PS: What piece is that?

JP: It's called *Bloodshower*. You end up with this weird, sort of sadomasochistic relationship between the two performers, working with very everyday objects and a drum kit. A whole ton of beer bottle caps, a lot of water, buckets, chairs, jars—all that kind of stuff—and the text itself from Marinetti. The final scene they're just sweeping the floor, cleaning up, singing a bizarre kind of love song, in which the text is something like, "and yet it feels so sweet to cause you pain." It's actually a painful text, but the way I present it is in a humorous way, so that it sneaks in, and you can digest it later.

PS: Kind of like how some games are really borderline funny, but also disconcerting?

JP: Yes, disconcerting is a very good word to use. I think someone else had said about my music that there are pieces that kind of groove, but they don't. Either I'm really bad at grooving or, more to the point, I'm interested in riffing on the idea of grooving. How do you set that up and then swat someone's expectations, so that they're disconcerted; so there's a gap between what you expect and what you get? And in that gap, people enter into the piece. I think if something is too expected, there's no room for anyone enter into a dialogue with the piece. You want to have some kind of discrepancy or some flaw, you could call it.

PS: Do you think things like timing and expectation change with the decades?

JP: I'm just thinking of acting and singing styles changing. That's a very theatrical artistic expression. And certainly, timing is key to a lot of those changes. So, yes, it's certainly possible. There's an earlier piece called *Self* for three percussionists and the text for that is by a Chinese poet Gucheng. It's a very physical piece, and the challenge is to run as fast as they can around the entire battery—there are three percussion stations. And they have to hit specific instruments while they're saying words from this text. In some pieces, I've enjoyed giving performers a challenge, and setting them as players in a game.

PS: When you're talking about the pieces, it's as though the elasticity of thinking and that quality you're looking for really is concentrated more on theatre than it is on how you deal with materials.

JP: No, not necessarily. I think it manifests itself that way in a music theatre piece, but if you're looking at a purely instrumental piece, I would think of *Mother Hubbard*, in which the process by which I wrote that was very playful and irresponsible. I wanted to see what happens when I intercut instrumental materials with found audio materials from the internet. How if I took them into small enough pieces and mixed them, they would start to form a new substance. In a way, I'm playing a game with these materials, and the listener and I get to judge what the result of that game is. Does that seem gamey to you?

PS: Yes. It has that quality.

JP: It was an experiment as to how much I wanted to edit that process before it's presented. And that would be one of the more raw examples that I have unleashed to an audience. With that piece, I say it's intercut, but it's different every time because the ensemble is not chained to the tape or CD part. They're just hitting on/off separately and when they collide, they collide. If something happens in the sounds, that's just serendipitous. If I did that piece again, I'd like to deal with separate sound files and audio tracks, and maybe have some triggering happening so that there are more connections. Still playfulness and unpredictability, but more causality.

PS: One consistent factor in your pieces is that they constantly look outside of themselves.

JP: Yes, absolutely. For me to sit down and just play a chord on the piano, like that's the beginning, and then go from there onwards deciding pitches from the beautiful pure soundworld where they are all hovering around me... I don't work like that. There will be something that strikes me in my everyday life. Take the sound in *Mother Hubbard*. The computer part all comes from this one little audio clip that comes from the Quebec Summit protesters, anti-globalization protestors. There was a little CNN video clip on the internet, and I just took the sound off that and worked with it, and the digital distortion that resulted in some of the sound machinations. What put my ear in that particular clip was this incredible emotional depth to such a flattened sound. I mean the sound quality is really wretched, but in it is this amazing sense that so many people were gathered and so many people wanted to stop this machine of globalization. Just the sounds of their voices, and sounds of drumming, were incredibly moving. In the orchestra piece I just wrote for Orchestre Métropolitain de Montréal, it was the idea of things sandwiched between Stravinsky's *Firebird* and Tchaikovsky's *Swan Lake*, and I ended up writing a piece called *Buzzard*, which is this most ugly bird that doesn't even sing. The music is completely scavenged from those two pieces.

PS: So, in looking outside of the pieces, you're wanting to tap into signification?

JP: Yes, I'm not interested in a pure music. I'm very engaged in the world around me. I don't know if it's a political music. That's a very uneasy sort of term, whether political music exists even. But, I certainly can't separate my political concerns from the way I would approach music or what would motivate me to write a piece? You don't want to beat people about the head on an issue, but I also don't want to be putting my time and energy into something that is simply entertaining or decorative.

PS: Each of the pieces you've mentioned also deals with juxtaposition?

JP: That's true. That's an essential condition of how we live. Particularly now. We're not living in a holistic, agrarian culture where I grow the tree and I make it into the chair and it's beautiful and I eat my bowl of barley that I grew. We live in such an age of juxtapositions where geographic and temporal realities are constantly colliding. Those kinds of juxtapositions in music... to me, it's sort of inevitable.

PS: Can you talk a bit more about that, specifically in relation to *Secret Arnold*?

JP: *Secret Arnold* is the first orchestra piece of mine that I like. At the time, I said, "What am I listening to?" And I was listening to Portishead, this fairly obscure dub album with Randy Chin. And I was also reading the Leonard Bernstein lectures that he gave at Harvard. He was writing about the Schoenberg string quartet in the movement where the soprano suddenly comes in out of the blue, and the language took us into this new realm of twelve-tone. So, in that piece, I wanted to create a space where these three very different musics could cohabit. What was fun about it, once I started to break them down, was there were so many areas of overlap. It was kind of spooky. The Portishead and the dub clip, this wonderful little harmonic space, and then the Schoenberg... it was a really nice experience because of the way they opened up to each other. That's how I sort of thought of them, as characters finding things in common and making music together.

PS: Do you try to achieve a unity between them or separately amongst them?

JP: At times, they're playing with each other, so to speak. And other times, one strong identity interrupts. So, there is that juxtaposition of very different musical materials. That being said, some of them are extreme juxtapositions in that piece; are materials derived from the same composer. I'm not keeping one person's identity so intact that they're the same throughout the piece. It's more what happens if you speed the Portishead and slow down the Schoenberg... Do they start to ooze into each other? I think of that process as a way of re-listening and re-hearing music that's already familiar to you.

PS: Are you seeking out connections between them despite their disconnection?

JP: Yes, but I don't want to homogenize them into each other. It's more an experiment of what happens when they share the same space.

PS: How do you want it to be perceived?

JP: In that piece, I felt that there were elements of humour to do with timings of different qualities of material. But also there are moments that turned out to be very beautiful, where you heard something that in dub is quite raw and funky, but when you orchestrate it can become luscious and Mahlerian. That is very fascinating to me, the process that something like a character shows another side of themselves that you hadn't realized was there.

PS: That's a recontextualization thing?

JP: It could be recontextualizing. Another aspect of it is that people who might think of these musics as having nothing in common would maybe think again, and have more open ears about how they hear things.

PS: What would Schoenberg have to say about that?

JP: I'm sure he'd be fine with it. I followed dodecaphonic procedures throughout *(laughing)*.

PS: How have these ideas come together in your recent work?

JP: I just had a new piece played in New York two weeks ago, which was for piano and percussion. The texts were by Dennis Lee, from his new book *UN*. They had wanted something theatrical, but in fact, the theatricalities ended up being pretty subtle. They don't really move, other than to play their instruments. But they do sing and they do speak because there is text.

PS: What is the subject matter of the texts?

JP: It's a cycle of poems that are very short. There are about fifty of them. The language is breaking down and reconstituting itself, into words that don't exist, but you kind of know what they mean because they come from the familiar. It's about the destruction of our world. There's a fibre-apocalyptic bebop kind of feeling to the whole thing. To me they're very musical and very dark poems, so it seemed nice that the players would sing them. They either sing or speak at the same time as playing. The performers were up for the challenge and they really responded to the energy in Dennis's poetry. It's very bleak, but the energy of the poems sustains you through that bleakness. I'm also writing a piece for Continuum for February. Each of the players now has a dream diary. They have to write down any dreams where they dream of music, and that's the starting point of the piece.

Christian Wolff

CHRISTIAN WOLFF was born in Nice, France, in 1934, and moved to the United States in 1941. He studied classics at Harvard, and taught there and at Dartmouth University until his retirement in 1999. Wolff is often associated with other magnificent American experimentalists, including John Cage, Morton Feldman, David Tudor, and Merce Cunningham, among others. His work bears their influence and inspiration, yet is also unique in many respects. Christian Wolff has composed for professional and amateur musicians, and through his music seeks shared freedom, self-determination, and democratically-spirited collaboration. This interview was commissioned by Arraymusic, for the programme of their second Scratch Festival (2004).

PS: The degree of specification in your music—the degree of freedom and constraint—varies from score to score. What types of variation are there?

CW: Types of pitch indication vary. They might be specific, they might not be. The notation might be variable; for example, you might have a stave where you can read either treble or bass clef. As far as rhythm is concerned, they may be specific in the conventional sense; they may be determined by the time it takes for a sound to decay to nothing, dependent on the resonance characteristics of the sound itself. They may also be determined by cuing systems. That is, you have a sound that starts and continues, then is cut off by the next heard sound coming from another player, without knowing when it will occur. Sometimes tempos are variously indicated, sometimes with precise metronome markings, sometimes nothing at all. Dynamics are also variable, perhaps the most often left out. There are also pieces where the instrumentation is not fixed, where actual colour of the sound is open.

PS: What necessitates this variation, and the variety of approach between pieces? What's behind that?

CW: Various factors. Within a given piece, there may be a whole gamut of these. It may go from quite precise to quite variable, and there you might say it's a compositional choice. Of wanting things that are precise, and others that are variable in performance, things that feel variable to me when I imagine them. It might be a situation where I know the performers involved, and they may or may not be performers who are familiar with the situation of working with open elements in notation. In that case, I may make a more conventional type of score.

PS: Is it the context, then?

CW: Yes, exactly.

PS: What is the ideal context for your music? The performers, the performance situation?

CW: There is no single one. I recently did a piece for the Arditti String Quartet. They've never done my music because they didn't want to deal with the indeterminate elements. They're extraordinary performers, and I was asked to make a piece for them, so I made a short string quartet. Towards the end, there is a section where there are choices involved, but as far as notation is concerned, it's relatively straightforward and conventional, because they don't want to deal with anything else. I'm looking forward to hearing it.

In other situations, there are performers with whom I've worked on and off over the years, ones who I know how they function, and what kind of musicality they represent. With them, the element of indefiniteness is intrinsic to the whole situation, and I'm very happy with that.

PS: Do you welcome these constraints? Do they stimulate you creatively?

CW: Yes. Music is already so abstract, so anything you have *(laughs)* that gives you some focus, is very helpful.

PS: In the Scratch Festival, your piece *Burdocks* will be performed multiple times. What interests you about this prospect?

CW: No two versions of it will ever be alike. In this setting, you get a demonstration, in a day or two, of how that might work.

PS: Would you agree that you engage performers not so much in the recreation of your music, but in its varyingly unpredictable emergence?

CW: That sounds like a good formulation of it. I enjoy that unpredictability. On the other hand, it's become a way of thinking such that it's almost as though it's not unpredictable to me. And of course, when it's played for people who are maybe not aware of the conditions in which the performers are playing, do they hear that what the performers are doing is the result of something that's not predictable? What is the specific effect of writing that way? I think there is one; otherwise, I wouldn't do it. I think that what you get, among other things, is a kind of rhythm, of the succession of events, and even the shape of individual events—you get a kind of rhythm that you can't get any other way. I don't think you could notate it. If you were to play one of these indeterminate pieces and then transcribe it into score form, which would then presumably be played to sound exactly like the indeterminate version... I suppose you could do it, but it just wouldn't work, it wouldn't sound right.

PS: They would approach it differently. Is it also the togetherness of the process, of the approach to making the work, and the communal decision making of the performers that makes the work?

CW: Yes. It's a little idealistic, but you get a kind of sound image, I imagine, of collaborative work.

PS: For you, what's the origin of this approach to music making?

CW: I'm trying to think back to when I started doing this, in the fifties. I was with other composers—John Cage, Morton Feldman, Earle Brown, and David Tudor, in a way, all of whom were working with various kinds of indeterminate procedures. I was interested in doing that too, but I didn't want to duplicate what they were doing. The thing that had occurred to me that was not covered by what they were doing was this possibility of using the performance situation and the performers themselves as the way to go about making these indeterminate situations. It was in the air, and in a way, it was by elimination that I started doing it, since the others weren't.

In retrospect, it occurred to me that one model for it is performance as such. I hung around a lot with pianists when I was young. I was struck by the fact that they tended to learn a piece of classical music in a certain way, and then try always to play it in that way. That always seemed a little odd to me. Not long ago, I asked a pianist friend, if when she went out to play, does she actually know when she walks out on the stage how she is going to play this Beethoven sonata. She's a very good pianist, and she looked at me and said, "No." In other words, even though she was playing from a score, which in every way was quite fixed, she approached it in the spirit of an improviser. That doesn't really answer where my intentions came from, but it suggests a kind of parallel situation, and an interest in the process of performance itself.

PS: Given that in some cases you involve decision making from the performers, how has the interpretation of your pieces changed over the years? Is a performance of *Burdocks* today different from a performance of *Burdocks* when it was first composed?

CW: That might well be, yes. With that piece, when you look at the material, it seems amazingly free and open, but in fact, each part has very distinctive characteristics, and I can almost always tell exactly which one is being played. There are differences, but it seems to me that you can't say they're historically determined. I haven't noticed that much difference from a performance in the seventies and from a performance now.

With other pieces, it's different. I have noticed it, definitely, that the pieces sort of take on the colour of the time in which they're being done. The *Piece for One, Two, or Three People*, for instance, I heard it played by John Zorn, and umm, it sounded like John Zorn. That piece has a number of pages, and he chose the one that is most adaptable to an individual kind of take. That's when the difference struck me most strongly, partly because in that case you had a very strong musical personality—himself a composer—with a very specific kind of style, rather different from mine. His work has an aggressive, hard-edged quality to it, which is not quite my way. That's a style that emerged in the eighties—I wouldn't have heard that piece that way when it was written back in the sixties. Otherwise, it's not as strong as I would have expected—that shift through time.

PS: So much composed music is about repetition, variation, and sequential development. Ultimately, memory. To what degrees are memory and the present moment active in your work, and is there a stress between them?

CW: I have a stretch of work, in the middle to later seventies, early eighties, where I did a lot of pieces that involve variation. Variation on pre-existing material and tunes. There, memory is obviously important, because the tune is the basis of almost everything that goes on in the piece. So I have the memory of the tune in my head as I work, if not actually in the notes that I worked from. Cage once volunteered the difference between his work and Feldman's and Brown's and mine, and he characterized mine by the fact that it was musical, which for him was not necessarily a compliment *(laughs)*. Then he explained that it's because it's involved with repetition and variation. It's true, but only for this limited area where I've worked, but tend not to do so much anymore. If I do work with tune material, it tends to be buried, so you don't hear it. It becomes almost only a technical procedure, or just material, rather than a sound image that is elaborated and where pitch is recalled.

PS: What about in the indeterminate pieces?

CW: That would be a different story. There, I think the element of memory and variation would tend to be related to the limitations of the materials that are being used in the piece. For instance, because of the way the notation works, it's unlikely the repetitions would be similar, but there would be a shape. The simplest example of that is one of the sections of *Burdocks*, which involves three players at a time, making what is essentially a kind of chorale. The notation indicates no pitch; it indicates simply rhythmic movement from relatively short, to variable for about four chords, then back to relatively short. That makes a phrase, and then you just repeat that over and over. That's repetition, if you like, but that's repetition with a great deal of flexibility to it. There's a kind of scaffolding of a rhythmic shape. Pitch itself is quite distortable and variable, but it doesn't take you too long to catch on to what the shape is, and then you relate to that, if you like. It's a memory, and/or variation situation at that rather abstract level.

PS: Can you identify some connections between your work and anarchist thinking?

CW: It's hard. It's a jump. When we were talking a little while ago about collaborative and communal activity, where you have what you could call a democratic situation, where it's very difficult for one person to dominate. That's not so much anarchy as it is a kind of communism. Anarchy... I'm very sympathetic to it, but I don't quite see it in the work. It has more to do with collaboration and with getting rid of hierarchies. That's not quite anarchy, is it? It's close, clearly. Maybe I'm taking the term too literally.

PS: You do explicitly seek a political connection in some work, though.

CW: Let me begin with a simpler notion, which happened to me in the seventies, which was when I explicitly took on a political stance, and underwent a kind of political awakening. I went at it very directly, by using material that had political connection—songs, or texts which I used in the music in some way. The notion that the actual way the music is put together is set up for performance and is performed, that that can have a political suggestion to it, and can be a kind of political model... I never pursued it. I mean, I do now, because I've been made aware of it, but when I first began making those pieces, even *Burdocks*, I didn't particularly think of them that way. It was just a way of putting the music together. It was more a question of temperament, or attitude, rather than some kind of ideological program. Now that the connections have been made explicitly, I can't help but be aware of it, but I still don't about doing a politically correct piece, doing this, that, or the other. If it happens, it also reflects certain views I have about ideal forms of social life.

On a more pragmatic level, many of these pieces that are indeterminate are not, in the conventional sense, difficult to play. That had a lot to do with the fact that I myself am not a virtuoso by any stretch of the imagination, but on the other hand, I very much wanted to be playing. These pieces were originally done at a time when it was very difficult to get professional performances. We had almost no resources. To make music that was available for performance to a wide range of performers, not necessarily professionals, that was definitely a factor. It's a little paradoxical, because I was hanging out with people like David Tudor. It really pleased me to be able to make a music that on the one hand would be interesting for somebody like Tudor, who could do wonderful things with it, and at the same time, would also be available for people like myself, who were basically amateurs, as far as performing went.

Mauricio Kagel

MAURICIO KAGEL was born in Buenos Aires, Argentina, in 1931, and is arguably the most prolific and respected Argentinean-born composer. On Pierre Boulez's
urging, he moved from Buenos Aires to Cologne in 1957, where he became associated
with Stockhausen and Ligeti, while working at the Electronic Music Studio and
attending the Darmstadt Summer Course for New Music. His music, films, and
theatre works break virtually every supposed rule of musical conduct, and leave the
receiver with a double-edged impression of both gentle humour and dark madness.
On February 2, 2004, a day after the New Music Concerts event that concluded a
multi-day quasi-Kagel festival, I had the opportunity to speak with him about his
vast body of work, and share an hour of his bright and nervous energy.

PS: I vividly recall being at the Concertgebouw in Amsterdam in 1991, witnessing the orchestra play a long, thickly orchestrated, and strongly Germanic music, your *Variation and Fugue*. Slowly, from the raised stairway at the back of the hall, there emerged a costumed figure—Brahms. While the orchestra kept playing, he walked down the stairs and through the orchestra, looking quizzically at the musicians. As he arrived at the front of the stage, you could see his yellow, cadaverous skin. He looked at the conductor, sat down on the podium, and put his head on his hand, depressed. Why?

MK: The piece was written for the 140th anniversary of the birth of Brahms. In this piece, he appears to come back to Hamburg. He had been rejected from Hamburg, and this was a kind of symbol for all composers, who always have trouble with their own town, their own land, be it Hamburg, Amsterdam, or anywhere. After Brahms's monologue, Handel appears, dressed in eighteenth century costume, and took him away to the paradise of composers—let's say this paradise is nowhere.

PS: It sounds like they represent something personal for you.

MK: I'm reflecting very intensely what I think about musical life and musical history, what happens to us, and our relationship with musical history and styles. This piece is a kind of X-ray perspective of these thoughts. It's very difficult for me to think that music is "pure" music. It *never* works like that.

PS: It was as though he were asking a question of the orchestra as well. He was confused.

MK: He (Brahms) was hearing his music, but through my "glasses." For me, this was one of the most interesting pieces I wrote in that decade, because the task was to take the music of Brahms and not distort it. I superimposed negative and positive, like with film and photographic technique. Over-exposed and under-exposed, but together. This seems for me very important, to clarify my relationship with the past. And of course, Brahms is *hearing* this. He recognized his music, and at the same time felt that there were things going on that weren't from the plume of his pen. I'm a perfectionist and, in addition to the music, only through the roles of Brahms and Handel and their accurate costumes can we take perfection into the field of ambiguity. Irony, ambiguity, and comedy are much more difficult than pathetic things or drama in the classical sense. We have no tradition of humour in music. Music itself isn't humourless, but the people administrating music are. They don't understand the diaphone of certain pieces and composers, the happiness of being touched by comedy. I don't mean in the American English meaning of only "entertainment," but as in the classical Greek comedy.

PS: The *Variation and Fugue* is an excellent example of two streams in your work. On the one hand, a commentary on tradition, and on the other, the implementation of theatrical elements. How does tradition inform your music?

MK: The problem of the avant-garde in the sixties was that it tried to be avant-garde at every moment, always the opposite of the rearguard. In each of us belonging to this curious society of composers, you can discover traces of conservatism that are more-or-less strong. The difference in these composers was how extreme their conservatism was. This is very important to me—how conservative was the avant-garde of the sixties, and how conservative has experimental music become today? I could speak about academic experimental music, but then I'm talking about killing all of the possibilities that an experiment can have. In an experiment, the end result is very difficult to predict. Certain processes are unpredictable, but experimental music has become very predictable. I'm not interested in the old opposition of avant-garde and rearguard. I'm a classic example of someone who did things that weren't in the mainstream during the time of the avant-garde. To obey the rules of style, I was always absolutely against that. Pieces that are written without anarchy, without going *against* style, *against* the stony dimension of style, are more-or-less impossible to hear.

What I'm trying to do is something that I love, like, and think I need. In that moment, you have to be very honest. A few months ago, during a podium discussion in Scandinavia, I was asked to give advice for young composers, and my only word was to be honest. If you try to be honest with yourself, and write what you think you need—not what you think *other* people, like music critics or colleagues need—you will then be trying to communicate your truth. If it has a trace of truth, then it will be interesting.

PS: So for you, in the middle of the avant-garde, the truth was to explore the past somehow?

MK: *No, no, no*, I wasn't saying that. The past is a very important dimension of the present, but it's *not* the present. You can't neglect the past. We are composers today because there is a lot of music written before us, and we have to be aware of this. If that is what you mean by tradition, *then* I will accept it. Tradition is made by a large number of traditions. If a university in a town has a very strong trumpet teacher, you can be sure that after a number of years, this town will have a tradition of very good trumpet players. "Tradition" can be used in a very superficial way.

PS: When it comes to performance practice, in many instances you establish a type, or mode, of listening, and then disrupt it. You change the hierarchy. How do you do that, and why?

MK: You never know exactly how the audience hears music. You ask ten people what they hear and you have ten different answers. Very often, it's a matter of plural interpretation. I'm not thinking about reaction, or success or failure, but the very rare moment of hearing music. What does it mean to hear music? You never know what your neighbour perceives from the same piece you are hearing at a concert. Let's transpose this problem to the performers. I think the ideal is to get, in the performer, a kind of double personality. One is the technician, and the other is reflecting his cultural behaviour towards a piece. These are two absolutely different things, and we know this. We speak of a pianist who is a good technician, yet we say his playing is "cold" *(laughing)*. It's not only about being *passionate*, but also reflecting the cultural behaviour to the piece of music.

How do I do this? For example, when you're walking along the street, and see a stone on the ground, and then trip or stumble, you will become very conscious of where you are stepping after that. Before the danger, your progress was naïve, or unconscious. After the accident, you're *very* conscious, for a certain number of steps, that you're continuing to walk. This is a way of describing, in very brief form, the triangular relation between the work, notation, and the performer. My idea is that the performer starts his thinking machine on a higher level, changing to a higher gear. I try to make them ask themselves, "Why is the piece being done in this way? What is my *real* function in this musical context?" How you can arrive, through mostly traditional music notation, at something that is an absolutely *non*-traditional context, is an invitation to think about musical performance, and musical language? Many performers are concentrating on the technical field of reproducing the musical score. The musical perception is condemned to a lower level, and this is a pity.

PS: So you change, and disrupt things to keep everybody *super*-conscious.

MK: Yes. *Aware* that they are a very complex mechanism. The simplest things can become theatre. A classical example of that would be if you're sitting in a bar, reading a newspaper, and notice that someone is staring at you. You stop *reading* the newspaper, and you then *look* like someone who is reading the newspaper. The same can occur in music. Speaking with performers, I was very happy to learn that this awareness has a function.

PS: What about the listener?

MK: I'm often surprised by how sensitive listeners are to what is going in a piece. For example, the public can be very conservative and never want to hear any more dissonance, and so on. But after fifty years of going to concerts and making concerts, I can tell you that, most of the time, the public is not unjust. If you measure minutes, or seconds of applause, you will see that the perception or *real* importance of the piece has a relative number of seconds measured in applause. We can look at the opera companies and complain that they are always playing the same fifty operas, but, well, they are the best. Even if they are badly played, even with horrible scenery, even if the staging is impossible, they function, because they are so good that they're very difficult to ruin.

PS: You can say that as a composer living in Germany, but here, don't you think that the insistence on those same fifty operas could exclude the creation of another great new one that's being written now?

MK: *(Loudly) No, no, no*, I'm not saying there is no place for the new, I'm not an idiot conservative. I'm telling you something that's related to the history of opera. Of course, we have to do new operas! The success of *Madame Butterfly* or *The Marriage of Figaro* shouldn't be used to reject any kind of adventure with a contemporary language. I want this to be very clear. You know that I am an example of the responsibilities of musical theatre, and an example of saying "No" to this world of opera. I've never written for the applause—you know this.

PS: Yes.

MK: At the same time, I'm regarding, as an historian and cultural geologist, what happens with opera and that repertoire. I'm regarding this and asking why this mixture of conservatism, pragmatism, and very poor instinct for adventure that is part of this world of opera? This, for a certain nucleus of people, can be very provocative.

PS: Are you also mocking convention?

MK: I'm *composing*. I'm breaking conventions, it's true, and I'm using this as dialectical material for my compositions.

PS: But there is also a certain amount of absurdity in what is going on.

MK: Absolutely. The *world* in which we live is absurd, from the beginning to the end. It's full of magical absurdity. If you have the sensibility to see this, you become very aware of it. The musical world is trying to be very rational because music itself is inexplicable and irrational. Music is a rational discipline that communicates irrational substance. Can you define music? I can't. *This* is what makes music so extraordinary. Nobody can define it, and because of that, we insist so much on the rationalism of our thoughts, and craftsmanship, and tradition. All this is done with a comedic rationalism. Music is inexplicable, and I'm very glad about that *(hearty laugher)*.

PS: What is the political subtext?

MK: Practically all of our actions have political implications. It depends upon how strong our actions are. We are placed, by definition, in a political context. If you get on the subway without a ticket, you will be punished, because without paying, the city can't continue the subway. Money is part of political convention. All that we expect from the government is related to politics. We take it for granted, of course, but we, ourselves, are part of this political strategy. Non-political actions don't exist. The only question is how conscious we are of the political substance of our actions. Related to music, I can tell you that the simplest piece of music can become a political manifesto if the political context of the country is against that music. In the time of apartheid in South Africa, I was sure that the Ninth Symphony of Beethoven wasn't played very often, because the words are revolutionary, and anti-apartheid. For example, in South America, in Argentina, I was astonished that the folk music (which is much more important in certain countries than the classical Western music), was suddenly forbidden because the words are against the present government. You see how political that non-political music can become. This was a revelation for me, of the relativity of one message or another. Each message can be translated, and in the translation, perhaps you're not translating the words, but the meaning. These meanings can become flexible, and stress certain words over others, and you get a different message.

At the same time, I'm not naïve. I know that it's not possible to write a piece for piano and think this is political. In the sixties and seventies, I found it absurd that the political content of the piece was explained in the programme notes, while the piece just sounded like the Darmstadt school. This was not only naïve and absurd, but treasonous to very serious ideas of political communication. In this way, intellectuals have, almost by definition, bad conscience, because they know this is the tradition of the twentieth century, they know they are speaking about the proletariat, but they are not a *part* of the proletariat. They're trying to educate the workers, but the workers are in the *factories*. They make pieces that say that the system is bad, and there are crimes to humanity and the world, but to write it about the people who don't listen to it, who hate it, is eminently absurd. It was an escape from reality, and has nothing to do with politics. I was against that, but wrote a piece like *Der Tribun*, which is about a politician preparing a speech, using applause from a tape and march music that is impossible to march to because the rhythm changes all the time *(Ten Marches to Miss the Victory)*. I prefer to write music instead of manifestos. I am only a composer, and I'm not preparing something that will be effective in the political field, but I am conscious that musical language and musical style are two different things. We have to work to develop a very fine grammar and semantics of musical language. This is a part of my work.

John Rea

JOHN REA was born in Toronto in 1944, spent time studying in California and Princeton, and had sojourns in Berlin and Mannheim. Since 1973, he has spent the majority of his time living in Montreal, where he teaches at McGill University. On January 31, 2004, Toronto audiences heard the Esprit Orchestra play his work Treppenmusik (1982), for ensemble and tape delay on a concert entitled Les idées fixes. As well, his work Man/Butterfly (Homme/Papillon) was performed by Esprit in November of 2002. Rea describes this work as an "engineering feat" to assemble, with its thirty-minute duration, implementation of Disklavier,[1] and multifarious compositional concerns to keep order of. That work, and numerous others of his making, has struck a sensitive chord among listeners, myself included.

PS: This series of interviews is called "composer to composer." Yet with you, the term "composer" is sometimes blurry. In fact, when asked *if* you're a composer, you have on occasion answered that you're not sure.

JR: *(Laughing)* Right...

PS: When applied to you, I see this term through a lens covered in Vaseline, where you're perched, posing as any number of interchangeable identities. I know that you're a composer, because you write music, and I listen to your music. Why is the term so unclear for you?

JR: The answer is designed to be provocative, and asks the interlocutor to question the answer, which is what you're doing—questioning my previous answers. The whole answer circulates around a profession, a way of being, *un métier*, literally a capacity to do a certain thing, in this case in the world of sound. Sometimes in our country, you tend to act like a composer, to work like a composer, even to be perceived as one, but you don't necessarily feel you are one. Certainly I don't, sometimes, because these things in our country are missing: follow-up and continuity. You're often starting from zero all the time, in many endeavours. That's not only the case for people my age, but even for young people. So, unlike the practice of art in other cultures, ours is a perpetually fragile one. That's how I answer the question—some days I am a composer, some days I'm not.

PS: But doesn't it also have to do with how you approach the *act* of composing?

JR: Every artist, every composer comes to some kind of understanding with what it is that they do. Some types of artists learn very quickly that they can make a "product." Some do it very, very well, some polish the products, and continue to have a significant output. Sometimes painters work this way, whenever they find a kind of *groove*, or a *brushstroke* that really works. In composition, in the concert music field, although there is something similar, I have always pulled away from that, and made each successive piece challenging to me in a different way. I've always liked to change a little bit each time. These are modest things—I mean, I still use pencil and paper, but I try to keep the projects variable, and to not have too many of them, in a way to avoid the problem of getting into a rut with brushstrokes.

PS: The difficulty in using the term "composer" is also somehow about the identity *within* the pieces, in the sense that the pieces are very layered, internally and externally. There is often a significant cast of others whose identities are present in your work. So the role of you as composer has changed—you're like a conduit, a conciliator.

JR: This is a good intuition. It means one is channelled to listen in a particular way. Sometimes, what one describes is put into the piece to be more perceivable than other elements. I appreciate multi-layered literary, cinematic, and visual works, and I also try to respond to them in my way. Maybe it's communication—one sends the messages. Artworks are messages in some ways. It's not ambivalence, or ambiguity, but polyvalence. Not everything is located at the same meaningful level; I like these multi-channelled messages.

PS: Does *hybridization* apply to your work?

JR: Yes, it does. I'm conscious of it, and of the approach and movements in the arts that involve it, but there are other words that can be used too, some technical, some poetic. For a while we were using the word "impurity," like there was something *(chuckling)* contaminating the entity. If there were impurities in the work, then there must have been a time when the work was "pure." There were even books written on the topic, in the eighties. Hybridization is certainly a fair rendering of part of my approach.

PS: You've also used the word *transcultural.*

JR: Some of my colleagues have taken this very, very seriously. If the word has any meaning, it means that within the artwork, at least two things have come together. In popular culture, there's world music, where we can sometimes recognize a number of streaming elements that bring together various cultures. Whereas in concert music, the transcultural elements are sometimes very subtle, and produce a different kind of alloy. I think of my colleague José Evangelista, who, for more than twenty-five years, has mixed Indonesian music, particularly traditional musics from Bali, from Burma (Myanmar), and from his native Spain. So you can really have a transcultural co-mingling of the streams. In my case, it's a bit different, because I've tried not to go overtly towards borrowing from one culture or another, or searching for isomorphisms that could be placed within the context of our Western culture, but it's true that it interests me as well.

PS: Given the many different sources that inform your pieces, I sometimes think they can be musicologically *read* as much as heard.

JR: On a good day, some people say I'm a didactic composer. On a bad day, they say I'm just lecturing to them. Maybe this has something to do with the fact that I've spent so much of my life in the classroom, and that part of the professional residue bleeds over into the composition. I'd hate to think that such an approach was "academic" in my music however, but it's true that I'm instructing sometimes... showing something, and therefore, the reading might be musicological.

PS: As much as they may be "academic" or didactic in some way, they're rarely conclusive. You present possibilities more than you resolve problems. Would you agree?

JR: Yes, I would, and if I were drawing some conclusions, then it might really be terribly academic. I think I do it playfully nevertheless. It's a playful inquiry and positing of possible answers. What come to mind are some *lieder* I've composed—call them melodramas. Once you accept that they're melodramas, then you have to accept that there is some kind of narrative, an accounting of a story or historical fact, or even a fiction. But to draw conclusions or to apply formal answers, I would usually recoil from that, and let the artwork ask all the questions, and let the audience make conclusions on its own.

PS: Your pieces must then require you doing significant preparatory compositional detective work. Is that the beginning of the compositional process, or is it when pencil meets paper?

JR: It starts earlier. It's conceptual, after all. Once the ideas start circulating (I've heard it said before, and it certainly applies to me)—I'm already composing. There are ideas that come to mind involuntarily— they could be concepts, notions, let's call them intuitions, little things that you put together, atoms of thoughts that produce a nexus of some kind. Sometimes you take notes on the ideas, and later go back to see if there was resilient genetic material in those thoughts. That can happen sonically, and the composition is well underway before the commission comes, or before you put the pencil to the page, or, shall we say, the mouse to the screen.

PS: It seems that you involve this early conceptual element a great deal. What is it that attracts you to it?

JR: I don't know what attracts me, but I know that I do it. The energy is channelled into at least two manners, or two personalities. I'm attracted to one type of music that could be called narratological, that has some type of intrigue, or human element, that involves human destinies. They're upfront, and they may be programmatic, or overtly theatrical, but human. There's a whole other part of my work that I would say, for lack of a better word, might be called geometrical, or structural, figurative. Not that it's inhuman, but it involves musical elements for their own sake, and for their own relationships, probable or improbable among themselves. The parameters of this music become the subjects themselves—harmony, et cetera, processing, in some sense—numbers, chains of numbers, entities, all sorts of things that translate eventually into sound. So I have these two manners, and each is always circulating in my head. Some days I'm more attracted to the human one, other days I'm attracted to the more abstract one.

PS: Where does a work like *Treppenmusik* fit into this?

JR: That is an abstract geometry piece, with a few winks, whimsical things that happen in it. Essentially, it's about sonic metaphors linked to visual images and the underlying techniques required to represent them. In this case, the inspiration comes from the visual illusions of the Dutch graphic artist Maurits Cornelis Escher, and finding parallels to such things in the world of sound.

PS: Is this type of thinking what you mean when you describe something as a *project*?

JR: A project to me is really a *projection*, and here I'm being a musical psychologist. I would say that whether artists know it or not, they're always projecting something. I'm very conscious of the fact that I throw against the screen, shall we say. I'm a projector and I throw against the screen of your ears, sound images. A project might be a hypothetical result, but I like to think of a project as the *result*, the concrete *evidence* you have and know something of the projection.

PS: How does this apply to your set of piano pieces, *Las Meninas*?

JR: There's no question that a project is involved in this work, and I would say that here I worked like a painter on it. That was my principle artistic approach to the task. I made a series of tableaux, in this case twenty-one. I worked as painters do who sit inside museums in front of paintings, trying to copy them and to be inspired by them. They treat a painting as if it were a still life, and they're rendering them in their own hands. This is somewhat the method I play with in the project of *Las Meninas*. My title, in some sense, is a carrier of the project, in that I was making a double reference to not only a painting of the same name by Velázquez, but also using it to serve a musical composition. I'm asking the listener to imagine that the composition *Scenes from Childhood*, by Robert Schumann, could be the equivalent of a tableau by Velázquez called *Las Meninas (The Lesser Royals)*. Like a painterly composer, I made variations on the musical tableaux, on various sections of the tableaux of Schumann, and I call up this image directly by asking the listener to know that painters have worked like this in the past. In the particular case of the painting *Las Meninas*, a number of painters, including two great ones, Dali and Picasso, were obsessed throughout their working lives with this Spanish master. Dali, in particular, continued to make reference to the achievements in that painting for most of his life.

PS: So you made the variations almost through the voice of Velázquez?

JR: It's a "double thing" again, because there were two approaches. One is the approach that Picasso takes. As an artist commenting on the work of another, Picasso cannibalized the Velázquez. It looks violent, destructive, and recompositional. He dismantles Velázquez in his images, and does almost fifty variations on this one single painting. But those images are rough. They sometimes look like body parts on the canvas, whereas Dali's work is respectful in a surprising way. He goes after various structures and images in this painting, and translates them in a wide variety of new settings, often whimsical, but often surprisingly new settings in the typical Dali style. He doesn't let you know the tricks. He doesn't let you know that he's making a reference to the Velázquez. I find myself working a little bit more like Dali in this piece, in that throughout the twenty-one little compositions, I adjusted, arranged, composed, transformed, and made it appear that it wasn't in fact me who was composing them, but somebody else.

PS: So where are you in this work?

JR: I'm the puppeteer, you know? You could ask the question of Dali as well. Where is Dali in the things he's doing? When he does this transformation of the Velázquez, you're sometimes unaware. We know now, because we know the style and playfulness that everyone recognizes, he puts on the mask of another painter. He's so inventive that sometimes it seems as if his work was done by someone else. This is what interested me too. Of course, everyone knows that I'm the author of this piano cycle, but it's also clear that I'm pretending to be other people. For the listener, it's like hearing two things, or even three things, simultaneously. One can hear the original "painting" by Schumann, and one should be able to hear the approach that I claim someone is taking by listening to the original "painting," and then one hears my "take" on that approach. So one is hearing three musics, or points of view.

The first piece is dedicated to José Evangelista and composed from his point of view, his "analysis" of the Schumann—I mean, where am I? I'm another party in this entire circle. It's a fourth level to it. And Evangelista's music is itself commenting on Spanish folk music by way of Burmese and Balinese music. So it gets a little twisted. I find this really fun. When the idea for the project came to me, it really charmed me. I had a lot of fun writing the pieces, and with the *debate* around them that certainly ensued right from the very beginning. Some people thought that I had done a great disservice to music and to Schumann, and it was appalling, while other people thought it was the greatest thing. It was a wild and kind of strange debate here in Montreal when that piece was performed.

PS: This is what I was getting at earlier, where you pose as different characters, with many other figures behind you.

JR: Right.

PS: You've described postmodernism in concert music as "the progressive dismantling of the precepts of European modernism since 1945, and to signify their progressive replacement with other precepts, however loose or untidy they may be." Do you agree with yourself?

JR: *(Laughs)* Well, it's a big word, a catch-all term. Postmodernism had, and still has, a certain kind of currency. It's a bit different now, but what you've just read, I would still agree with that. One thing is sure: If you accept that the so-called grand narratives in Western European civilization have come to an end... (I suppose liberty is one, liberty at all cost. Marxism, Freudianism... no one has said capitalism has come to an end), if you argue that the grand narratives have come to an end, even though everything has transformed itself, somehow the narrative, the historical projection remains an obligatory destiny. If you transfer this notion to music, one recognizes very quickly that in the twentieth century there was some type of obligatory destiny that music would have to evolve toward. It comes a little bit from Schoenberg, and by way of the post-Second World War composers like Boulez, Stockhausen, et cetera. If one accepts that the narrative underlying this obligatory destiny has come to an end, then that which comes after it is *post*. We usually associate these narratives with the modernist project. There's still a debate about this, whether it has finished, or is still at work. I would say it's still at work, actually, because capitalism is like a medium that keeps on transforming itself and transforming ideas. But many things have changed, so I'm prepared to say we live in postmodern artistic times. But these words are illusory, and slippery, or journalistic sometimes. They can get you to think a little bit, and then they fog you over.

PS: Interestingly, many of the reference points in your works remain the historical European ones, what I'll call the "distant belovéd."

JR: That's wonderful... beautiful. Yes, there's a type of nostalgia, a longing, a looking back. I must say, now that I think about it, this makes my skin creep a little bit.

PS: Why?

JR: As they say, people who are condemned to look backwards are death obsessed, and it's only people who look forward who are looking to tomorrow, who have greater success in survival. Why look backwards? Why look at the doors that have just been closed? But it's true that many of my projects are of that nature. On the other hand, one could look at these pieces by saying maybe they're looking at places that have never been looked at before, looking at things differently, that we missed things, so we need to look at them again. We see things with a fresh light, and illuminate them differently. We turn them around and see the back. That is a much more positive and optimistic view than the nostalgia-laden one.

NOTE

1. A Disklavier is an electronic player piano; essentially a cross between a computer and a piano.

Gary Kulesha

GARY KULESHA was born in 1954, and was raised and still lives in the
Etobicoke area of Toronto. He teaches at the University of Toronto and, since
1995, he has held the position of Composer Advisor with the Toronto Symphony
Orchestra. Gary Kulesha has long been a contributor to the Toronto and Canadian
music scenes, as composer, conductor, teacher, and in various administrative roles.
His 2004 activity included a July return to the Banff Centre as Guest Composer, a
new Trio for Horn, Violin, and Piano for the Winnipeg Chamber Music Society,
and the composition of his Second Symphony, premiered by Oliver Knussen
during the TSO's New Creations Festival in March and April of 2005.

PS: When banning Jean Cocteau's 1929 film *The Seashell and the Clergyman*, the British Board of Film Censors said, "This film is apparently meaningless, but if it has any meaning it is doubtless objectionable." Cocteau, on the other hand, described this and other films as "a petrified fountain of thought." It may seem unusual to begin your interview with a statement about film, but I know that you're well versed in this medium, and seem to take inspiration from it. How does cinematic art inform your music?

GK: I was very deeply influenced by film when I was younger, but it's not so much the case anymore. The earliest impact it had on me was in the way of structure, and my earliest memories of the greatest films that I've seen are all about the way in which they manipulated time, and all about concepts of simultaneity and multiple perspectives. This is also kind of cubist, so it's interesting that you mention Cocteau. In particular, I remember being deeply impacted by a movie called *Il conformista* (1970), by Bernardo Bertolucci. It still seems to me to be a completely brilliant approach to structure, in that there are two streams of events unfolding simultaneously—the present and the past. The way he intercuts them, they gradually switch places, so when they meet, that becomes the present, and from that moment, we move into the future. I remember being so struck by that. It occurred to me that structural control in music has a lot to do with the flow of time and multiple perspectives, and I became very intrigued by simultaneity, time compression, and intercutting. All of those things led naturally toward composers like Ives and Carter, and I became interested in trying to apply those things to some of my own music. Ultimately, that led to having two conductors in my *Symphony*. The structural procedure of film is central, as well as the plasticity of it, and the way in which it deals with time.

I wrote a piece for the Toronto Symphony called *The True Colour of the Sky*, and the image that I had in my head throughout the entire composition of the piece was a moment in a movie called *The Right Stuff*, which is about the early space program. The pilot manages to get his jet *just* above the atmosphere, and as he's getting above it, the colour of the sky changes completely and he begins to see stars. That image really struck me. It's not at all uncommon for me to maintain movie images like that in my head forever. The way they impact me is sometimes very direct, as it was in that particular case.

PS: So it's a technical influence, as well as narrative and imagistic.

GK: Yes, but while this is true, I think that an artist emerges through the combination of psychological factors that create our unique personalities. I don't think you can be a musician first and a human being second. So the impact that both film and poetry had on me was more about me maturing as a human being, and me coming to understand myself, and perhaps to question my own role as an artist and human being. That probably had a far deeper impact than the technical side of film. In that sense, literature also influenced me. There are books that literally changed my life. It's safe to say that we're a product of everything that we absorb as we're developing and continue to live and grow.

PS: Can you give a few more detailed examples of how film has influenced your music? I'm thinking specifically of *Book of Mirrors*, your *Second Essay for Orchestra*, and *Syllables of Unknown Meaning*.

GK: The influences range from fairly arcane to fairly trashy. The *Second Essay for Orchestra* came about as a result of my admiration for Coppola's *Apocalypse Now*, which is based on Joseph Conrad's book *Heart of Darkness*. I was trying to explore how we can be drawn toward the dark aspects of our own nature, and that it may or may not be controllable. The difference in that piece is that I assert that there are things that continue to make us human. It's also influenced by my readings of T. S. Eliot. He dealt with the same things, and found a way through the darkness.

Book of Mirrors came about directly as a result of Peter Greenaway's *Prospero's Books*. I was struck by the image of the book of mirrors that comes up in the film. I saw it and thought '*That's* a piece of music.' Because my music is based on argument and developmental process, each mirror reflects the primary material, which has been modified to suggest what the mirror is. It's a semi-programmatic concept, although at times it gets quite abstract. It's a continuous variation principle that again suggested strong structural procedures to me. The ending is an enigmatic and epigrammatic series of mirrors, the meaning of which is not known. It also relates to a film by Luis Buñuel called *Tristana*, the end of which is a flash recap of the whole movie in a series of very brief still images. It's a technique I also used in my *Concerto for Bass Clarinet, Marimba, and Orchestra.*

Syllables of Unknown Meaning is sort of a trashy story. I was commissioned by Vancouver New Music to compose a piece for the millennium. Ten composers were commissioned and each was supposed to choose, and deal with, a century of the last millennium. When Owen Underhill asked me which century I wanted, I said I didn't really care. Needless to say, I got the first century, because nobody knows anything about it. I began to poke around the writings of the day—there's not a whole lot of music, a few chants and things. One of the things that was happening at the time was experimentation with notation. Back then, there was no standardized notation; it was highly variable from composer to composer, region to region, and there was a lot of learning by rote. I discovered a beautiful and famous little chant by Hermannus Contractus (Hermann the Cripple, 1013-1054), entitled *Alma Redemptoris Mater.* It's even mentioned in Chaucer's *Canterbury Tales.* I had the idea to reprocess this chant into a genuinely contemporary piece of music. By a technical trick, I derived a twelve-tone row from it, and I treated the material partly as chant, and partly in a very strict serial manner. I was driven by an image from a John Carpenter horror movie called *Prince of Darkness*, in which Satan may or may not be in the basement. He may or may not be about to emerge and assume control of the world. The people who are there researching this are having strange dreams of him emerging, and it turns out that it's the people of the future who are beaming back information, trying to warn them, but they can only reach them in their dreams, through a tachyon beam. I had a very strong notion of being asleep, of dreaming, and having Hermannus Contractus beam his message forward to me, but only in a dreamlike state. So the whole piece has this quality, in which hallucinatory fragments of the chant circle around clouds of twelve-tone and totally atonal passages. The original image from the movie is kind of cheesy, but the piece itself is very delicate.

PS: Although you're very interested in film, you've written only a small amount of film *music.* Why?

GK: I have a friend who was a student at the same time as me, and when he was taking a film course at York, I was very much involved with the films he was making, and I scripted and directed a few, and acted in one. I wrote the scores for those tiny little movies. I also grew up with a guy named Blaine Allan. When he made his first feature-length film, *You Are Not Alone*, he asked me to do the score for it. That's the total extent of the work I've done in film. I worked at the Stratford Festival for many years, providing music for their productions, and while I don't mind being an assisting artist, if I have a choice, I'd prefer not to be. Although it's perfectly all right to be part of a creative team, and I've enjoyed working on things as a co-producer, it's much more satisfying to work on my own projects, with my own parameters. I consider myself almost lucky that nobody has asked me to do any more films. The other thing is, there are people who do film music really, *really* well, and I'm not sure that I do it that well. Drama is one thing, and film is another thing altogether. I think it takes a very special kind of discipline, and a special sense of what's required. Mychael Danna, who does the music for Atom Egoyan, or Howard Shore—these guys *really* know what they're doing. My specific interests are not in thirty-second cues, or mood music. I admire it very much, but it's not for me.

PS: Despite your interest in a modern medium such as film, many titles of your work are taken from older, classical forms. For example, you have pieces called toccata, symphony, sonata, concerto, et cetera, and often use traditional instrumental groupings. How do you reconcile your respect for tradition, and interest in the modern?

GK: My output has been extremely schizophrenic. In my youth (and here I'm quoting Lutosławski quoting Bartók), "I did not write the music I wanted to write, I wrote the music I *could* write." When I was young, and people were asking me to write pieces, I wrote quickly. I wrote a lot of light music, and I was working in very traditional forms, attempting to learn my craft. There's a fair bit of music in my output that is quite traditional, and quite backwards looking. I consider most of it to be light music. Most of the composers I admire have written light music, and I feel there is room for it in the world. At the same time, the structural procedures were attractive to me. I'm a very "structural thinking" kind of guy. That doesn't mean I turn to traditional forms every time I write, but they are the forms that I continue to devolve back towards.

PS: So you're following the structural patterns implied by the name of the form?

GK: If I use the title *Sonata*, then yes, somewhere in there, there's a sonata.

My symphony is called *Symphony* because it is one. There *is* such a thing as symphonic form. For example, Shostakovich is a symphonist but Copland is not. There is a kind of discipline and structure that goes beyond the title. I used the term symphony because I was trying to write something that I considered *in* the tradition of the symphony. I think of Busoni as being a kind of paradigm for myself. While I'm totally and completely interested in everything that's going on, my own aesthetic is somewhat narrower than that. While I've premiered (as conductor) works using all kinds of aesthetic approaches, my own aesthetic is much more closely related to traditional music and traditional forms than a lot of the music I've conducted and promoted, and a lot of the music that my students write. I don't see any particular contradiction there, but in the end, my own work comes down to expressing *me*, although my interests are more broad and intellectual, or all-inclusive.

PS: You said that you were learning your craft by writing music that is more traditional. Do you view that as necessary for younger composers?

GK: Hmmm... necessary... well, it's how I was taught, and is certainly how I teach, but I can't make a sweeping generalization and say it's necessary. I think it's worked for me. As you know, what we struggle with as composers is some kind of *line*, some kind of throughput on the piece. The piece has to go from the beginning to the end, and be somehow convincing. When you're young, and learning, the obvious thing to do is to imitate, and that's what I did. Then you begin to discover how to write lines, and how to make structures that hold together, even if you're doing them in the most traditional possible ways. Over time, you learn to hide those forms, that approach to form, concepts of repetition, and periodicity, sequence, et cetera, but the underlying structure may make sense because underneath it all there are these concepts.

PS: You talk about "line" a lot. What do you mean?

GK: The concept of line is something performers *all* understand, but composers are usually the last people to get it. Line for me is not melody, or harmony. It's the succession of one sound after another, in a manner that the ear can follow the logic, and that there is some kind of journey involved. There are many levels on which that can happen. It can be purely visceral, as it would in a pop tune or in a highly rarefied way as it does in the Boulez *Structures*. Nevertheless, there has to be some kind of aural logic to follow what is going on.

PS: Continuity?

GK: Continuity is part of it, but it's also that the composer has made sense of why two sounds happen side by side. The ability to continue that, and make it into something somewhat longer, is a comparatively rare gift. Even when you get into polystylism, it's the abutment of all these styles that forms line.

PS: How would you describe your creative process?

GK: Varied. I'm driven by personal needs first. It's the old cliché that composers essentially create for themselves, and if we're good artists, other people react to it. I'm simultaneously driven by mutually exclusive opposites. On the one hand, I think that what we're doing is probably fairly trivial and unimportant and that if we didn't do it, we'd be unhappy people. And at the same time, I think that art, if it's done well, is supposed to change people. It's supposed to make people's lives into something else. So on the one hand I have this pompous, self-important view that artists are significant matrices interpreting human experience for all of humanity, and at the same time, I know that I'm not Beethoven. Even then, if you *were* Beethoven, does it really matter? Is he really that important? My artistic process is a kind of selfish thing, but with a view to broader issues.

PS: You've said, "Like most young composers, I'm no longer interested in writing things which are 'new' and 'revolutionary.'" What did you mean by that?

GK: That's an old quote, from an era when people thought that it was still possible to do something that nobody had heard before. As it happens, I now think that it probably *is* possible to do. In that infamous kafuffle,[1] John Corigliano said that finding things that are new for *him* is more important than finding things that are *new*, and I agree with that. I think you have to be new and inventive and different and start-ling—to *yourself*. But I don't think that you have to reinvent the wheel. I think people *will* do that. There's the whole world of microtones, and we've barely just scratched the surface with rhythm. Somebody will come along and do things that are revolutionary and new, but I personally am not interested in doing that. I'm only interested in keeping myself fresh, and in finding things that keep me stimulated.

PS: There's an element of conservation in your music. Conserving certain streams of musical creativity. Although it's incomplete, is it fair to describe you as a conservative composer?

GK: If conservative means traditionalist in some sense, then yes, sure. I still espouse and respect the traditional values of concert music. I still believe in the concert hall. I still believe in the traditional forms. Conservative implies somebody who's writing in E-flat major, and I don't do that, or have particular admiration for that, so I'm cautious about the term. Musically, I'm far less conservative in some of my pieces than a lot of people you might not call a conservative, so I'm a little uncomfortable with the term being applied to me. In some pieces, I'm completely a classicist, or a romanticist, or a modernist, so I'm trying to resist the pigeonhole. In different pieces, I have different stances. I could even be comfortable with the term "structur-alist," which used to be a really bad word, that people would apply to composers they didn't like, but I'm not really comfortable with words like conservative, or classicist, or romantic. Those are words that have a lot of baggage that doesn't particularly apply to me.

PS: I'd like to talk about your other activities. One of the things you do, besides composing, teaching, and conducting, is work as composer in residence. What are your responsibilities?

GK: At the moment, I'm the composer advisor of the Toronto Symphony, where I've been for many years, and I have renewed my contract for one more year. The role there is not really composer in residence. The fact that I write a piece for them every several years is a perk of the job. But it's not part of the job. I will produce a piece for them next year, but it's my first one for them since the year 2000, and it's probably my last until the year 2010. At the TSO, my role is to advise on new music in general and Canadian music in particular. Since we have a new Music Director, Peter Oundjian, it's my job to make him aware of what is going on in this country. He has some roots here, but he's not aware of the whole new music scene, so what I've been doing is bringing to his attention things that I feel he should be aware of. He's a very interested guy. Little by little, you learn people's tastes. It took me a while to learn Jukka-Pekka's tastes, and now I'm learning Peter's. You don't want to inundate him with things you know he'll hate. My job is to be a conduit, through which the orchestra becomes aware of important things that are going on that will fit in with the programming needs of the conductor who is there at the time.

I'm also with the NACO (National Arts Centre Orchestra). I don't have a title—basically we're called Awards Composers. The job there is much simpler. It's not administrative in any sense. It's composing three pieces across four years, including a chamber piece, a large chamber piece, and an orchestra piece, as well as one summer of working with young composers as part of their summer training program. There's no input on programming, or anything like that. I'm really not there very much. It's not really a hands-on, day-to-day situation.

PS: With your various associations with the orchestras, what's one thing you haven't done that you would like to do?

GK: There's not a whole lot that I haven't done. I've been at the COC (Canadian Opera Company), the TSO, the NACO, and it's worrying me a little bit, because all of these situations will end, and then I really don't know—how do you continue to go upward from there? I suppose the short answer is that I'd like my career to go international, because at the moment, there's no Canadian composer who has substantial international presence. At this point in my career, I'm flickering at the edge of that, but others have done that before me. Murray Schafer is not a household name in Europe, and he lived there for a while. I guess the thing that I haven't done, is gain access to the Chicago Symphony Orchestra, or the London Symphony Orchestra, or Staatskapelle. Those are the things I'd like to do, but I don't know how practical that is, given the situation that we find ourselves in.

PS: How do you respond to the criticism that the orchestra is simply a museum?

GK: Several years ago, we did Berio's *Sinfonia*, and he came to town for it. He responded to that very question by saying, "Many people think that the orchestra is just a museum, but I think that's good, because we *need* good museums." You need to be able to go back and see treasures of the past, and they need to be well looked after, and they need to be kept alive. Orchestras need to serve their whole constituency, and they need to serve both their public and their artists. To me, that means keeping the music a living art. Music is a living art, we're still creating it, and it still seems important to people. And that means covering the entire repertoire. You don't just serve Brahms and Beethoven; you also serve Kulesha and Steenhuisen. But at the same time, many contemporary composers think that the orchestra should be serving *only* Kulesha and Steenhuisen. That's simply a misconception about what the orchestra actually is. The orchestra is an instrument with a culture. There is a way of approaching it that is based upon its tradition and its repertoire, and good orchestras serve all the repertoire. The proportions that the Toronto Symphony finds tend to reflect reality. Some small percentage of the programming is contemporary Canadian music, a slightly broader segment is music from the twentieth century, and then the bulk of it is the traditional symphonic repertoire. Anybody who argues that it should be different really doesn't understand the kinds of audiences that we serve, and the kind of job that they're trying to do. That reflects the reality of what the players want, what the conductors want, and what the public wants. There's a kind of necessary tension there, between the traditional structure, and what we as composers want. That tension, if it is properly dealt with, can be very healthy. Orchestras that don't play any contemporary music are doing the wrong thing. I think it's even necessary for composers to agitate. We can't ever stop saying, "You've got to do more," because if we ever stop, if we're ever satisfied with how much is being done, they'll stop doing it. The orchestra is a living instrument that is not going to change dramatically in the near future.

PS: If the orchestra is reflecting a balance of what composers, conductors, and the public want, why do you think that the orchestras are all struggling?

GK: Because the government isn't giving them enough money. Art costs money. There's this mythology that's trickled down from the 1980s that somehow art and entertainment are interchangeable, and although art can be entertainment, and entertainment occasionally rises to the level of art, it's important not to get into this mindset that a symphony orchestra is a musical, and that it should be able to pay for itself. It can't. The government has to accept its responsibility and recognize that music is part of our culture, even if it is serving only a fairly small percentage of the *voters*. It needs to be supported. The less it is supported, and the physically weaker it gets, the more difficult it is to present interesting programming, and take some chances, and the less the audience is interested in it, and they begin to back away from it. It's that same old thing—nothing breeds success like success. Similarly, if something begins to show signs of weakening, the public turns its back on it. We're really between a rock and a hard place on this. The *only* real solution for new music in this country is more government funding.

PS: Do you think that an orchestra would recognize a success if it had one?

GK: It depends entirely upon the conductor, and entirely upon the situation in which the conductor finds himself. Ultimately, I don't know. Some conductors would, and others would not. There are circumstances in which the conductor is just a figurehead, and the actual work is being done in other ways. In those circumstances, it depends on the will of the orchestra as an organization, how they would perceive success or failure. As we get driven back further and further on the money issue, the question of ticket sales becomes extremely important. Is success ticket sales? To some people it is.

PS: Success could be having a good development person in the organization, getting suitable sponsorship for the orchestra.

GK: Absolutely. Success could also be premiering an extremely fine new piece. The orchestra players know when a piece is good, for the most part. Making the players happy that they've done something of substance and that they've premiered a new work that is good— even if the response isn't so good, or if the ticket sales aren't good, or the critical writing about it isn't so good. The fact that the performers like it is also success, and in some orchestral cultures that would be perceived as being success.

PS: Here, we're talking around the balance of the artistic and the economic.

GK: Well, that's the problem. As I said, there's a necessary tension, which also fits in with the concept of new music versus old music. The old music, although it is artistically necessary to serve it as well, is, let's face it, where the tickets are sold. There are constant tensions that all orchestras, and all performing organizations, live with. There's economic necessity, and artistic necessity. A good balance is difficult to achieve. I think we have it at the TSO.

PS: How does that search for balance apply to being a composer in Canada?

GK: It's worth noting the difficulty of having a career in this country. When Murray Schafer says that he's not as famous as he should be, he's totally right. It's very frustrating to be a Canadian composer, and to feel like we're completely isolated, even from what's going on in the United States. I remember when Glenn Buhr was at the peak of his success with the Winnipeg Symphony. He was running the festival, he was helping program the orchestra, he was writing big orches- tral pieces, and he had a recommendation from John Corigliano to publisher G. Schirmer. He sent the music, and they said they weren't interested. I remember talking to him shortly after that, and him saying, so plaintively, "*What* do they *want?*"

I feel the same frustration as him. It's not a question of how great we are. It's the kind of double standard by which people who are as good as we are, or not as good as we are, somehow get that kind of representation (through publishing), and that kind of international success. You understand what I'm saying? It's not that I'm so great, it's that I'm at *least* as good or better than a lot of people who *have* the things that I do not have. That's a source of great frustration, not just for me, but also for all Canadian composers. I don't know if there's a solution, it's just a kind of comment, that it's an irritating thing to live with, especially when you're hitting the age of fifty in a few months.

PS: There's no Canadian composer that's published internationally, correct?

GK: Well, Claude Vivier has some of his catalogue with Schott.

PS: But he's not living anymore.

GK: True, and his exposure cooled off a little too. A number of Glenn Gould's pieces have been placed with Schott also. Again, at first, it's a little bit of a buzz, and then it cools off. Don't forget that Murray

Schafer, when he was young, had a contract with Schott and Universal Edition. Several of his pieces were placed with that catalogue, and he eventually had to buy them back. The fact that you are placed in their catalogue of works doesn't mean that you're going to be wildly successful. What needs to happen is that the machinery behind it, the financial and promotional machinery, has to go to work for you. Frankly, it's not happening for Vivier, although it would certainly be easier if he were alive. If you look at Schott's newsletters, they never mention him. It's a little... almost cynical. The truth of the matter is that to become a better artist, you have to work with better and better people. You really need to expand your horizons. It's great that I can work with the Toronto Symphony, but I also would like to work with Krystian Zimmerman. In order to get to that point, you really need the kind of publicity and visibility that the professional connections make for you. We do not have that in this country. For whatever reasons, the Americans and the English have consistently ignored us. They'll sign some totally unknown Australian composer to a contract with Boosey & Hawkes, but not us, and I don't know why. It's the great frustration of my career, and many people my age feel the same.

NOTE

1. In 1998, the Toronto Symphony hosted a panel discussion moderated by Gary Kulesha. Participants included John Corigliano, Eric Morin, and Paul Steenhuisen. Corigliano stated that he wouldn't write complicated music for certain audiences because he felt they would not understand it, and Steenhuisen questioned how Corigliano was able to gauge the intelligence of his audience. Corigliano became defensive and aggressive, hurling insults and expletives at Steenhuisen, and later, Morin. Eventually, Morin rose to challenge Corigliano physically.

Howard Bashaw

JUNE 2004

HOWARD BASHAW was born in White Rock, British Columbia, in 1957 and received his Doctor of Musical Arts degree from the University of British Columbia. After stints at the Banff Centre and a short time in Nice, France, he has lived in Edmonton, Alberta, since 1992. The work of a composer is often intensely solitary, and few composers embody this more so than Howard Bashaw. When not busy at the University of Alberta, where we both teach composition, he works long hours in his basement on an old, refurbished, and steadfast grand piano. In 2004, he travelled to Toronto to attend the premiere of his new work Minimalisms *(written for New Music Concerts and pianist Roger Admiral). Upon his return to Edmonton, I was able to corral him for an interview, trying to get to the heart of the matter.*

PS: Morton Feldman wrote a piece entitled *The Viola in my Life*. Using the title alone, it would be appropriate for you to write a piece called *The Piano in my Life*. Why do so many of your pieces feature the piano?

HB: I recall that long ago, in a composition lesson, I expressed a great reluctance to write for the piano. It had to do with the simple fact that I wasn't a pianist—not to mention the dauntingly enormous range of repertoire for the instrument, and the extraordinary compositional minds behind that repertoire. It was a very large world that I didn't feel comfortable getting into. But when I was at the Banff Centre, I had a specific opportunity to write for piano. I worked in one of those secluded huts, just me, the piano, and the great outdoors, and it was there that I first really came to terms with the instrument. I realized then that it wasn't so much a problem of writing for piano as it was about teaching myself new ways to compose. It was an important time for me. The piano connected me to things that I wanted to do and say as a composer, things I hadn't reached, or formalized yet. I was searching for certain types of harmony, certain technical ideas, reaching thought processes that had been swimming around in the back of my mind. It was at this time that I really started to find my voice as a composer. And in a sense, the piano actually became my composition teacher. It was then that I wrote the piece *Hosu* for Barbara Pritchard, and there has been no turning back since. That work generated my interest in the instrument, and it certainly generated interest in my music from other pianists. And now my solo piano music has been performed in national and international piano competitions. Twenty years ago, I would have been the last even to imagine this possible. Looking back, I have this strange feeling that I didn't choose the piano so much as that pivotal piece chose me.

PS: You didn't *have* to agree to the requests for more piano music.

HB: True. But why leave it? In retrospect though, the piano may have replaced what might have been an interest in the electroacoustic medium. Given my sense of focus and direction, and my position at the time as an emerging composer, I very well could have gone in that direction, but I went to the piano instead. I could never have predicted that. I suppose it was the result of circumstance, but it also has to do with the way I work. I enjoy working in complete isolation, working directly with the instrument that becomes the voice of expression. It's very meaningful for me, and I think there's a parallel here with those working in the electroacoustic medium.

Returning to the subject of Feldman, I recall him speaking about how important it was for him when he bought his piano, having just the right instrument to get the sounds he needed, the sense of time and space he wanted, and how the instrument itself is so important for the compositional process. That made a very big impression on me. Taking the sense of how you're composing, and what you're composing for, to a very refined, specialized space. It's not just about the piano; it's about a sense of focus, and a real sense of association with the medium you're working with. I can't imagine getting away from this medium now. I've even considered writing *only* for the piano for a number of years, and nothing else. I communicate one-to-one, directly with the instrument and its performers, which for me is more effective than working and rehearsing with large ensembles.

PS: What is it about the piano that keeps calling you back?

HB: The instrument is inspiring on a number of levels. Take the technical aspects of the keyboard itself, composing through a direct connection with finger patterns or chord structures—discovering those patterns, and their physical relation to the instrument, and how that, in itself, becomes part of the creative process. For me, that was very interesting and inspiring. Or take the deep and diverse sound resource of the instrument, one you can't *really* know about until you start working with it. It's about understanding shades of pianissimo or forte, or balancing textures through discovery. It's the kind of composing whereby musical ideas are extracted from the instrument rather than imposed upon it. And I'm speaking here as a non-pianist. I don't have any classical piano training to speak of, but I think *not* studying the piano has freed me to find my own way around the instrument. I don't have a pianist's *default* setting in my hands or ears, as it were, and I'm grateful for that.

PS: So you were initially reluctant to write for the instrument because you weren't a pianist, and now you feel that not being a pianist became your advantage.

HB: Exactly, but I had to get through the difficult stage of composing for the piano to find that out.

PS: You mentioned the vast piano repertoire. What do you extract from that and involve in your music?

HB: If you're asking whether I deliberately model my pieces on specific piano works, then the answer is no, or at least not intentionally so. But I would say *genre* and idiom in the general sense could be seen as influences. For example, I regard bagatelles, preludes, and other short keyboard works as a genre, and one that has inspired me.

PS: Why have you written so many short pieces?

HB: I've always found it appealing to have information compressed, focussed, and stated within a very short time span. To make a singular statement where emphasis arises through brevity itself.

PS: Over the course of your career, your music has changed quite a lot. Initially, there was a physicality, or rawness to the pieces.

HB: Parts of them, yes. Perhaps I was just an angry young man.

PS: Now, they maintain that physicality, but it's icier, more measured.

HB: There is certainly an imposed rationality on the physicality, but I look at it as *refining* that musical energy, and directing it in different ways.

PS: In that sense, there could be a relation to the martial arts. Controlled physicality.

HB: I've studied martial arts, and I think that's an interesting parallel. There is so much energy and concentration underlying the effectiveness of each action. I think that also speaks to my interest in short forms. Everything can be brought into a quick, brief, concentrated... *(Snaps fingers loudly).*

For a while, I became deeply, deeply interested in the works of Leonardo da Vinci. In particular, *The Last Supper.* There are intense, diverse, and complex energies within that fresco. Consider its immediate impact, its emotional dimensions, its sheer drama, but all co-ordinated with that day's underlying science of perspective and geometry. Studying and researching that fresco likely became the biggest single influence on my compositional perspective. Taking what I may have felt, as what you call the raw, physical composer, and recognizing the potential of still using that level of energy and impetus—but now through strategic kinds of filters, controls, structures, or just ways of modifying expression to redirect the energy of a piece. This happened in the early 1990s, when I was getting out of the raw energy phase. I'd brought myself to a point and asked, "What can be... no... what must be, the next step?" And I wasn't exactly looking for it there, but by going back five centuries and studying Leonardo, the extraordinary lesson was offered to me. Interestingly enough, I feel it was my training in musical analysis that allowed me to understand that fresco. But in the end, it was the fresco that subsequently inspired, if not guided, my new compositional perspective.

PS: Your music is tighter, both technically and expressively.

HB: I try to increase the effectiveness of the musical voice that energy can take at various times. This raw energy is not just a bubbling cauldron that has to burst. It has to find the right way out.

PS: In some pieces, you take what is very much a maximalist approach. Maximal expression, maximal physicality, maximal virtuosity. And yet, your most recent piece is called *Minimalisms*.

HB: If you were to ask me to compare *Tsunami*, my most aggressive piece from the early days, to *Minimalisms*, occurring close to twenty years later, I would say the minimalisms here have only to do with stylistic derivation of pattern, process, and repetition. There's still a maximal degree of virtuosity involved for the two soloists. It's taking the kind of energy we have been talking about and pushing the envelope, as it were.

PS: Is this piece an example of you applying the types of geometries you mentioned, those that were inspired by Leonardo?

HB: No, not geometries as such in this work. That's an interesting question, however. Now that we're talking about this, I can see that I've never lost, and probably never will, the desire to push those envelopes, to drive things further. I don't always deliberately set that as the agenda, but when I'm in a piece, if I don't feel I'm pushing towards something—usually taking some form of virtuosity—I feel I'm missing something. It's important to mention that virtuosity can take different forms in my music. As you know, it can also be intensely quiet, spaced moments, which can be extremely difficult to play with exact precision.

PS: So you mean virtuosic *energies*, rather than simply playing fast, or a plethora of notes.

HB: Both virtuosic energies and technical facilities. The lightest pian-issimo touch, with exactly the right depth of key, and sound, that's... (*Trailing off*).

PS: Can you provide another example of how you connect your ideal performative energy with the geometric?

HB: Let's take the recent piano piece, *Form Archimage*, that I wrote espe-cially for Marc Couroux. The movements in that particular work represent excellent responses to your earlier questions. Here, the middle movement is all about pulse streams and co-ordinations of layered tempi. Sure, that's not new in music, but a lot of them combined in a work for solo piano, requiring a refined, controlled touch with quiet dynamics, which is an extremely virtuosic thing to pull off. The last movement, a roaring, powerful statement, has a direct link to the raw energy of my earlier compositions. *Form Archimage* combines this energy, but unlike my earlier works, with underlying structural processes or strategies.

PS: What types of processes are you talking about?

HB: *Form Archimage* contains expanding, pattern-based processes that I would never, could never, have written in earlier years. The second movement unfolds a strategy of macro-level acceleration. The collective texture accelerates in carefully managed phases throughout the movement. The metronome-like pulse streams we referred to earlier, those simultaneous different speeds, collectively create a region that modulates to a faster tempo-region. This happens several times, with the whole movement ending up being twice as fast as it started. The third movement is completely different. It's a pattern-based process using continuously ascending and descending lines in alternation, traversing the entire piano register with an unrelenting drive. However, extremely brash, dynamic chord passages interrupt these linear continuities with ever-increasing intensity, interruptions that gradually take over the movement. It's a large-scale process that not only expresses virtuosic energy in two different forms, but more importantly, also creates tension and conflict at the level of structure itself. Here's the directing of energies we discussed earlier.

PS: What other types of compositional strategies do you employ?

HB: Here is where the lesson from Leonardo really shows up. What I did not clarify earlier was my specific interest in using structure itself as an important, or *the* important, aspect of a musical statement. Structure not just as a static background container for foreground activity, but rather as the element of primary interest. And I have some works that are all *about* architecture, and nothing else. When listening to these movements, the foreground material becomes subordinate to an emerging structural design. Consider my *Seven Spheres*. Here, there are several movements where relatively simple, surface, collage-like activity is used to reveal structure. One of my favourite examples is the movement "Double Convergence," where eight voices, each playing a higher and lower part, combine for a total of sixteen voices. All sixteen voices start out playing one motive at different speeds. In the opening field or region of this short movement, you have both the fastest and slowest statements (with a range in between), which are a long way apart in terms of tempi. In their reiterations, the faster voices get slower, and the slower voices get faster. Every voice does so independently, until they all arrive and converge at the rhythmic unison. As the voices become close in relative speeds, they collect-ively create an area or region of structural tension. They're not quite lined-up enough to be heard as being rhythmically co-ordinated, and they're not quite far enough apart to be heard as being comfortably independent. Direction and expectation is created, and the resulting tension is released with arrival of the unison. The main point is not recognizing the underlying process as a pleasing formal abstraction; it's the perceived *effect* of this process.

PS: So how much pre-planning, or pre-composition do you do, before you start writing pitches? Do you plan all of the tempi in advance?

HB: If I'm working on a short, structuralist piece, it's all about planning. In a case like that, I don't know where the line between composition and pre-composition would actually be. This is music of measure-ments. I make calculations and designs, and I don't do this at the piano.

PS: What do you calculate?

HB: Rates of speeds, placements for entries of voices, overall form, or, if it's a process of convergence, where and how voices align, things like that. Finding the motive, finding a musical *idea*, one that will work in collaboration with the structure, might be as much a pre-compos-itional element as all the calculating. Then, it's a question of designing the piece. If I'm looking to create a motivic or harmonic symmetry, I'll find, at the piano, the right tools to demonstrate it, but then the rest of it, the composition, will be away from the piano. Often I'll design things using graph paper. And as you know, I use my grid-score notation to write these movements.

PS: The point remains the transference of the structural ideas into sound.

HB: Yes, that is the compositional objective. And I think I first realized the need for the appropriate notation when working with multiple tempi. For example, having three, four, or five simultaneous tempi in canon. Conventional notation was holding me back, so I had to evolve a new system for myself. I say new, but proportional notation is hardly new of course. My particular version facilitates my particular needs.

PS: So it opened up different avenues for you as a composer?

HB: For sure.

PS: Given these interests, why *didn't* you become involved in electronic music, where all of these things can be measured and performed with complete precision?

HB: Because, at the end of the day, it's not just about finding ways to realize, in sound, exact measurements. For me, it's also about generating a special kind of "live" performance energy—that which the musicians convey when they are engaged in this music. The sense of precise co-ordination, the sense of ensemble, the playing *into* the complex textures. Live performance is not about detached, statistical realizations. There's a particular type of association between score, performer, and ensemble that arises. This association generates an unusual interpretation *space* that is revealed to the listener.

Christopher Butterfield

CHRISTOPHER BUTTERFIELD *was born in Vancouver, British Columbia,*

in 1952. After many years away (in Toronto and New York, as well as travelling),

he now resides in Victoria, where he teaches at the University of Victoria. Although

the majority of interviews were conducted over the phone, Christopher Butterfield

was one of the exceptions that requested the interview to take place in person.

Excited at the prospect of our interview, I drove from Edmonton to Victoria in the

early summer of 2004. After a daylong drive, and the ferry ride from Tsawwassen,

BC, to Swartz Bay, I found myself in the garden of his house. Before we could sit

down and talk, there were large rocks that needed moving. Inspired by the fatigue

of the day and the buzz of his active household, I decided to start the interview on

a topically absurd note.

PS: The apron rarely exceeds seven inches in length.

CB: If ever I speak again, I'm going to try and face up to my audience squarer, to take courage to let my eyes go right over them to the very corners of the room, and feel the space my voice has to fill and then to meet all those bright young eyes.

PS: Its belly is a greyish white.

CB: There they are, two to each, some boring through you, waiting.

PS: This method of presentation may be applied to all fruit.

CB: It must be very wonderful to be a real speaker, and to feel one's audience as a unit, to feel them sitting there, and feel them responding, at first quizzically, and then interested, finally opening up, giving whole attention to what you yourself have dug up, what you have riddled out of nature, and what nature has riddled into you.

PS: Turn it out into a shallow glass.

CB: Suppose you got up with a mouthful of shams to give them, and you met all those eyes.

PS: Small, toothless mammal.

CB: How you would wither up in shame.

PS: Covered with scales.

CB: What a sneak and an imposter if you did not believe sincerely in what you were saying, and were not trying, yourself, to live up to that standard.

PS: It's about the size of a guinea pig, but more highly esteemed as meat. (We close our books—the *Larousse Gastronomique*, and Emily Carr's *Fresh Seeing*.)

PS: How does what we just did relate to your work *Pavilion of Heavenly Trousers?*

CB: (*Laughing*) Oh! My piece is an installation, with six hundred pages of yellow foolscap, and they tile the wall of the 25' x 15' x 10' space. It involves two texts, interleaved, rewritten by hand, one sentence after the other. Meanwhile, a recording of me reading the text plays. I was interested in making a long text piece that would use existing material, but I wouldn't have thought of doing it had I not had in mind these two particular books, both of which are novels and take place in China (*The Maker of Heavenly Trousers*, 1935, by Daniele Varè, and *Pavilion of Women*, 1946, by Pearl S. Buck). They're both love stories of a certain kind. In these books, a lot of space is given over to just description of day-to-day life, customs, events. I call it an endlessly self-complicating story. It appears to be a narrative, but if you listen to it for long enough, it doesn't appear to have a clear thread. If you did give it time, you have a chance to hear sentences as single images, so it becomes a kind of poetic experience. It becomes a long poem, or an opera without music.

PS: And the process of making the work was one of discipline, wasn't it?

CB: It was an absolutely arbitrary process, which I set out and followed, without any deviation. I wanted to see what would happen with an absolutely rigorous process, rewriting three pages a day for two hundred days. It's interesting when you compare this to a musical process. We could take a Brahms symphony and a Mahler symphony and interpolate them, measure by measure, but I don't think we'd get the same hypnotizing quality that comes out of this particular job. Then there's the reading of it—thirty hours of recorded speech, which is playing back in the space the whole time as well.

If you read any of the gallery guides, or descriptions of various biennales, and shows in major centres, there's so much time-based art now. It's become a commonplace, whereas once upon a time, video, or sound art was really exceptional. It's now a given that you go and you'll be expected to spend *time* experiencing something, something that is *in* time. My piece is like that, with the only difference being that you don't expect to hear the whole thing. Nobody has thirty hours to spend listening to the whole business.

PS: Why was the rigor of the process important?

CB: It's like panning for gold. You go through a lot of dross in order to find one or two interesting things. But you include all of it. You have to, because you ultimately end up with this artifact. You have to understand that this gallery is a small space, and whatever goes in it will transform it. I could have just placed a single speaker in it, but I was interested in the whole thing being covered.

There's also the idea of writing—I love the idea of writing. It's a lot like walking. I love Hamish Fulton's walking pieces, where he goes on, say, a seventeen-day walk across the Andes. There's a map of the walk, and then a single photographic image. You know that he's done the walk, but the fact is that there was this certain kind of work he did that was represented in the single, big image. There's something quite attractive about the simple idea of labour, and of seeing what kinds of correspondences could result from this kind of a process. And it worked. If only for the couple of moments that were so staggeringly beautiful that it made the whole thing worth it. There are certain confluences in the text which, to know that they're there, are sufficient to justify the whole thing.

PS: And they're arrived at completely by chance.

CB: Yes. There's no way you could have predicted it. No way. This is what makes assessing materials in advance very important. Cage could not have been as successful, working the way he did, without a very clear understanding or feeling for the materials that he set in motion. Even in the most abstruse piece, where there's nothing given, he's still very aware of how things are going to be set in motion, of what's going to result from it. I think you have to be terribly confident about setting up a process like this, and that something good will result from it. But you can never be absolutely sure. What I had on my side was extremely clear prose, in both these novels, and a lack of any self-consciously literary writing. There wasn't much reliance on fancy metaphor. Things were plainly descriptive and expository. Sentences tended to be very clearly formed, so the thing married together quite beautifully because of this transparency.

PS: I'm interested in the labour of the work. Was it transformative? Did it affect how you consider things subsequently?

CB: Yes, hugely. The aspect of the *quality* of time. I don't think we think of time as having a quality? It made me aware of how easy it is to waste time. If I did my three pages, writing the sentences out, just going back and forth, it would take one hour. It made me keenly aware of how careful one has to be in the use of one's time, especially if one is an artist. It's very easy to let that time flow away from you. That was a very telling lesson.

PS: When you read the text for the recording, did you read what you had re-ordered and re-written, or did you read from the texts separately, and edit it together?

CB: I read from my re-written yellow foolscap pages. That changes the delivery completely, and that's what I love about it. It's like playing Satie or something. You don't even try to make sense, you just play the notes, and everything else will be taken care of. The moment that you try to enforce any kind of movement, or direction, you've ruined it. It's the same thing. All one could do was simply let one sentence lead to another one.

PS: So far, we've talked about compositional parameters, but not music directly.

CB: I think that, early on, I got really interested in the way that artists visualized thought. I'm thinking about people whose ideas were based in a more conceptual world, working in a singular domain, making choices about how to render it, and subjecting it to a process of some kind. Even starting with Cézanne, going on to the cubists. Duchamp kind of wraps the whole thing up and says we can operate on a fully literary level, and start playing all sorts of games with language and with the image and the juxtaposition of the image. Nobody's quite sure what they're experiencing any more. You're open to several kinds of interpretation. I like that, the really vague place where you're not really sure how to define a work of art, whether it's music or painting, or sculpture, or poetry, or whatever.

PS: With the *Pavilion*, it's as though you treat this visual and literary installation *musically*.

CB: The whole thing is a kind of massive isorhythm. One book is about two and a quarter times the length of the other, so you have these two and a quarter times tropes repeated under the singular "melody." It makes purely musical sense to me.

PS: Let's talk about travel, in relation to your pieces. My father was a sailor, working on the Holland America Lines. Yours was too, and the sea seems to have some importance in your work.

CB: I don't think it was terribly obvious to me until I wrote a piece called *Empress of Russia*. It's a short piece, with a beautiful title, but it also happens to be the name of the ship that my father sailed on. He was a midshipman on one of the Canadian Pacific line's "White Empresses," and it went from Vancouver to the Far East. I find the whole nineteenth and twentieth century idea of steam ships to be very romantic, and very attractive. They were extraordinary machines and seem to carry a lot of resonance. I wrote another short piece, using the name of another ship, called *Crusader*. The piece *Convoy PQ-17* was a collaboration with choreographer Bill Coleman, and that came about because of his own father's involvement in the Second World War, where he was a hand on a freighter. Bill, of course, made a dance work out of this impossible subject—a Second World War arctic supply convoy—but you know, he did it, and I wrote the music for it. Other than that, I don't think there's any clear acknowledgement of the sea. It's just part of my life, part of the things one refers to, and it finds its way into the work you do. It doesn't seem to be conscious. That's the weird thing—you recognize these things after the fact. I've been aware of it, but *after*.

PS: And *Port Bou*?

CB: That's a homage to Walter Benjamin. I'd started reading Benjamin's extraordinary book *The Arcades Project*. It's one of the greatest books ever written. It's about a thousand pages long, and consists of entries he made on file cards, as notes to a possible study of the shopping arcade, which first appeared in Paris in the 1830s, and changed a whole set of behaviours, and developed a whole new class of how people spent money and how they used the city. It's almost oracular in its essence. It's almost like the *I Ching*. You open it anywhere and it will comment directly on something. It doesn't matter if it's fashion, Baudelaire, prostitution—you name it. After reading that, and being, a few years ago, in Port Bou, on the Spanish side of the border from France, I made the piece. Port Bou is where some of the people went, during the war, while escaping from the Germans to get to neutral Spain and to America. If you drive there, you'll see a sign saying, "This way to the Walter Benjamin memorial." I knew that he'd died just over the border, while waiting for his papers. Legend has it that they arrived the morning after he died from an overdose of morphine.

It's been very interesting thinking about Benjamin and Adorno, because they were very close. Reading Adorno is like eating peanut butter by the tablespoonful, whereas Benjamin is endlessly light. There's nothing heavy about it. He was writing the beginnings of cultural theory, but in a poetic way. It's great fun reading Benjamin, and hard work reading Adorno. Not that you don't get stuff out of Adorno, but with Benjamin, there's no sense of an enforced dialectic. It's playful. He was interested in speculation, and not taking things too far. Setting things in motion and seeing how ideas would interact.

You asked if travel has much to do with things, and I would say it does. I wrote this long piano piece, years ago, called *Pillar of Snails*. It refers to an afternoon I spent looking for an old monument in an orchard on the coast of Syria. I never found it, but it's a big, black, basalt cube that I think had simply fallen into a swamp. The guidebook I had was written in 1935, and there were no guidebooks to Syria when I was there in 1984, so I had this antique, and I think in the ensuing fifty years, the cube had been covered over by the swamp. I also like the idea that along the pre-Islamic sects in the Eastern Mediterranean, the object for a way of objectifying the divine was a black cube. If you go to Petra, you see these black cubes. The Kaaba in Mecca is a black cube. I love the idea of the deity being represented by this kind of solid. It doesn't have to be any more than that.

PS: I listened to *Adrenochrome-E* (electronic music, 1976), three scenes from *Zurich 1916* (composed between 1985 and 1991), *Clinamen* (eighty mobile fragments for solo violin, 2000), *Four short pieces for violin and piano* (2001), and the ensemble work *Port Bou* (2001). You said there was an underlying secret between these works. What is it?

CB: Everything is process-based. The tape piece is an incredibly ugly piece based on every possible four and five-note chord, using square-wave generators. I screwed one part of the results onto the other. That interests me quite a lot, setting process in motion and simply accepting the consequences. I do that with text a lot, and I did that in the opera. I would just attempt to destroy text by subjecting it to all sorts of vicious and nasty treatments, and again, just taking the consequences. With all those pieces, especially the older ones, there is, at bottom, a reliance on a process of some kind. In the later pieces, like the ones for violin, and *Port Bou*, there is a really klutzy sort of half-serial, half-chance method that I came up with. It's really crude, but I'm quite happy with the results. It gives me counterpoint, it gives me pitches, and what's interesting about it is that it tends toward a kind of triadic idea of harmony, but with all the voice-leading really messed up, so you can never predict what's going to happen

I'm also much taken by the French group of writers going by the name Oulipo, which stands for *Ouvroir pour littérature poten-tielle* (Workshop for Potential Literature). It's like Messiaen, based on extreme limitations. Mathematical ones. Rigorous formal ideas. How you move around the apartment house. A list of words you have to use in a certain chapter. You set out pre-compositional materials in advance and work with those.

PS: So it's the process and the restrictions that interest you?

CB: Pretty much. It's about how you convert an extremely limited idea into something that is possibly poetic. You could do that through setting up some kind of fairly strict conceptual idea and following it as closely as you can. You trust that you've done your homework properly and that you're sensitive to the objective materials that you've selected in advance of the whole project. If you've got the right materials, it sure helps towards a successful outcome. It's hard to do stuff with bad materials.

If you're me, you still can't know what the outcome is going to be. There's endless thinking about how to get an attractive musical object, one that I find interesting, out of the process of composing. I never trained well as a composer using conventional materials, and I wasn't very good at doing conventional musical things. In fact, I was pretty bad at it. I have no great imagination within commonly acceptable musical conventions.

PS: What does taste have to do with it?

CB: Working the way I do, I manage to avoid issues of taste most of the time. Taste implies something that everybody will acknowledge. We know what the signs are. I'm happy working this way because I'm not sure if it's vulgar or not. I rather hope that it's vulgar, but not an easily recognizable vulgarity. It's back to the idea of doing something beautifully... maybe there's this sort of ideal place that is very alluring and beautiful, but that is actually free of taste in some way. It's a late, late, late modernist idea and forgive me for letting the word cross my lips, but if you can talk about postmodernism in music (and it's something I try to avoid), it's all about taste and irony, and irony and taste, and the iron taste of irony.

It's self-reflexive, self-knowing. Maybe it could be said that that's the best that modernist painting has managed to prevail, that somehow the taste in those artists was unconscious. I immediately think of American painters. Pollock and de Kooning come to mind—especially de Kooning, Barnett Newman, the enormous elegance of his paintings. Joseph Beuys had no taste whatsoever. Everything is usable in an attempt to reflect the world. You make sculpture of ideas, or air, or honey, or dead animals. Everything is a usable material. The idea of lightning is usable. And yet it seems to me that in everything Beuys did, there wasn't a conscious avoidance of taste—it simply didn't enter into the equation. Nothing is well finished. It has its own intrinsic qualities. It's interesting to think of music in those terms.

Hildegard Westerkamp

HILDEGARD WESTERKAMP was born in 1946 and raised in Osnabrück, Germany, emigrating to Canada in 1968. Since then, she has lived in Vancouver, British Columbia, where she taught at Simon Fraser University, and has served on the boards of World Forum for Acoustic Ecology, and the Canadian Association for Sound Ecology. Since her early involvement with the World Soundscape Project in Vancouver, Westerkamp has been listening closely to the world around her— working with it, and for it. She is a composer, radio artist, lecturer, sound ecologist, and adventurer, as well as a pleasure to speak with.

PS: If you could *remove* any sound from the world, what would it be?

HW: Motor sounds.

PS: For me it would be signal sounds, like cell phones.

HW: Yes, there are those types of signals, and there is also the train one, which I love. But I think that the problem with these sounds has to do with the continuous droning of modern society, which doesn't give us access to silence. I don't mind sound stimulation or loud sounds once in a while, but it has to do with the balance between the absolute silence that we can experience and the energizing stimulation that sound can give. Even muzak, the ongoing music that we hear, is to me like a motor sound. It doesn't allow us to go deeper into a silent state.

PS: In twenty years, what sound of today will be absent?

HW: I think there will be animal sounds that will be absent, but I wouldn't know specifically which ones. The really morose part of me thinks that the wilderness sounds that we have in Canada will be absent in many more places. I hope there will be enough wilderness left, in the vastness of Canada, to be able to experience it for days on end, but that possibility is shrinking more and more. I'm not saying that we can't find silent places. I'm always astonished in Europe that you can find quiet at night that is much quieter than anything here in Vancouver. In many older places, like India or Egypt, and parts of Europe, you can still find these nooks and crannies with quiet, and perhaps even sacred quiet.

PS: What is the quietest place you've ever been?

HW: Camping in northern BC, around Prince Rupert, but also the Zone of Silence in northeastern Mexico. I was there with a group of artists for three weeks in the eighties, and that was probably the longest time that I experienced quiet, without any kind of motor sounds. There were no cars, and I heard only two jets during that time. It was called the Zone of Silence because it has a particular magnetic quality that creates places in the area where technology won't function. Batteries will empty, and you can't make photographs or recordings. Acoustically, it is also a very quiet place, but the name stems from the fact that you can't communicate with the outside world if you're in these spots within it. You knew you were going to be completely on your own there, and not disturbed by any form of contemporary life, including the media. The silence from media and commercialism is an incredible rest, and I experienced an incredible alertness there that is very difficult to access in the daily life that we lead now.

PS: What is the loudest place you've ever been?

HW: In terms of decibels, I've been in factories that are excruciatingly loud. I remember going into the bottling section of a brewery here in Vancouver, where the motor noises and the clinking of the glass on the conveyor belt were unbelievably noisy. But when it comes to loud sounds in terms of continuous business around you, and the continuous output of sounds that are social sounds, and part of the way the society runs, I would think India is the loudest place I've been. You are constantly barraged there, with something coming from all sides. That could include voices talking to you all the time, people always coming up to you, traffic, car horns, beggars... life comes at you relentlessly.

PS: What drew you to India?

HW: Nothing drew me there, in fact, and I always had a fear of going there, but I was invited by the Goethe Institute to do a soundscape workshop in New Delhi, and couldn't resist the invitation. I got thrown into an environment that was very foreign to me, and I laugh when I think of it, because it was so extreme. I brought recordings, sound examples, and my experience in soundscape work and trust in the listening that I do. The Goethe Institute didn't really know what they were getting, either. To me, it was a meeting of resources. I came with what I had, and they came with *India*, their knowledge of the culture and the city, and I began with that premise, each meeting what the other could bring to it. But it was chaos, from my perspective.

The first problem was how we would stay together as a group and meet, because people in India are not really prone to forming groups. They're very individualistic; I would say "creative anarchists." Groups don't really stick together. But they were very engaged in it, and there was a great deal of curiosity about what I was speaking about, because it was very new there. To ask someone in Indian society to listen to daily life and open his or her ears to what is going on there is much more of a challenge than I knew at the time. They have an incredible ability to *not* listen, and focus in on what they need to. They're very strong in terms of listening to their inner voice, and to what is neces- sary at that moment, rather than listening to the environment around them, because the environment around them is so difficult to listen to.

PS: So for them, not listening was a way of coping with their environment.

HW: Yes, and it's a way of focussing in on what's essential. But it's taken me some years to understand this. I now understand why it was so difficult to take them on soundwalks. They would simply not be quiet. In a way, it is socially rude to walk through New Delhi as a silent group, and not engage. I'm only now beginning to understand this much more deeply, because I'm doing a lot of soundwalks in different cultural contexts, and it's different in each location. What does it mean to take a group through a different social environment and ask them to listen to their home environment? It's quite complex. Here in Canada there's nothing strange about that, but in other cultures, there is.

PS: Isn't closing off from one's sonic environment the opposite of your goal?

HW: I'm not sure whether I have a goal in that regard. Over the years, having many international experiences with this, I've become much more humble about what I think is important about listening. Initially, when I started with the World Soundscape Project, it was very much an environmental issue to me, a noise pollution issue. We listened to the environment because we wanted to find out what we were doing to it. We wanted to know why we are putting so much noise into the environment. The courage of Murray Schafer to ask us to open up our ears to noise pollution and find out what it means, I think it's a big, courageous thing to do. We're then facing the dark side of society, the side that is more destructive and doesn't pay attention to what we do with this kind of noise—to ourselves and the environment. It was an ecological question.

Over the years, having been in different cultures, it became more complicated. India really turned me around in that way. The noise pollution problem in India is *way* worse than it is here. The luxury of making machinery quieter economically doesn't exist there. So, you have to find ways of creating a lifestyle that protects you from that. The religious environment, the ritual environment, the temple, the practice of meditation, is what provides that. The practice of meditation is that you're not going to ignore the noise pollution, but you're going to include it in the sense that you know that it's there. It passes through, as you meditate. The aim, of course, is to find stillness.

India has shaken up all of my experience of what is right and wrong, and what is good and bad. I can't, now, easily say that urban noise is bad. We have it, it's there, and that's the reality. I can now also never say that silence is good, because we know that the silence people experience in an empty life, without a social context, is worse than the worst noise. We know that from the Western world, and it's something that the Indian people don't know so much, and they're lucky. There is a type of happiness and encouragement towards life there.

PS: A number of times you've mentioned stillness, and said, "Of course, the goal is stillness." What do you mean by that?

HW: Personally, I enjoy the space of mind that is connected to the world in a way that comes from an inner calm and sense of love. It's what we experience when we create a composition. You know that moment when you are composing and everything in you says "Yes"? You've *got* it, and everything resonates.

PS: Those are good days.

HW: *(Laughing)* Yes, and the rest are torture! But that feeling is what I'm talking about. That is an inner stillness while, at the same time, everything vibrates. You're in resonance with what has just happened. I think it's the same as the sound in a temple bowl, which resonates just in that space, and has a stillness in its sound.

PS: You said that we have noise pollution, and that's the way it is, but at the same time, there is activism in your thinking.

HW: It's an area of conflict for me, actually. I started out very much as an activist, and was involved with fighting the expansion of the airport at the time, and being involved with the new noise bylaws, et cetera. That part is still there, but it has not stayed on the level of the concrete daily activism. It has moved into an educational arena, where soundwalks are an activist thing. You're taking people out into your environment and noticing what goes on. I've noticed that the effect of that is quite powerful. Most people are touched by it. The activism that can come from it is the important part. Because they have noticed things on the soundwalk, they can go and change things in their own life, in their own community. I am in constant conflict between the part of me that wants to fight the noise, and the person who wants to work on the not-so-obvious activist level that you can influence the world by how you yourself work and listen.

PS: So it was external and now it's more internal?

HW: It's definitely that...

PS: With a bit of noise between the two.

HW: *(Laughs)* Yes. People notice you listening and experiencing things all the time. It always rubs off on them.

PS: What happens on a soundwalk?

HW: It's not just going on a walk; it's deciding to listen to everything that meets your ears. And I now include listening to one's inner voice also, as it distracts you, and takes you from the outer world. You can do it by yourself, with your children, or with an organized group. We've done it with groups of three through to groups of sixty-five. The only rule is that one is not to speak. I present it as an opportunity to be in a group that does not communicate on a word level. My idea starts with experiencing your own sound environment. I find the sound-walks are always creative moments. Ideas spring up no matter what. Soundwalks create a relationship with the environment and the people, creating a connection between listener and environment. Deep down, that is my interest in everything I'm doing with sound. Knowing the relationship, understanding the relationship, and deep-ening the connection. That's why you want to include your inner world. That's where the creative source is.

PS: Most of the composers I speak with deal with pitches and rhythms and notes on paper. Soundscape composition is so different.

HW: I created soundscape compositions at a time when that term didn't exist. The pieces I made had to do with experiences in life. The first piece I did in this way was called *Whisper Study*, and it came out of my work with the World Soundscape Project. At that time, I was very concerned with the idea of silence and what it means. I had never really thought about it in my life, and I was experiencing it in a new way. I began to do some studio work, and I decided I wanted to explore the voice, so I recorded my whispered voice saying the sentence, "When there is no sound, hearing is most alert." To me, this captured all of the philosophical thinking around silence. I'll have an idea for a piece, and the sounds that will be involved in it, from the place that is connected to it, or the theme of the work. Then I get into the nitty-gritty of pitch, rhythm, and things that composers think about, and I'm then in complete shock *(laughs)*.

PS: What do you mean?

HW: It's at that point that I'm getting to know the material in a different way; to know the instruments that I'm working with. Maybe it's the same thing that every composer goes through in the end, when it becomes concrete.

PS: Yes and no, because the themes and the characters in your work are unpredictable sounds that you've documented yet don't control.

HW: That's right. To me, this is the essence of soundscape composition, in that you don't ever know what is going to come out in the piece. I think soundscape composition is an extreme case of not planning a piece in a nitty-gritty way. What happens is that when you take a recording and begin to process the sound of it, every recording behaves completely differently. It depends on the angle of the microphone, et cetera.

PS: It's similar to getting to know materials for acoustic composition, but the process of obtaining the materials in soundscape composition may be less isolated, and more open.

HW: It's that connection with making the recordings—experiencing the place, having lived in the place—that makes it fascinating to me. It's very inclusive.

PS: Who is your audience?

HW: I think that my audience is not the regular contemporary music audience. My pieces are played in that context, but I feel that there is also an audience that comes from people who aren't involved in contemporary music. Recording technology, and the fact that everyone can listen to things through headphones has created an enormous interest in the soundscape work, because people are listening with the microphone ear that searches for sound.

PS: Does the interest in soundscape composition make you feel optimistic about the sound environment?

HW: Not really. People often listen to recorded sound more than to their own direct hearing of sound. The microphone and the loudspeaker have become very important aspects of this society, and have the capacity to cover up what our own ears and voices can do. It can have a debilitating effect on hearing and human sound-making.

PS: Is this an admission of defeat?

HW: In a way. It's blocking it out and making a so-called better world. It's no longer clear what is precious. Everybody can document the world now, and a lot of it claims to be soundscape composition, but the aspect that is missing is that of *relation*—and the compositional aspect. In my darkest moments, I think that what is forgotten is Schafer's initial inspiration of "What are we doing to our world?" We have so many recorded sounds now that we don't have enough time to listen to them, let alone to the world around us.

Keith Hamel

KEITH HAMEL was born in 1956 in Morden, Manitoba, raised in Toronto, and studied at Harvard University. Since 1987, he has lived in Vancouver, where he teaches at the University of British Columbia. On October 2, 2004, The Hammerhead Consort performed at The Music Gallery, in a concert featuring, among other pieces, the premiere of Keith Hamel's Kolokolchiki (for two pianos and two percussion). I travelled to Vancouver and spoke with him in his office, the same room I once had composition lessons, and in which twenty-year-old Macintosh computers serve as bookends, while monitors, a stockpile of newer machines, recordings, and cables fill the room with the look and feel of activity.

PS: I'd like to talk about your onomatopoeically titled piece *Kolokolchiki*. What is the background of this work?

KH: *Kolokolchiki* was the first piece I wrote after the composer Nikolai Korndorf died, and the piece is a memorial to him. He was very much in my thoughts at the time I was working on the composition. *Kolokolchiki* means "little bells" in Russian, and Nikolai was very fond of bells—they had a spiritual significance for him. He used them quite often in his pieces, but unconventionally. For example, he uses chimes in his string quartet, and has the quartet play them. I decided that bells would be my way of evoking the memory of Nikolai. Bells are played by all the performers at various times, and the pianos are used in bell-like ways as well—with sharp attacks in the upper register. By invoking bells and bell-like sounds, I was trying to capture some aspect of Nikolai's spirit. Unlike many memorial pieces, this piece is light and optimistic; it's not a grieving piece.

PS: Why didn't you make any quotations of his music?

KH: Well, that's his world, and this piece is coming from me. When you pay homage to someone, you do it in your own way—it's very personal. I think that's true of any kind of grieving process. It's something one has to work through oneself in one's own way. I wanted to make this piece a very personal reflection of my relationship with Nikolai and not to try to recreate something he might have done or to quote from his music.

PS: What was Nikolai Korndorf's background?

KH: He was a professor of composition and musicology at the Moscow Conservatory. When he left Russia in the early 1990s, he moved to Burnaby, British Columbia. He was an extremely talented and inventive composer, and a fascinating human being. He came to the university (University of British Columbia/UBC) to learn something about electronic and computer music, which he had never done before, and we became friends. He had a vast knowledge of art, musical repertoire, and literature, and everybody who had contact with him felt they were in the presence of someone truly extraordinary. He was also a very warm and kind-hearted man. Later, he worked at UBC with some of the composition students. Nikolai and I regularly attended concerts together and spent countless hours discussing every imaginable topic. He died suddenly and tragically of a massive heart attack while playing soccer in the spring of 2001. It was a tremendous shock to everybody, since he was only fifty-three.

PS: It's interesting to hear you talk about spirit, and the soul. As a composer and researcher, much of your work involves technology, which is stereotypically seen as the antithesis of spirit and soul. Is there any discrepancy for you, between your goals as a composer, and the media you use to achieve it?

KH: No. For one thing, I always involve humans in my pieces. I'm not a tape music composer—someone who writes solo electroacoustic music for performance through loudspeakers. Almost all of my music involving electroacoustics is interactive—compositions in which live performers interact with electronics, so the human element is very much part of the equation. I use technology as an extension of human beings and their musical instruments, rather than as a sterile alternative to human performers. In my compositions, there is usually no electroacoustic sound unless there is a human being to create it, either directly or indirectly. The sounds from their instruments will be triggering electroacoustic sounds, or the sounds of the instruments themselves will be processed, mixed, and turned into something quite different. I really enjoy working with performers, and for me, it's a very important part of the creative process. Also, I think that through computer technology, I am able to take performers to musical places they've never been before and to extend the sound world they're capable of creating. In fact, it sometimes changes the relation that they have with their instrument.

PS: Would you call this a supernatural extension of the instrument?

KH: Yes. Hyper-instrument is also a valid term for it. You can affect the sound of the instrument in ways that aren't possible on the instrument by itself. For example, in my piece *Faded Memories, Faded Jeans*, there is a lot of live processing of the instrumental sounds—various kinds of modulation, chorusing, sound stretching, et cetera are used, so that the instrumental timbres are colourized in a wide variety of ways. As well, the roles of the players change. For example, there are times when one instrument will control the volume of another instrument, or control the volume of pre-recorded samples. In rehearsal, the player suddenly realizes that they're not just playing the cello, but also controlling the level of the other sounds they are hearing in the distance. As a performer, their roles and responsibilities become different.

PS: Why do you find this particularly interesting?

KH: I think that composers are always interested in seeing what else can be done with an ensemble, or instrument. One could say that much of twentieth century music is involved with timbral and instrumental exploration. We know already how instruments sound when they play in a nineteenth century fashion, and that they are capable of certain kinds of extended techniques, so what else can be done? As a composer and researcher, I'm interested in pushing the timbral world of instruments forward, and I use technology to try to create sounds that haven't been possible before.

PS: So your implementation of the technology is fluid, and part of progressive research.

KH: Yes, exactly. That's why every piece is a little different. I'm not the kind of composer who will stop and say, "This is what I do well," and then do a series of similar pieces. Technology changes so quickly, and with every passing year, technology and software are capable of doing more. I guess I want to be on the cutting edge—looking to see what we can do this year that we couldn't do last year, and couldn't even have dreamt about doing two or three years ago. I have a real interest in being part of that evolution. And if you want to be on that edge, then you have to get involved, in a fairly deep way, so research and development is an important part of my compositional work.

PS: Whether it's implicitly or explicitly stated, there is a quest for longevity in artistic works, yet with technology, there is a virtual guarantee of obsolescence—sooner than later. In composing this way, you are virtually ensuring a brief lifetime for your piece. Is that a concern for you, and how do you deal with it?

KH: Longevity and long-term archiving are certainly important issues when dealing with technology. If you were really worried about those things, you would probably stay away from technology completely, because you're right, there is a built-in obsolescence of almost all pieces that involve technology. But it's not a huge concern of mine. I think of most of my music as having a relatively short life, in every respect. When I write a piece, it's not for posterity. I want the work to be gratifying, but the lifespan of the piece is not important to me. It's

certainly not enough of a concern that I would consider comprom-
ising and, for example, deciding that I'm only going to write for
conventional instruments, which would ensure the greatest chance
for longevity. My creative work is more tied to the moment. I'm
currently working on a piece that uses a lot of technology, and I have
no idea how long its life will be—I guess I don't really care that much.
After that piece is completed, I will be ready to move on to something
else anyway.

PS: Even though it's for two percussion and two pianos, *Kolokolchiki*
also uses technology—the notation software that you built—Note-
Ability Pro. There's another interesting dichotomy to explore here,
between notation and interactive music. On the one hand, you
specialize in developing software to notate complex musical ideas,
and on the other, you work with technology in a way that is relatively
un-notatable.[1]

KH: *(Laughing)* I'm working on that. It's something that I think about a
lot. Strategies for enhancing our notion of what a score is. The truth is
that in an interactive piece, or any kind of electroacoustic piece, the
notion of "score" becomes an insignificant part of the piece. It's hard
to represent the piece in any meaningful way in a conventional score.
This is especially true of interactive pieces, because the kinds of events
that happen are based on musical actions that occur in performance.
In a sense, it's like an improvisation, yet it's not an improvisation,
because a certain action in performance often has clear responses in
the electroacoustic world. So, it's important that those relationships
be represented in some way. One of the things I'm working on now,
on the research side, is to develop ways in which the nature of inter-
activity can be embedded in the score, as well as other important
elements such as the electroacoustic components.

PS: So not only to represent audio information, but also to deliver it?

KH: Yes, and deliver it remotely, through networks. For example, in
a notated piece, you'll have a conventional score with notes and
rhythms, but you will also have a lot of control messages that effect
how the sounds of the player are to be processed—that will be
changing all the time. So, you have many layers of control streams, as
well as the note information. I'm looking at ways of trying to encapsu-
late all of that information, so what you have is not just the depiction

of the notes, with the remainder is in a separate piece of software. Instead, you have a score that encapsulates the nature of the inter-activity as well; the score becomes more complete.

A score is a graphical representation of a piece of music. Black dots on a page are interpreted by a performer, and you get music when that is done. When you start dealing with electroacoustic elements, you also need something else. Dots on the page aren't useful, because the kinds of information you need have to do with what is happening to the sound of the instrument, and when it is happening in the score. Often they are control messages, indicating what happens to a particular effects unit, or where the audio information is channelled. When you look at a score you need to be able to see that the clarinet sound is channelled to a digital ring modulator, and that is passed on to a panning module that is shifting the sound around in a circle, et cetera. This kind of information is necessary if you want a complete representation of what is going on in the composition.

PS: Has your work in software development affected your creative thinking?

KH: I feel like I have the rare situation where I can build my own music software tools. Most people use the technology that they can buy, or that other people have built. I make whatever tools I need. This puts me in the situation where I'm less constrained by the availability of software. The downside is that I have to take the time to do it, but the upside is that I don't have to use someone else's software and be impeded by its limitations.

PS: So it's the opposite then. Your creative thinking directs your programming work.

KH: Exactly. If I am working and I come across a software limitation, the solution is to go into my own software and extend the program to work the way I need it to. Of course it takes some time, but in the end, I've got something that is a better tool for me. It's a huge advantage to be involved in the development of the software tools. The result is that I rarely feel that I'm constrained by software—my level of frustration is probably lower than almost anyone working with music software.

PS: And in the end, you have the potential for more individualized musical results, and over time, you compile a large set of tools. You're not translating your ideas through someone else's software.

Is that why you choose to remain independent in your software development?

KH: Yes. I've had software distributed by other companies. There are many benefits to doing that, but the software ends up taking on the vision of the company, and the vision of the company is usually commerce, and who they perceive their user to be. I perceive my user to be me, and other people whose interests are relatively similar to mine. In terms of notation software, it's for composers who are writing contemporary music for instruments, and increasingly, it's for interactive music environments.

PS: Whom do you see as your predecessors in working this way, with technology and composition?

KH: Grisey comes to mind as someone who did a lot of scientific exploration, which had a huge impact on the kind of music he wrote. I guess I feel a close affinity with several of the composers who worked at IRCAM—composers such as Tristan Murail and Kaija Sariaaho. For them, technology was used to push their art forward, and without the technology, they wouldn't be creating the kind of music they create. In these cases, and for me, technology is not used to make something more efficient, or to help you to do something you already know to do. It's used to open up a new aesthetic world. I often come across composers who are mostly concerned with efficiency, who are looking for tools that will let them work faster. That's a valid objective, but it's not what motivates me. I'm interested in developing technology in order to expand the art form.

Other important composers who worked with technology are Stockhausen and Berio. They were primarily acoustic music composers who began to work with electroacoustic sounds. Working with that technology had a huge impact on how they conceived of music and how they wrote their acoustic music. Berio's music of the 1960s and '70s would never have developed the way it did if he hadn't worked in electronic music studios in the previous decade.

PS: Do you think it's important for all composers to study electroacoustic music?

KH: I think it is. It helps composers to think about sound in a different way. It comes back to the idea of little black dots on the page. Composers who don't see anything smaller than the black dot on the page are not really thinking about sound, because within that dot, a world of micro-changes takes place. There's an attack, an envelope, pitch fluctuations, and changes of timbre. All those things take place *within* the black dot on the page, and those microscopic details of sound are a huge part of what music is. Electroacoustic music forces you to think that way. Most of the time there are no black dots. When you look at a waveform, you are actually looking at the microstructure of sounds. It takes your focus away from the symbolic objects on a page. Notation doesn't tell you what is going on within a note, how a timbre changes with a decrescendo, and how in the low register of the flute, the breath becomes more audible. So much of composition is about orchestration and being attuned to the timbral subtleties of sound—I think this can be stimulated and sensitized by the study of electroacoustic music. Composers shouldn't take electroacoustic music simply because they want to make tape pieces—it's a way of encouraging them to think about music in a different way.

PS: Although you work with electronics so often, you have made almost no tape pieces. Why is that?

KH: I'm surprised that I don't make tape pieces, because I am a bit of a control freak, in terms of the way I approach composition. My scores tend to be very detailed and tape music would seem to be the ultimate in control since you can fix almost everything before you go to a performance. But for me, two aspects of tape music are problematic. One is that the piece doesn't involve performers. For me, a piece only comes alive when you have performers involved. The second thing is that in a concert situation, tape music doesn't make good theatre. Loudspeakers on stage are not very engaging for me.

PS: How do you distinguish between electroacoustic and acoustic sounds in your creative thinking, or is it a matter of different means?

KH: Different means, yes. The larger compositional objectives are quite similar, whether I'm writing an interactive electroacoustic piece, or a solely instrumental piece. The resources are different. In acoustic music, my timbral palette becomes broader, because I do not have the electroacoustic enhancements. In an interactive piece, the instrumental parts often become slightly simpler, because I've got the additional electroacoustic world as well. That doesn't necessarily mean that the interactive pieces are easier to play because there are other responsibilities that the player has in those pieces in addition to playing their instrument.

PS: As you said, it's quite rare to find composers comfortable working with acoustic instruments and technology. If anything, there may be a diminishing understanding of acoustic instruments.

KH: I think that is probably true. The availability of music software tools makes it relatively easy to put together a musical composition. But it's just like every other discipline—the tools don't make art. Tools help, but you only get art if the tools are the hands of an artist.

NOTE

1. Although Hamel is an expert programmer who devotes a vast amount of time to his music notation software, conversely, he also works with technology and electroacoustic music/live electronics to create sound that is impossible to notate. The notation of his live electronics parts could only be a hint at the sound, and a vague, ambiguous description, compared with the greater precision of his notated instrumental parts.

Jean Piché

ELECTROACOUSTIC *composer Jean Piché—born in Trois-Rivières,*
Quebec, in 1951—has been an active contributor to the vital Canadian elec-
troacoustic scene since the mid-seventies. In 1988, he joined the faculty of the
University of Montreal, where he continues to teach and do research in electro-
acoustic and computer music. One of his areas of activity involves the combination
of electroacoustic music with video images, of which his piece Sieves *was the*
most recent new work when I interviewed him. As part of SOUNDplay, *between*
November 4 and 7, 2004, Piché was in Toronto to present a talk (November 4) and
premiere his new piece (November 5). I took that opportunity to speak with Piché
by phone at his home in Montreal.

PS: Tell me about the soundworld of your piece *Sieves*. Is there a primary sonic idea for the work?

JP: I'm using 1930s recordings from a Southern Baptist preacher, as well as the communications tapes recorded during the 9/11 attacks on New York. But the identity of the sound sources isn't obvious in the work. I'm using the material as dramatic texture. You get the dramatic content without actually understanding what they are saying. There is urgency to the sound materials, which comes across in the spectra of the voices. The other sound material is from my rather large bank of sound processing that I've accumulated over the years—mostly granular textures and stretching of acoustic materials.

PS: But the soundworld is only *part* of the story with this piece. Tell me about the visual component. What are the primary visual materials in the work?

JP: I'm using HD video for the first time, and the precision of the image is quite extraordinary. I've pulled my images from close-up shots of the ground—the earth, forests, and paths in the countryside—so what you see are the intricate details of the soil as I walk with the camera pointing down. I compose with the images the same way I do with the sound material, in the sense that I will distort and process them with varying degrees of recognizability. The complexity of the image is associated with the complexity of the sound. By putting them together in the ways I do, it's really a new paradigm for composition, in that I compose the image and the sound together.

PS: Is the ambiguity of a recognizable form important?

JP: It is. The more I do of this, the more I realize how important it is. The reason this new form works is because meaning is extracted from these connections between the sonic and the visual. I'm not exactly sure what the meaning *is* yet, but I think the aesthetic experience comes from recognizing that there are conjunctions. They do not work based on narrative, but because of how time drives perception. It comes down to what Michel Chion called *synchrèse*—a theoretical construct of synchronization where you unequivocally know that the sound you have just heard is produced by the object you are seeing. The idea is to lead to those points of *synchrèse* in the work in the same way a chord progression leads to a resolution on a tonal centre.

PS: How do the sound and the visuals interact in your piece?

JP: In this piece, it's a little more complex, because the *synchrèses* that I am working with are a lot looser. As a simple example, if you have a beat structure in the music you can cut the images to the upbeat or the downbeat. It's an element of grammar that you can go further and further with by saying that a high-pitched, slow-moving sound will visually translate into a form of a straight line that flows slowly across the screen. But to be interesting, the metaphor has to go a lot further. It's very hard to describe the mechanisms that lead to *synchrèse* points that go beyond this direct anchoring. We don't have a grammar to describe it, so the problem of electroacoustics is transported to the visual. Synchronization points are an obvious way of having the parts interact. Where something in the sound also happens at equivalent time and speeds in the image. You'll see it right away. Even though those moments will typically only compose ten to twenty per cent of the work.

PS: Why is the piece called *Sieves*?

JP: The close-up shots of the earth look like you would want to take a sieve and sift out everything but the rocks or the greenery. That's more or less what I do with the image processing—I go in and take the colours out, take the movement out, and the forms of the objects I filmed. It's a metaphorical process of sifting and filtering through the raw materials.

PS: We know you primarily as a composer, sound designer, and programmer. How do these skills prepare you for work in the visual domain?

JP: That's the first question I answered when I started doing this kind of work. I was doing a lot of sound design for video artists such as Tom Sherman. We'd go into the studio together and he would do his capturing and processing of images, and I looked at it and realized that this is exactly what I do when I work with sound. It's the same workflow that I use when I'm composing with computer. You have your timeline, your sounds, your processing chops, and with the time-line, you organize a coherent discourse. I started doing it and it was a pure joy.

PS: So your training as a composer is transferable to your work with video.

JP: Directly. Composers deal with time, like video artists and filmmakers. In this new form, we're also talking about design, which can be very intuitive, as long as you have the techniques to put them together, and through electroacoustic music, I have that. I work with some visual artists, and many are completely confounded by the issue of time. They're not used to it. When design becomes movement, it's a very different set of skills that apply.

PS: Does your experience as an electroacoustic composer give you a unique perspective on the visual?

JP: Yes, absolutely unique.

PS: How is that different from someone who is trained in film?

JP: If you're trained in film, you're trained in storytelling, first and foremost. Fiction, non-fiction, documentary—in ninety-nine per cent of film, the central concern is storytelling. That's not what I do. I provide an audio-visual experience that uses coherent language but is non-narrative, or is semi-narrative. This form has a lot of promise, and technologically, it's feasible now to do credible images that can be supported by music only, and don't need narrative. The means of production for visuals now are extremely interesting, catching up to what we've been doing with sound for over a decade. It's an exciting new form that has a lot of depth to it, and is linked to a technology that is highly available. I think it will grow.

PS: What do you call this new form?

JP: I call it Video Music. To distinguish it from Music Videos, and Visual Music.

PS: What is Visual Music?

JP: It's actually a very old field, going back to Scriabin, whereby the colour organ would give you shades of blue in the high pitches, and shades of red in the low pitches, and so on. It's a very simplistic way of considering the relation between image and sound, but over the years, with the work of Stan Brakhage, Norman MacLaren, and James Whitney, et cetera, a lot of people have worked on the idea, developing that relation in a semi-scientific way. They would say if the image of a square is small, it's a quiet sound, if the square is big, it's a loud sound. Many people have tried to work with those one-to-one correspondences, same with Lissajous figures. Lissajous figures are what happen when you take an oscilloscope and you put one signal in the X-input and another one in the Y-input. You get figures that are directly proportional to the frequency and amplitude of both signals.

It was a way of generating mandala types of images. Whitney has become known as the father of the form, and what it has given rise to in the sixties and seventies was a kind of psychedelic, very colourful mandala image moving to the related sound. That type of work has become visual music, and it has picked up again in the U.S. because of the opening up of the means of production. Theirs comes from a representation of sound by image, and vice-versa, but I think that's an unsatisfactory way to go about it.

PS: So how do you negotiate that difficult balance between sound and image?

JP: The music has to be able to live on its own. I should be able to take away the image, and listen to the sound and it would be fine as a piece. That's not true for film music. There, if you take out the image, the music loses its reason to be. It's important that the music have a certain complexity— that it can work independently—but when the image is present, you get the immediate impression that one cannot be without the other. The video will be worthwhile on its own too, but the work will assume its complete sense when the two are together.

PS: How did your work as an electroacoustic composer evolve into working with video?

JP: I did a few film scores, and worked with video artists, but I think the evolution was rooted in a profound dissatisfaction with the public space of electroacoustic music. It wasn't enough for my personal enjoyment of the music to go to a concert and just look at speakers, to listen to sounds in the dark. At the same time, I don't want to short-change the decision to go into visuals as a kind of *ersatz* for lack of visual support in the concert stream. But it was a considera-tion. The other reason is that in the late seventies and early eighties I did some collaborative work with a San Francisco video artist who had worked at the Art Institute of Chicago with Dan Sandin, who was one of the first people to build a modular analogue video processor. We had a Sandin Image Processor and while we were working on the piece, I plugged the output of the music into the image-processing unit. *Whispers in the Plane of Light* had the control signals of the audio synthesizer control the switches on the output of the image processor. At that point, I realized that video and electronic music are one-and-the-same, in a very elementary sense, because the compositional paradigm is the same. It's only with narrative that this type of connection falls apart. Images tell a story, but sounds (at least musical sounds) don't. What I'm aiming for is to accommodate the problem of narrative so that the form can develop a discourse where image and sounds are more than a direct commentary of one by the other. It's a thorny problem and I am trying to push the issue in every successive work.

PS: But it's also interesting to try to describe the type of process you're involved in.

JP: Yes, it is, and the most satisfactory description for me is through process. Music analysis is really process analysis. You do this that way, and you get that. The best way to explain the work I'm doing is by explaining *how* I am doing it, and the processes, in a streamlined way. I collect data, I treat the data, and I reorganize the data, and get an art piece at the end. Like with electroacoustic music, you work from the material up. One thing suggests another, and you pull out from there.

PS: With the realization that the description is not the whole thing.

JP: Yes, of course. As I said, the problem I am currently struggling with is the one of narrative and how to deal with that. You can't do without it, and, at the same time, after looking at the work you're left with the impression that this is not what you've seen or heard. It goes beyond narrative, and is more all encompassing, or, depending on the point of view, it doesn't reach narrative.

PS: Is your work with video a response to the problems of "Cinema for the ear?"

JP: My discomfort with electroacoustic music, since its inception, has been the problem of performance. No matter how many loudspeakers you put into a room, there is something that is not engaging. There is a bit of a fallacy in a performance of that kind, because the music is composed in the studio, and ninety-six speakers in public performance don't render the correct signal. It has been considered heretical for an electroacoustic composer to say this too loudly, but every composer has felt it and felt a need to address it. To me, the legitimate output of electroacoustic music is the CD, which you listen to at home. There are other solutions to performance, such as mixed music and live electronics (though these have their own problems). No matter how it is done, it will never be like a cellist sitting in front of an audience, and knowing that the sound is coming from the pressure she or he is applying to the bow at that moment. Electroacoustic music is abstracted by its very nature. Video music restores the visual link I find essential to public presentation. However, that's not the primary reason I moved into visuals. I did it because the combination of abstracted image and sound make a fertile ground where an entirely new poetry can grow.

James Harley

JIM HARLEY was born in 1959 in Vernon, British Columbia, has lived in Montreal, and spent many years abroad in London, Paris, Warsaw, Los Angeles, and Moorhead, Minnesota, before returning to Canada in 2004. He now lives in Guelph, Ontario, where he teaches at the University of Guelph. He brought with him a wealth of experience and interests, including many engaging pieces, and a new book on the music of Iannis Xenakis. His piece Portrait, *for solo flute, was performed December 3, 2004, at the River Run Centre, Guelph. His music was also featured on February 3, 2004, at a Noon Concert at the School of Fine Art and Music, Guelph. At the latter concert, listeners heard* Voyage, Chaotika, *and the eight-channel audio and video version of his recent piece* Wild Fruits.

PS: Your book *Xenakis: His Life in Music* was published in June 2004. Why did you feel it was necessary to add to the body of work on this important composer?

JH: I didn't think there was a great deal of work about the composer. There are certainly some written publications *by* him, but he barely talks about his music in specific terms, and he pretty much gave up talking about it at all after about 1969. There also wasn't anything out there that gave you a chronological overview of what he'd done from start to end—a guided tour through his music and some reference to the ideas and techniques. It came out of me wanting to understand more of his music better, particularly as a lot of his work is never performed in North America.

PS: Why do you think it's rarely played here?

JH: That's a good question, because anybody who's heard his orchestral music live knows that it's incredible music, and some of it is not out of the realm of being performable in the usual amount of available rehearsal time. Xenakis's music isn't really on the radar in North America in the same way that other European composers are, like Magnus Lindberg, or Harrison Birtwistle. The number of North American orchestral performances of Xenakis's music in the past fifty years could probably be counted on your digits. It's really a shame, because we have good orchestras over here.

PS: Did you consult directly with him for your book?

JH: At times, yes, but he's never been really interested in talking about his music, although there was the *Conversations with Iannis Xenakis* by Andras Balint Varga (Faber, 1996). In the period that I knew him, he was really more interested in what he was doing right then, and less interested in dredging up details from decades earlier. He was most helpful gathering the materials though. It is non-trivial tracking down all those recordings and scores. He also let me make copies of sketch materials. But to go in and say, "What did you do in bar six in that piece from 1962?" was not something you could do with him at all. When I was working on the book, he was pretty much at the end of his ability to be communicative. The last time I remember having a long conversation with him was with his wife, Françoise, in 1996. It was easier for him to remember things when she was there to help him.

PS: Why wasn't he interested in discussing his older pieces?

JH: Well, he wanted to look forward. He wasn't interested in dealing with things he'd already done. I remember going down to Pittsburgh in 1996 to hear one of his rare orchestral performances. Somebody was interviewing him onstage beforehand, and he literally wanted to talk about the piece he had just written that hadn't yet been performed. Something new he was enthusiastic about. But the interviewer kept trying to take him back to studying with Milhaud in 1949, et cetera. It was such a shame, because he so rarely talked publicly about what he was doing.

PS: You heard a performance of *Dämmerschein* there?

JH: Yes. It was great to hear live. The music really doesn't come across the same way in the recording at all. It was incredibly intense, with its forty-note clusters and so forth. There's nothing really shocking about any of it, but when you hear it acoustically, the volume of sound and the way it travels around the orchestra is much more spatial and three-dimensional.

PS: I wish someone in this country would perform it.

JH: Exactly. Orchestras in Canada tend to do their obligatory amount of Canadian music, but rarely anything else. When an orchestral score you or I write is performed, it's always in a context of dead European music.

PS: Tell me about Xenakis's UPIC system and what it's like to work with.

JH: It was a computer for creating sound, where the interface was a large electromagnetic drawing board and an electromagnetic pen. You designed your notes and your timbral waveforms. There was a little technique to it, but no programming. In the mid-eighties, that was a unique way of working. It wasn't a good system for doing traditional music. A traditional note was represented by a horizontal graphic line, but you could also draw lines that weren't horizontal, and the computer would translate your design onto whatever frequency map you set up. For Xenakis, who was into glissandi, he could just draw them and they would be realized by the computer. I did two pieces there—*Voyage* (tape), and *Per Foramen Acus Transire* (flute and tape). It was a real luxury, because I had open access to the machine. The UPIC is really easy to use, but it takes a long time to do something that doesn't sound like everybody else's UPIC music. I learned a lot there. Some of the ideas in my acoustic music tied into it as well. I was trying to control textures graphically that were generated using serial procedures. It overlapped with the idea of designing textures graphically.

PS: What role does chaos and chaos theory play in your music?

JH: It came out of those years in Paris immersing myself in Xenakis's whole approach to music. I was working through prototypically algorithmic compositional procedures, but I wasn't programming any computers. I was involved with serial procedures and sieve techniques, and then read an article about "strange attractors"— non-linear chaotic functions. It wasn't in reference to music, but I wondered about how it might apply. I managed to get my little programmable calculator to run one of these reiterative chaotic functions. It just produced numbers, but when I looked at it, I realized that the kind of repetition and variation of numerical patterns seemed similar to musical patterns of repetition and variation. You'd get a series of numbers, a pattern coming back, but one of the numbers was different, or one was added on, then it would be like the original again, and so forth.

I thought about how it could be applied to music, and I quickly realized that it could be useful to get it off the calculator and onto a computer, where you could have a printout. At that time, I was living in Warsaw, and I worked on the procedure with a composer friend of mine. We generated some values that I could work with and apply to a compositional procedure. I then moved to Montreal and worked on it more intensively at McGill, developing compositional algorithms using a chaotic generator as the basis, and then figuring out ways to map those values in ways that would be useful to me as a composer.

PS: What is an example of a piece in which you employed a process like that?

JH: *Piano* (1989) is one of my first pieces to be written using a chaotic algorithm. For each section of the piece, a fixed set of pitches is determined in advance; the algorithm draws upon that set to create an ordering, and another procedure determines the temporal organization of this succession of pitches. On another level, the algorithm was also used to determine the tempo of the section and the resolution of the temporal grid (for example, eighth notes). There's more to it, but in this case, the unfolding of a quite restricted set of notes, in essentially a monophonic texture, makes it easy to hear how the chaotic process unfolds, with repetitions of notes and phrases, variations, temporary closed-loops where a three-note phrase is repeated a number of times before moving on, et cetera.

PS: One conception of algorithmic music is that it is amusical—that it doesn't breathe, and isn't organic. How would you respond to that criticism?

JH: I'm willing to argue that all music is algorithmic.

PS: What do you mean?

JH: Well, what do we mean by *algorithmic*? Everybody composes following rules of some kind. Some people work in a more subconscious way, but they nonetheless follow some rule in order to put one note after another. It's never utterly intuitive. Therefore, there are rules, which means there can be an algorithm that describes the rules. The question, then, is "How algorithmic is it?" There are, of course, examples of music that are completely algorithmic, where you program something and you push the button and the music comes out, and the extent of your involvement is setting up the parameters for the algorithm to run. Xenakis did that back in 1962 with the ST algorithm and series of pieces. That's one extreme. I've written music that is more along those lines, but I'm not scientific in that sense. And that's not what I consider a definition of algorithmic music to be, necessarily.

Being able to use algorithms to produce material that you then may work with in a more interactive or intuitive way is probably where I'm at now. I don't have any difficulty calling that algorithmic music either. The criticism is that something generated by a process can be inflexible, I guess, but you could say that about John Cage, too. I would argue that his music might be the *most* algorithmic. He sets up rules and follows them, and the music is the outcome. There are many ways of thinking about it. Can you build flexibility into it, and "breathing," or phrasing, give-and-take, or what you may call "musical" values? I think you can. Most of the music I've written over the last fifteen years is algorithmic, but in many of my pieces, you would never guess it. I think that's a good thing.

It's really interesting to work in that realm. It involves thinking about what music *is*. When you have to create rules, processes and procedures, and figure out a way to program them so that you can work with them, you have to think very deeply about what you're doing. These are tools to help me think and explore. But in order to get to that point, you need a certain level of technical facility in order to translate the ideas into computer instructions.

PS: Do you find that working this way provokes you creatively?

JH: Yes. There have been many cases when I pose myself a question, and try to work it out this way. One of the examples is a piece I wrote for Arraymusic, called *Kaleidarray (Jazz III)* (1994). One of the starting points for that piece was rhythm. When you subdivide a beat, what if you wanted to change tempo in the middle of a beat? In terms of notation, it's easy to change tempo on the beat, but if you were playing by ear, without a score, you wouldn't have any trouble shifting tempo at any point in a beat. Notationally, that is difficult to convey. If the whole ensemble is doing that, you're trying to co-ordinate a complex flux of tempos that don't have anything to do with a common beat. So I was thinking about it for that piece, and how that ties in to improvising musicians who aren't locked to a score. So, the problem was how to get at that with the score. That was a really difficult and interesting piece to write. I had to figure out a way of controlling the rhythms in reference to a time frame as conveyed by a conductor. It was fun. In order to get the piece done, I had to solve many logistical problems.

PS: I've heard it said that you reinvent yourself with every piece. Do you agree? Is that a goal, or a consequence of how you write?

JH: I guess I would agree with that, to an extent. It's not something I consciously try to do, but I do think of music as asking questions. Wondering about something in music... "Can it be done? What would it be like to do this?" If it's something I've already done, then it's less interesting to me. There are composers who try to cultivate a consistent style, and that's not a concern to me. It comes out of wanting to explore with a piece, rather than do something that I already know how to do. I don't feel like I have any innate Mozartian musical gift that just rolls out, but I love sound and I love the adventure of working with it.

PS: In his article on you, Marc Couroux tried to apply the non-linearity of your work, and wandering creative personality to a Canadian identity in music. I'd like to know your thoughts about Canadian identity in music.

JH: I haven't perhaps thought about it as much as he has, but when I lived in Europe, I certainly was aware that I was not European. There were people who told me my music sounded North American, and I wasn't ever sure about that. But I did write a few pieces, such as *Memories of a Landscape*, in order to become more aware of where my aesthetic sensibility came from. Of course that's a big question, which comes not just from the country you grew up in, or the place you lived. When I was away from Canada and was thinking about it, I realized that it wasn't so much Canada, as my specific environment in the interior of British Columbia, growing up overlooking a lake, looking down the valley to the glaciers. I'm sure that is much more important than some abstract sense of country. But at the same time, those elements do factor in.

The fact that I am from Canada means all kinds of things, including the whole geography that is part of it. The great North, and having grown up in the West, where civilization was new, but there were people living there before—Native traditions and cultures that are part of what I grew up with. And the French/Quebec element, which I grew up studying. It was part of who I was, especially since I lived in Paris for two years, and then Montreal for eight years. It's a complex network of things, and it's not the same for everybody. I've also spent a lot of time living in the States, and I'm surely not American. Without being blatantly political, I'm thankful for that. I didn't have any problem living there, but it wasn't part of my identity.

PS: As a composer, what's it like to be back in Canada?

JH: I'm quite happy about it. In terms of looking for opportunities, there are more for me in Canada. As a composer, I have a lot more connections in Canada. My work as a composer is all about relationships with musicians and organizations. My last two larger ensemble pieces were written for the Montreal group Kappa. *Bien serré* is one of those—twenty minutes of dense, complicated music for big band. They rehearsed every week for five months before they did it. That's about a relationship between me, the group, and the music. I'm much more interested in that than the glory of having an orchestra play a piece that they've barely rehearsed. I love the orchestra, and I wish that we could all hear this music live, so we could believe in it more.

As we were talking about with Xenakis—when you hear new orchestral music live, acoustically, it's really amazing. I'd never want to give that up, but in terms of what I find most fulfilling as a composer these days, it's the interaction with the other people who are part of the process. Being able to be there, to provide feedback, and make adjustments, is something I find quite rewarding. I had a longer time to establish those musical relationships in Canada.

As a general comment, my impression of the United States is that it's much more product-driven, even in the new music world. There's not very much support from arts councils, and there are fewer situations where ensembles program pieces because they find them interesting musically. Rather, they program a piece because the person who wrote it is politically important, or has an institutional connection. That was my sense of things when I lived as a freelancer in Los Angeles—if you don't have anything to offer except your music you don't have a chance in hell of people playing it. The music is not programmed because it's good; it's programmed because it's useful. I know there are exceptions to that, but the scenario I describe is alien to what I'm interested in as a composer. I'm quite willing to earn my living teaching, which I love in any case, rather than "do what it takes" to be successful commercially. Maybe that's partly what makes me... ummm... Canadian?

Afterword

SEVERAL FACTORS taken into consideration regarding the pre-
compositional and directly compositional phases of my music provide
a perspective not only on my pieces, but also insight into the questions
that I asked of the interviewed composers. I have always been drawn
to "complexity" and multiplicity in music, as it expresses itself in rich
and rapidly changing orchestration, extreme density, polyphony and
counterpoint, the many simultaneous layers at work in a piece, and far-
reaching networks of structure and expression. Examples of this can
be found in the music of the *ars subtilior*, Renaissance polyphony of the
Netherlands school, and richly ornate Baroque music. Examples that
are more recent include some music by Michael Finnissy, as well as that
of Brian Ferneyhough, Richard Barrett, Helmut Lachenmann, Tristan
Murail, and others. Complexity is everywhere in music and sound,
although not exclusively according to the definitions actualized by the
above-mentioned composers. The multifaceted issues of the performance

of new music, the concert ritual, reference and quotation, electroacoustic music, computation and music, and selected influences in contemporary and other music are issues I was addressing and seeking to resolve at the turn of the twenty-first century, and ongoing. These are some of the topics that permeated my thoughts, and took their place in my music as well as conversations with other artists, both formally and informally.

Having written several orchestral works and functioned as composer in residence with the Toronto Symphony for two years, I am particularly aware of orchestral music and the context in which it is performed. I heard the orchestra play often, sometimes twice a week, in rehearsal and concert. Every performance is different, dependent upon the communication, the day, the ensemble, conductor, venue, and the specific requirements of the music. The same piece could be performed three times and be different each time, with slightly different tempi, balance among the instruments, and nuance led by the conductor. At the time, the TSO's conductor was Jukka-Pekka Saraste, and on some nights, he danced on the podium, every subtlety and dynamic carefully connected in an elegant stream of revisiting the known. Following my residency, the orchestra commissioned a new work, entitled *Pensacola*. The piece is for orchestra and narrator (absent and disembodied voice, played back from the computer), with additional electronic material. The narrated texts were fragments of poetry by Michelangelo Buonarroti, recited in Italian by composer Giorgio Magnanensi. To date, the piece has been performed by three different groups—the Toronto Symphony Orchestra, with Jukka-Pekka Saraste conducting, the Orchestre Symphonique de Montréal (OSM) with Roberto Abbado, and Toronto's Esprit Orchestra, with Alex Pauk at the helm.

The OSM and TSO performances of *Pensacola* were similar in that they were both by large Canadian orchestras. The context was similar—on programmes of old music in a very large hall, and based on the response when walking onstage, I felt that the bulk of the audience was mostly there to watch the soloist in the piano concerto fling sweat from his brow after the cadenza. Or at least that's how the context was trained to function. Also similar was the nearly constant rule that on a large symphony orchestra program, the new work is played first, followed by a concerto with instrumental soloist. While the reception of the work at the TSO was warm and enthusiastic, at the OSM it was decidedly cool, except for

the sprinkling of young people in the Montreal audience. I recall one of
the Francophone newspapers in Montreal describing the work as "filth."
Having a work performed by the Esprit Orchestra is an entirely different
circumstance. Esprit is a new music orchestra. Because of this unique
difference, the mindset of all participants is different. With a conventional large orchestra, you may hear music spanning two hundred years.
At Esprit, you'll hear recent works, probably not more than twenty or
thirty years old. The musicians generally have more experience playing
contemporary repertoire. For the composer it means somewhat fewer
problematic variables, and for the audience, there is the implication
of awareness and an openness to how they approach what they hear—
generally speaking, they're differently sophisticated, and expect and
invite the new more frequently and excitedly. I think the large orchestras
also have the potential to access that openness in their audiences, if they
were to re-evaluate how frequently and the manner in which the music
is presented. Esprit is closer to street level, therefore closer to composers.

As wonderful as they sound, I had always felt a discomfort with
the conventional symphony orchestra—the historical weight, baggage
economics, and relation to class structure—and finally recognized that
it was a parameter I could work with in the music. I wanted to turn
some of it on its ear, and alter the roles and hierarchies of the orchestra
concert, shift them around and bring in new subjects that were closer to
me. Musically, it explains the quotations in *Pensacola* and how they could
be used to transform perception in the concert. In the final moments of
Pensacola, I quote the beginning music from the Ravel *Piano Concerto in G,*
which followed my piece on the TSO program. I wanted to work against
the Ravel, and funnel some of its weight into my piece. Some audience
members may recognize the Ravel in my piece, and others may hear
the beginning of the Ravel as a quotation of my piece. This would imply
that Ravel was quoting from a piece written several decades after his.
Either way, the boundaries of one piece expand into the next, and the
seam between pieces is put into question. Music of the common practice
period, or music involving predetermined forms, tends to resolve, or have
closure through cadence and/or recapitulation. But as we know, not even
Beethoven was content with that, and in his extreme coda sections began
to question the choice and balance in his music. I enjoyed this aspect
of writing *Pensacola,* thinking of it as a mental game, and look forward

to employing it in other ways. Originally, I had intended to rewrite the ending of the piece to make it the beginning of the subsequent piece on every program it would inhabit, but didn't have time to do so after the TSO premiere. The performance by Esprit diluted the impact of the end quotation, because it's a less ordinary, new music setting, and the historical baggage of the music on their concerts is, by nature of its relative youth, lighter. As well, Esprit performs in a much more intimate setting, so we are nearer to the sound, which is ideal. *Pensacola* is one example among many of how normative concert practice can be challenged and renewed.

Reference and quotation have also played an uncomfortable yet important role in several of my recent works. *Recipes for the Common Man*, for oboe and tape, is very unusual for me, in that the approach is quite unlike anything I had written before. In most cases, I've been very critical of explicit use of quotation. Most of the prevalent examples were, in my opinion, insensitive and unprofound, often some form of cultural appropriation. Being of Dutch/West Indian heritage and knowing that history, for a long time I maintained that the best approach was to avoid it altogether. Naturally, that didn't work, so I decided to try to resolve it, or at least approach it by moving directly towards it. I mentioned already that *Pensacola* contains some quotations—almost all of which were quotations that had already been referenced by others. One section contains references to the third movement of Luciano Berio's *Sinfonia*, which itself is quoted material, including Mahler, Ravel, Debussy, and many others. I wanted to make second generation quotations, so when hearing it, there was the potential for a layered network of references. Listeners who know the original works by Mahler, Ravel, and Debussy would potentially recognize those, and those who know the Berio piece would recognize its orchestration and sequence of quotations interrupted and augmented with other quoted pieces, with Michelangelo's text cued overtop. Conversely, hearing and getting to know my piece makes for an interesting re-acquaintance with Mahler, Ravel, Debussy, and especially Berio's *Sinfonia*.

In *Recipes for the Common Man*, however, I made full effort to be guilty of every musical crime I could think of. Insensitive pairings of sound sources, music I knew little about, blurring of proprietary issues, et cetera, and direct quotation was the most significant part of that. A "scratched" turntable recording of the oboe solo in the *Pantomime* section of Ravel's *Daphnis et Chloé* is paired with the sound of me writing in chalk on the brick sidewalk in Amsterdam, layered with some pygmy chants and American yodelling. Elongated fragments from Copland's *Fanfare for the Common Man* underlay the work, as a *cantus firmus*. Tasteless, unkempt, and crude, but unintended material similarities oddly and surprisingly revealed themselves as I worked on it—the musical contents of some of these semi-haphazardly chosen sources seemed to relate to one another, despite differences of original intent, function, culture, and geography. I worked with the similarities, blending one into the other, layering their connections with another in the written part that was completely derived from the material on tape. Nonetheless, I had become an employer of everything I disliked in quotation, in an effort to test my limits, boundaries, and responses as a composer. In doing so, I became a sort of "Sanford and Son" scrap music collector, sorting small fragments of sound, without necessarily any initial regard for their origin. My discomfort with the idea slowed the gestation process, and tempered the writing. I considered this new terrain, if not for others, then myself. I wanted to know what would happen if I worked with these unsettled musical questions, and where they would lead.

Another early decision was intentionally to not write a single original note. Every oboe pitch would either be randomly improvised, or absconded from the diverse source materials of the electroacoustic part. The piece wasn't about the notes I wrote, but about how the oboe part dealt with the obstacles placed in front of it by the tape part. The oboe writing could be ignorant of its musical surroundings, or incorporate, absorb, reflect, and reconcile their differences, aspects of musical material inherited from one part of the work to the next. In some cases, I treated recorded material I had made with the same intents as the quoted. While gathering sound materials for the tape part, I recorded Lawrence Cherney improvising freely at top speed on his oboe. Squeaks, squawks, and randomly chosen alternate fingers with unexpected pitch results were encouraged. I then imported the recording to the computer, slowed it down to approximately one twenty-fifth of its original speed, and carefully transcribed all of the pitches so they could be used on their own or in combination with other quoted material. In several sections of the electroacoustic part, very slow, ambiguous notes that sound like a distorted saxophone are renderings of the high-speed oboe improvisation. It too was pilfered for all it had. Structurally, the quotations and types of oboe responses at play in *Recipes for the Common Man* are organized into three sections. The first section is the patriotic one—the oboe part plays its material completely oblivious to every other organic material around it—it is an independent soundscape with only reference to itself. Ultimately, it fails to sustain itself. In the second section, the oboe slavishly tries to imitate its surroundings; it too, fails, exhausted by its lack of independence and role as lemming. The third section is conciliatory in nature, with the oboe attempting to cope through a balance of linkages, or striking out on its own related tangents. Each section of the piece is separated by bleeped-out cuss-words from television and the movies—things one doesn't hear so often anymore. The sound of a stylus on a dusty old record is frequently heard, as I retain nostalgia for some disappearing sounds.

About fifty per cent of my music contains electronics, which function as the tape parts or sound files played from the computer, alone or combined with live instruments, or, more recently, in the form of installation works, which are performed completely outside the usual concert setting. Initially, I was greatly attracted to electroacoustic music because of its potential for virtual velocity. The speed of air moving dynamically in space was a metaphor for the extremes of mechanical, computational, and psychological rapidity. I first came to electroacoustic music through two intersecting paths. One was my formal academic training and voracious study of composers like Stockhausen, Henry, Schaeffer, and Berio; the other was through an interest in pop music. Like many of my generation, my first exposure to electroacoustic-type transformation of sound and synthesizers wasn't the canon of electroacoustic music—it was from progressive pop music. In my case it was specifically the record *Fame* by David Bowie—I got the 45-RPM single in 1975, when I was ten years old, and listened to the vocal transformation over and over. When I was eleven or twelve, in addition to doing conservatory piano studies, I listened to Pink Floyd's *Dark Side of the Moon* literally thousands of times. Gary Numan and Tubeway Army introduced a predominantly synthesizer sound to my ears when I was fourteen, and led me to recognize that my piano studies were transferable to something "cooler." Pushing further from there, one finds Frank Zappa, then composers Edgard Varèse and

Iannis Xenakis, in whom a sought-after link between the intellectual and the physical can be found. The harder, guitar-based energies of punk bands like the Stooges, MC5, Hüsker Dü, et cetera also had a huge impact on me. In them, I recognized the recording of an unbridled energy. It was not a directly electroacoustic influence, even though amplification and the revolution of the microphone made it all possible. The rock and punk sources weren't unusual for a bored kid living in the suburbs, and in some cases, they weren't groundbreaking works, but they were available to me through other people's record collections, and the gateway from there to the potential for implied velocity, physicality, and motion in elec-troacoustic music remains.

With electroacoustics, I could access a seamless convergence of the energy and speed of the punk music, the synthesizers of electronic and extended pop music, and the structures of the European music I knew. I could pass through sounds, implied environments, and mind spaces so much more quickly than with acoustic instruments, and I coveted the idea of making something faster than we could play, something that would require a machine to do—even taking those to the breaking point. We experience that extreme mechanical speed on a daily basis, and I was constantly aware of giving control to machines and media that we had made, yet that moved or calculated faster than we could. We'd built some things out of our own reach, and I wanted to highlight that in sound. I was also attracted to the idea of using electronics to imply the most primitive form of the media behind it. For example, speakers are wire, paper and magnets, and these basic sound elements have never been too far from the pallet I was working with. As well, my interest in making fast electroacoustic music derived from the observation that all electroacoustic music is slow. With few exceptions, it corresponded rela-tively closely with the speed of either acoustic music, or the original and stretched/time-stretched speeds of the sound sources referred to in the work. This would have been around the late 1980s and early 1990s, when MIDI keyboards still ruled the airwaves, and a *klang* followed by a reson-ance was all too familiar.

I was using "obsolete" equipment (in the old Studio 1 at the Royal Conservatory in The Hague), where Stockhausen had worked once, and where all of the equipment was older than me. In order to achieve the desired velocity, I spent a year cutting audio tape on old Studer reel-to-reel decks and a one-inch eight-track, cutting them into the smallest segments possible and splicing them back together in a different order. Elsewhere I was using old, cheap gear because that was all I could afford, and made anti-obsolescence a topic rather than an economically determined flaw in the work. Sound-wise, regardless of the equipment, I wasn't simply speeding up the playback of the sound, but quickening the interpolation of sounds to fuse into a new morphology. The resulting piece was called *Tube Shelter Perspective*. Concurrently, the pace of editing in commercial media was quickening. Not like now, when Juicy Fruit gum commercials are cut the same as fight scenes in *The Matrix*. Everything is edited to make it fast now, even faster than it *is*. At that time, I felt like I was staying a step ahead of media in terms of implied velocity, maybe presupposing its direction (not that anyone was watching). It had value for me then, but a focus like that can't last, and was of its moment. Having tested my personal limits in that regard and recognizing that I probably had none, the impossible speed and velocity of the electronic parts submerged one possible option among many. I still highlight the technology and editor behind the sound, with harsh cuts and juxtapositions, and with the addition of "glitches" and "noise" to recordings, but now they're as much sentiment and textural hiccoughs as they are commercial media references. As well, I spent some time writing things like orchestra pieces that had no electronics at all, so the concentration changed. Gradually, the music became more about other music, rather than using electricity as a primary subject.

As my focus shifted just slightly away from the mass industrial sound of my early tape pieces, I increasingly wrote pieces for mixed media, such as trombone and electronics (*Now is a Creature*), or orchestra, soprano, and electronics (*Wonder*). As active as I have been in this area, I don't believe the acoustic source and the processed, amplified other can truly blend in a concert hall. The only exception would be real-time processing of acoustic sounds. Acoustic sound is precious and permeating while electronically-diffused sound is wildly different. Instrumental amplification is often quite disturbing—the distance between the source and the loudspeaker creates an experiential falsity that can't be rectified in concert. Composers often use amplification of acoustic instruments to cover their orchestration mistakes, and the sonic reality is almost unbearable to my ears. I will at times amplify an instrument, but then it's more about bridging the perceptual gap between electroacoustics projected from loudspeakers and material from the acoustic source. I suppose that's recognition of the imbalance and sound distribution in space. Some of the rare exceptions of successful integration are the synthesizer parts in pieces by Tristan Murail.

Instead of emulating acoustic sounds or true integration of electro-acoustics with instruments, through practical experience in the field I became interested in the prospect of making illusions and allusions through computer generated parts. I find it interesting to have moments when I would not be able to identify the specific contributions of either the instruments or the electronics—one could recognize the sounds, you could see the actions, but you weren't quite sure of the relations between them. It's a kind of "voodoo"—sometimes the electronics take flight from the instruments, and vice versa. You hear the violin play, and the material spinning off it is like a hyper-violin, or an unrealistic sonic possibility commenced by the acoustic instrument. It's not natural, and it can't be. Usually, nature rules, but this is an exception. The overall mind and soundscape can then be broadened and magnified significantly. The result is often the unconventional animation of the concert space. Sound projects unexpectedly. For me, this also connects to a renewal of listening and the concert experience. When you walk into a hall and see four chairs and a certain configuration of music stands, you know you are at a string quartet concert. If you see loudspeakers, it's a different scenario altogether—the combined possibilities are boundless. There's still plenty of terrain to be traversed with acoustic instruments and materials alone, but the addition of loudspeakers broadens it significantly, such that they can generate the seemingly impossible.

It's also about scale. In our commercial culture, scale is a source of confusion—with advertising, everything is manipulated in isolation to appear large and necessary. Electroacoustics afford the composer the opportunity to work with scale as a compositional parameter—we can work with the implied size and proximity to musical objects, and renegotiate scale on our own terms, suggesting size and space in any configuration. While electroacoustics and mixed media works occupy at least fifty per cent of my output, I also sometimes consider what I would do if there were a blackout that remained. No electricity. That makes me want to diversify things further.

Selected Discography

THIS DISCOGRAPHY is designed to introduce a reader to the music of the composers interviewed, and it lists for each composer up to five selected CDs that include recordings of his or her works. In many cases, the composer's discography is considerably more extensive; details will be found in recording catalogues or online.

The discography includes many recordings of Canadian music on the CBC or Centrediscs labels. These can be ordered direct from the Canadian Music Centre, which has an extensive catalogue of recordings of Canadian music [www.musiccentre.ca].

The discography lists the work(s) by the composer on the CD first, and then the CD recording number by which it may be ordered. Listed next are works by other composers on that CD (if any); the generic title of the CD (if any), and the names of the performers. Where no performers have been listed, the CD is of electroacoustic or electronic music created by the composer(s) themselves.

Howard Bashaw

Eolian Braid. ARKTOS 99032, with works by Allan Gilliland, Jeffrey McCune, David Scott, and Neil Weisensel; CD *TRAFFIC*, Hammerhead Consort.

Form Archimage; 12M-4P-15m; Preludes, Book II; 4T-XMP-14m. ARKTOS 200480, CD *Form Archimage*, various artists.

Horos: Horos. Al Segno AS 2009-2 with works by Steve Reich and Stephen Funk Pearson; CD *Electric Counterpoint*, various artists.

Hosu; Music for Organ and Piano; Music for Trombone and Piano; Preludes; Seven Spheres; Timepieces. ARKTOS 20039/40, CD *Compositions of Howard Bashaw*, various artists.

John Beckwith

Arrangements from Canadian Song Traditions; Avowals; Six Songs to Poems by e.e.cummings; Stacey; Three Songs to Poems by Miriam Waddington. Centrediscs/ Centredisques CMCCD 12907, various artists.

études; Keyboard Practice; Quartet; Upper Canadian Hymn Preludes. Centrediscs/ Centredisques CMCCD 5897, CD *John Beckwith*, Orford String Quartet, various artists.

For Starters; Circle with Tangents; Round and Round; A Concert of Myths. CBC Records PSCD2028-5 with works by Talivadis Kenins, Norma Beecroft, Barbara Pentland, Gilles Tremblay; CD *Ovation, vol. 3*, various artists.

Stacey; Synthetic Trios; Taking a Stand; The Trumpets of Summer; documentary on the composer. Centrediscs/Centredisques CMCCD 9103, *Canadian Composer Portraits: John Beckwith*, various artists.

Pierre Boulez

Anthèmes II; Messagesquisse; Sur incises. DGG 4776351, Ensemble InterContemporain, Boulez.

Dérive 1; Dérive 2; Le marteau sans maître. DGG 4775327, Hilary Summers, Ensemble InterContemporain, Boulez.

Dialogue de l'ombre double; Répons. DGG 4576052, Alain Damiens, Ensemble InterContemporain, Boulez.

...explosante-fixe...; NotationsI-XII; Structures II. DGG 445 8332, Pierre-Laurent Aimard, Florent Boffard, Ensemble InterContemporain, Boulez.

Pli selon pli. DGG 4713442, Christine Schäfer, Ensemble InterContemporain, Boulez.

Christopher Butterfield

Flamingo Limo. Artifact ART-003, with works by John Abram, Michael J. Baker, Rudolf Komorous, Claudio Pompili, and Owen Underhill; CD *Strange Companions,* Elissa Poole and Richard Sacks.

Music for Klein and Beuys; Pillar of Snails. Artifact ART-015, with work by Kurt
    Schwitters; various artists.

Empress of Russia. Artifact ART-006, with works by Michael J. Baker, Rudolf
    Komorous, Stephen Parkinson, Terry Riley, James Tenney; CD *New World,*
    Arraymusic.

Jappements à la lune. CBC Musica Viva MVCD 1109, with works by Michael
    Bushnell, Jo Kondo, Alexina Louie, and Michael O'Neill; CD *Tree Line,* Fides
    Krucker, Vancouver New Music Ensemble.

George Crumb

The River of Life; Unto the Hills in *Crumb Edition, Vol. 10.* Bridge Records 9218A/B,
    Anne Crumb, Orchestra 2001, James Freeman.

Makrokosmos I. Wergo 68042, with works by Claude Debussy; CD *Primeval Sounds,*
    Enrico Belli.

Quest; Songs, Drones, and Refrains of Death. Naxos 8.559290, Ensemble New Art, Fuat
    Kent.

11 Echoes of Autumn; Federico's Little Songs for Children; Vox Balaenae. Naxos 8.559205,
    New Music Concerts, Robert Aitken.

A Haunted Landscape; Echoes of Time and the River; Star-Child. Bridge Records 9174,
    CD *George Crumb Orchestral Music,* soloists, Warsaw Boys' Choir, Warsaw
    Philharmonic Choir and Orchestra, Thomas Conlin.

Omar Daniel

After the Panorama. Marquis Classics FDR 191, with works by Leo Brouwer, Antonio
    Lauro, Robert Pollock, and Manuel Ponce; CD *Panorama,* Rachel Gauk.

My Angel; Only the Eagle Flies the Storm; Piangiamo quel crudel basciare; Tientos.
    Marquis Classics FDR 209, Monica Whicher, Rachel Gauk, Penderecki String
    Quartet.

The Mechanical Advantage. Opening Day ODR 9319, with works by Roger Barns,
    John Burge, Charles Cozens, Gary Kulesha, and J. Scott Irvine; CD *Heavy Metal,*
    Beverley Johnston, Hannaford Street Silver Band.

Wild Honey. Atma ACD 22335, with works by Chan Ka Nin, John Lesage, Andrew
    P. MacDonald, and Kelly-Marie Murphy; CD *Wild Honey,* Nancy Dahn and
    Timothy Steeves.

Francis Dhomont

... et autres utopies. empreintes DIGITALes IMED 0682.

Cycle de l'errance. empreintes DIGITALes IMED 9607.

Forêt profonde. empreintes DIGITALes IMED 9634.

Frankenstein Symphony. Asphodel ASP 0987.

Jalons (various electro-acoustical works). empreintes DIGITALes IMED 0365.

Michael Finnissy

Independence Quadrilles; In Stiller Nacht; Necessary and more detailed thinking. NMC
   D107, CD *Independence Quadrilles,* Trio Fibonacci.

Folklore, part II. Metier MSV92010, Michael Finnissy.

Multiple Forms of Constraint; Plain Harmony; Sehnsucht. Metier MSV92011, Kreutzer
   Quartet.

Stabant autem iuxta crucem. ECM New Series 1614, with works by John Casken,
   Morton Feldman, Piers Hellawell, Barry Guy, Elizabeth Liddel, James
   MacMillan, Joanne Metcalf, Ivan Moody, Arvo Pärt, Paul Robinson, and Veljo
   Tormis; CD *A Hilliard Songbook: New Music for Voices,* The Hilliard Ensemble.

Eadweard Muybridge—Edvard Munch. Divine Art 25021, with works by Morton
   Feldman, Paul Newland, Paul Whitty, Max Wilson, and Iannis Xenakis; CD
   Decoding Skin, Philip Howard.

Keith Hamel

Traces. SNE/Techni Sonore SNE 652, with works by Denis Gougeon, Christos Hatzis,
   Jacques Hétu, Alcides Lanza, and Karlheinz Stockhausen; CD *Amours,* Louise-
   Andrée Baril, Jean-Guy Boisvert.

Lullaby; Salem, 1692. CMCCD 6800, with works by Peter Bjerring, Malcolm Forsyth,
   Ramona Luengen, David MacIntyre, Chan Ka Nin, Tobin Stokes, and Lesslie
   Uyeda; CD *Legacy,* Elektra Women's Choir, Diane Loomer, Lorna Edmundson,
   Centrediscs/Centredisques.

Each Life Converges to Some Centre.... Electra ECCD 2050, with works by Linda Catlin
   Smith, Alfred Joel Fisher, Piotr Grella-Mozejko, Ron Hannah, Alice Ping Yee Ho,
   and David Wall; CD *Stringtime,* various artists, Penderecki String Quartet.

James Harley

Canyon. Artifact Music ART 025, with works by 24 other composers; CD
   25 Miniatures, Arraymusic.

Édifices (naturels). Dame CQB 0805, with works by Denys Bouliane, Paul Frehner,
   and Ana Sokolovic; Brigitte Poulin.

Flung loose into the stars. Atma ACD 22180, with works by Sean Ferguson, Michel
   Gonneville, and Jean Lesage; Marc Couroux.

pLayer8. Veronika Krausas VK001, with works by 22 other composers; CD *The Player
   Piano Project,* Veronika Krausas.

Song for Nobody. Soundprints 9603, with works by Gustav Ciamaga, Kirk Corey, Bruno Degazio, Robert Del Buono, Karlheinz Essl, Rin Fein, Heinz-Josef Florian, Martin Guertner, and Karl Mohr; CD *Roads to Chaos.*

Chris Paul Harman

Globus hystericus; Midnight with the Stars and You; Procession burlesque; Theme and Variations. Centrediscs/Centredisques CMCCD 7201, CD *Chris Paul Harman,* Stephen Clarke, Christina Petrowska Quilico, Mark Sabat, Continuum Contemporary Music Ensemble, Rosemary Thompson.

Iridescence. CBC Records SMCD 5132, with works by Istvan Anhalt, Harry Freedman, Alex Pauk, and R. Murray Schafer; CD *Iridescence,* Esprit Orchestra, Alex Pauk.

Sonata for Viola and Piano. Centrediscs/Centredisques CMCCD 5798, with works by Michael Colgrass, James Hiscott, and Diana McIntosh; Rivka Golani, Stephen Clarke.

Poem. Centrediscs/Centredisques CMCCD 5395, with works by Brian Cherney, Melissa Hui, Bruce Mather, Chan Ka Nin, and Harry Somers; CD *The Charmer,* various artists.

Incidents in Transition. continuum CRCD 9801, with works by Jocelyn Morlock, Wendy Prezament, Micheline Roi, and Ronald Bruce Smith; CD *Continuum 1,* Continuum Contemporary Music, Rosemary Thompson.

Peter Hatch

And As He; Blunt Music; A Chopsticks Fantasy (Mildred's Thoughts); Eurhythmy; Reflections on the Atomic Bomb, in *Mildred's Thoughts.* Artifact Music ART 001, NUMUS Concerts.

Il Cimento dellármonia dellínventione; Endangered Worlds; Gathered Evidence; In a Vernacular Way. Artifact Music ART-028, Cynthia Hiebert, Penderecki Quartet, Canadian Chamber Ensemble, Dan Warren.

Festina Lente. Centrediscs/Centredisques CMCCD 4793, with works by Sergio Barroso, David Keane, Jean Piché, Steve Tittle, and Barry Traux; CD *Tongues of Angels,* Lawrence Cherney.

Fragments of an Unknown Teaching. Centrediscs/Centredisques CMCCD 6298, with works by Linda Catlin Smith, Barbara Monk Feldman, Anthony Genge, John Rea, and James Rolfe; CD *The View From Here,* Barbara Pritchard.

When do they is not the same as why do they. Centrediscs/Centredisques CMCCD 4592, with works by Harry Freedman, David Jaeger, Gary Kulesha, and Ann Southam; CD *Alternate Currents,* Beverley Johnston.

Mauricio Kagel

1898; Musik for Renaissance Instruments. DGG 459570–2, Peter-Griess-Strasse Hauptschule Children's Choir, Brugense Collegium Instrumentale, Koln Flittard.

Der Tribun. Wergo Wer 63052, Adam Bauer, Ingrid van Bergen, Dieter Hufschmidt, Georg Kröll, Carin Levine, Carin Levine, Christian Rode, Manos Tsangaris, Chor des WDR, Mauricio Kagel, Herbert Schernus.

Zehn Märsche, um den Sieg zu verfehlen, De Ereprijs. BVHAAST 8901.

An Tasten. Disques Montaigne: MO 782043.

Finale with chamber orchestra. Ensemble 2E2M, Paul Mefano. Accord: 201262.

Udo Kasemets

3/7 D'un Morceau en Forme de Poire; Feigenbaum Cascades; Music of the First Eleven Primes; Pythagoras Tree; Tangovariables on the word TANGO; Timepiece version I; Timepiece version II. Hat Art HAT 113, CD *Pythagoras Tree,* Stephen Clarke.

One Plus One, vol. 2. Studea Musica BR1336, with works by 63 other Canadian composers; CD *Canadian Compositions for Young Pianists,* Elaine Keillor.

Timetrip to Big Bang. Artifact ART 010, Chris Devonshire, Susan Layard.

Calendar Round: Megalcides. Editions Shelan ESP 9601, with works by John Celona, Micheline Coulombe Saint-Marcoux, Robert F. Jones, Alcides Lanza, and Bruce Pennycock; CD *New Music from the Americas, Vol. 3,* Alcides Lanza, Meg Sheppard.

Gary Kulesha

Toccata. Centrediscs/Centredisques CMCCD 4592, with works by Harry Freedman, David Jaeger, Peter Hatch, and Ann Southam; CD *Alternate Currents,* Beverley Johnston.

Angels. Centrediscs/Centredisques CMCCD 2786, with works by Serge Arcuri, Alexina Louie, and Jean Piché; CD *IMPACT,* James Campbell, Beverley Johnston.

Piano Trio No. 2. Analekta-Fleur de Lys FL 23174, with works by Christos Hatzis, Chan Ka Nin, and Kelly-Marie Murphy; CD *Canadian Premieres,* Gryphon Trio.

Concerto for Recorder and Small Orchestra. BMG (RCA Red Seal) 09026 68769 2, with works by Malcolm Arnold, Vagn Holmboe, Thomas Koppel, and Asger Lund Christiansen; CD *Moonchild's Dream,* Michala Petri, English Chamber Orchestra, Okko Kamu.

Mysterium Coniunctionis. Centrediscs/Centredisques CMCCD 4392, with works by Violet Archer, Gregory Levin, Phil Nimmons, and John Weinzweig; CD *Crossroads,* James Campbell, David Bourque, Gary Kulesha.

Helmut Lachenmann

Gran Torso; Salut für Caudwell. Col Legno AU 31804, Wilhelm Bruck, Theodor Ross, Berner Streichquartett.

Air; Intérieur I; Schwankungen am Rand Lachenmann : Orchestral and Chamber Music. Col Legno WWE 1CD 20511, CD *Lachenmann : Orchestral and Chamber Music,* Christoph Caskel, Christian Dierstein, SWF Sinfonieorchester Baden-Baden, Staatsorchester Stuttgart, Ernest Bour, Lothar Zagrosek.

...zwei Gefühle..., Musik mit Leonardo für Sprecher und Ensemble. Accord 204852, Helmut Lachenmann, Andreas Lindenbaum, Björn Wilker, Klangforum Wien, Hans Zende.

Das Mädchen mit den Schwefelhölzern (revised version). ECM New Series 1858, Tomoko Hemmi, Helmut Lachenmann, Mayumi Miyata, Eiko Morikawa, André Richard, Yukiko Sugawara, Nicole Tibbels, Experimentalstudio der Heinrich-Strobel-Stiftung des SWR, SWR-Vokalensemble Stuttgart, SWR-Sinfonieorchester Baden-Baden und Freiburg. Sylvain Cambreling.

Allegro sostenuto; Serynade. Kairos KAI 0012212, Lucas Fels, Shizuyo Oka, Yukiko Sugawara.

Alexina Louie

Starstruck. Carleton Sound CSCD-1006, with works by 11 other Canadian women composers; CD *By a Canadian Lady,* Elaine Keillor.

Music for Piano. CBC Records MVCD1064, with works by Linda Catlin Smith, Jacques Hétu, and Ann Southam; CD *Canadian Music for Piano,* Louise Bessette.

Cadenzas. Centrediscs/Centredisques CMCCD 2786, with works by Serge Arcuri, Gary Kulesha, and Jean Piché; CD *IMPACT,* James Campbell, Beverley Johnston.

Music for a Thousand Autumns. Centrediscs/Centredisques CMCCD 7902, Lydia Wong, Accordes String Quartet, Esprit Orchestra, Alex Pauk.

From the Eastern Gate. BIS CD649, with works by Louis Applebaum, Milton Barnes, Marjan Mozetich, Barbara Pentland, and Rodney Sharman; CD *Erica Goodman Plays Canadian Harp Music,* Erica Goodman.

Robert Normandeau

Rumeurs. Le Chant du Monde LDC 278046/47, with electroacoustic works by James Aikman, Paul Dolden, Ricardo Mandolini, Åke Parmerud, Gabriel Poulard, Vivian Adelberg Rudow, and Lothar Voigtlaender; CD *Cultures Electroniques 3.*

Bédé; Éclats de voix; Spleen; Tangram; Trope. empreintes DIGITALes IMED 9920, CD *Tangram.*

Ellipse; Figures de rhétorique; Le renard et la rose; Ventures. empreintes DIGITALes
   IMED 9944, CD *Figures.*

Clair de terre; Erinye; Malina. empreintes DIGITALes IMED 0157, CD *Clair de Terre.*

Le cap de la tourmente; Jeu; Matrechka, Mémoires vives; Rumeurs. empreintes
   DIGITALes IMED 9802, CD *Lieux inouïs.*

John Oswald

Grayfolded 10-Year Anniversary Reissue. FONY 68/92, Grateful Dead, (Book + CDs).

Aparanthesi. empreintes DIGITALes IMED 0368.

Plunderphonics 69/96. SEELAND 515.

Complicité. VICTO 074-075-076, Marilyn Crispell, John Oswald, Paul Plimley, Cecil
   Taylor.

Arc d'apparition; Whisperfield. OHM/Avatar AVTR 034, (DVD-V + CD).

Juliet Palmer

Egg & Tongue, Secret Arnold, Stitching in the Ditch, Trellis. Centre for New Zealand
   Music (available on-line for members only), with works by Lissa Meridan,
   Jordan Reyne, Gillian Whitehead; CD *NZ Women Composers Vol.1.*

Secret Arnold. Atoll ACD 100, with works by ten other New Zealand composers; CD
   Fanfares for a New Millenium, soloists, Auckland Philharmonia (available from
   the Centre for New Zealand Music).

Jean Piché

In Vertical Fire. UMMUS UMM 101, with works by Alan Belkin, Marcelle Deschenes,
   and Francis Dhomont; CD *Halogenes.*

Sleight of Hand. Centrediscs/Centredisques CMCCD 4793, with works by Sergio
   Barroso, David Keane, Peter Hatch, Steve Tittle, and Barry Traux; CD *Tongues of
   Angels,* Lawrence Cherney.

Steal the Thunder. Centrediscs/Centredisques CMCCD 2786, with works by Serge
   Arcuri, Gary Kulesha, and Alexina Louie; CD *IMPACT,* James Campbell,
   Beverley Johnston.

Yo Soy La Desintegración. Amberola AMBC CD7109, Pauline Vaillancourt.

Yannick Plamondon

Fil Retors, Forum 98. Amberolla AMBC CD7141, Nouvel Ensemble Moderne, Loraine
   Vaillancourt.

Post. Atma ACD 22208, with works by Sean Ferguson and Andre Ristic; CD
   Nouveaux territoires 2, Ensemble contemporain de Montréal, Véronique Lacroix.

John Rea

Kubla Khan. UMMUS UMM 105, with works by Michel Longtin, Bruce Mather, and Anthony Rozankovic; CD *Musique de Montréal*, Nouvel Ensemble Moderne, Lorraine Vaillancourt.

Over Time. CMCCD 3188, with works by Michel Longtin and Claude Vivier; CD *Orchestre Métropolitain*, Orchestre Métropolitain du Grand-Montréal, Walter Boudreau, Centrediscs/Centredisques.

Treppenmusik. CMCCD 5194, with works by José Evangelista, Denis Gougeon, and Claude Vivier; CD *Montréal Postmoderne*, soloists, Société de la musique contemporaine du Québec, Orchestre Métropolitain du Grand-Montréal, Evénements du Neuf, Serge Garant, Lorraine Vaillancourt, Centrediscs/Centredisques.

Offenes Lied. Les éditions Doberman-Yppan DO 135, with works by Denis Gougeon, Michel Longtin, and Edgar Varèse; CD *SMCQ*, soloists, Société de la musique contemporaine du Québec, Walter Boudreau.

Les Blues d'Orphée. Media Magic CDBR01, with works by Donald Crockett and Arnold Schoenberg; CD *Blue Rider Ensemble*, Blue Rider Ensemble.

James Rolfe

Come, Lovely and Soothing Death. Arktos 200149, with works by Allan Bevan, Gavin Bryers, Jean Coulthard, Bruce Sled, John Tavener, John Whitehead, and Healey Willan; CD *My soul, there is a country...*, University of Alberta Madrigal Singers, Leonard Ratzlaff.

Idiot Sorrow. Centrediscs/Centredisques CMCCD 6298, with works by Linda Catlin Smith, Barbara Monk Feldman, Anthony Genge, Peter Hatch, and John Rea; in *The View From Here*, Barbara Pritchard.

Worry. Eclectra ECCD-2074, with works by Roger Bergs, Omar Daniel, Peter Hatch, and Jascha Narveson; CD *String Theory—Théorie Des Cordes*, soloists, Penderecki String Quartet, NUMUS Cello Ensemble, Rosemary Thomson.

R. Murray Schafer

String Quartet 1-7. Atma ACD 2188/89, Marie-Danielle Parent, Quatuor Molinari.

Beauty and the Beast; String Quartet 8; Theseus. Atma ACD 22201, Julie Nesrallah, Jennifer Swartz, Quatuor Molinari.

Epitaph for Moonlight; A Garden of Bells; Gamelan; Felix's Girls; Miniwanka; Snowforms; Fire. Grouse Records GR 101, CD *The Choral Music of Murray Schafer, Vol. 1*, Vancouver Chamber Choir, Jon Washburn.

Minnelieder (original version). CBC Records MVCD 1073, with works by Luciano Berio and Igor Stravinsky; CD *Jean Stillwell*, Jean Stilwell, Canadian Chamber Ensemble, Raffi Armenian.

Magic Songs. Centrediscs/Centredisques C M C C D 4893, with works by Alexina
Louie, Srul Irving Glick, and Imant Raminsh; C D *Love Songs for a Small Planet*,
soloists, Vancouver Chamber Choir, Jon Washburn.

Linda Catlin Smith

Memory Forms. Artifact Music A R T-024, Stephen Clarke, Mark Fewer, Henry
Kucharzyk, Marc Sabat, Rick Sacks, Arraymusic, The Burdocks, C B C Radio
Orchestra, Owen Underhill.

Little Venice. Artifact Music A R T-004, with works by José Evangelista, Steve Reich,
Rodney Sharman, Kevin Volans; C D *Chroma*, Arraymusic.

As you pass a reflective surface. Eclectra E C C D-2050, with works by Alfred Fisher,
Piotr Grella-Mojejko, Keith Hamel, Ron Hannah, Alice Ho, and David Wall; in
Stringtime, Penderecki Quartet.

Versailles. Artifact Music A R T-014, with works by François Couperin, Jacques
Hotteterre, Henry Kucharzyk, and Jean-Philippe Rameau; C D *Gardens of
Versailles*, Les Coucous Bénévoles.

Zart. C B C Records M V C D1064, with works by Jacques Hétu, Alexina Louie, and
Ann Southam; C D *Canadian Music for Piano*, Louise Bessette.

John Weinzweig

Contrasts for Guitar; Private Collection. Centrediscs/Centredisques C M C C D 0582, C D
Private Collection, Philip Candelaria, Monica Gaylord, Mary-Lou Fallis.

Dance of Masada. Marquis Classics E R A D 215, with violin works by ten other
composers; C D *Elegies and Rhapsodies*, Akira Eguchi, Catherine Manoukian.

*Divertimento No.1 for Flute and String Orchestra; Divertimento No.11 for English Horn and
String Orchestra; 15 Pieces for Harp* (excerpts); *Refrains for Contrabass and Piano;
Sonata for Violin and Piano; Tremologue.* Centrediscs/Centredisques C M C C D 5295,
C D *Weinzweig in Concert*, various artists.

*Divertimento No.3 for bassoon and orchestra; Hockey Night in Canada; Piano Concerto;
Prisoner of Conscience; Red Ear of Corn (ballet suite); Wine of Peace.* Furiant records
F M D C 4602-2, C D *Wine of Peace*, soloists, Opera in Concert Chorus, C B C
Orchestra, C B C Vancouver Chamber Orchestra, Toronto Symphony Orchestra,
various conductors.

*Dummiyah; Concerto for Harp and Chamber Orchestra Pieces of Five; String Quartet
No. 3; Symphonic Ode; Violin Concerto; Woodwind Quintet;* documentary on the
composer. Centrediscs/Centredisques C M C C D 8002, C D *Canadian Composer
Portraits: John Weinzweig*, various artists.

Hildegard Westerkamp

Attending to Sacred Matters; Gently Penetrating; Into the Labyrinth. earsay productions
02002, CD *Into India.*

*A Walk Through The City; Beneath The Forest Floor; Cricket Voice; Fantasie for Horns II;
Kits Beach Soundwalk.* empreintes DIGITALes IMED 963, CD *Transformations.*

Breathing Room. empreintes DIGITALes IMED 9604, with works by 24 other
composers; CD *Électro Clips.*

Gently Penetrating Beneath the Sounding Surfaces of Another Place. earsay productions
ES 98005, with works by Rainer Burck, Andrew Czink, Damian Keller, Giogio
Magnanensi, and John Oliver; CD *Harangue II.*

Talking Rain. earsay productions 98001, with works by Andrew Czink, Susan
Frykberg, Damian Keller, Giorgio Magnanensi, and John Oliver; CD *Harangue I.*

Christian Wolff

10 Exercises. New World Records B000HD1MZ2, various artists, Christian Wolff.

Bread and Roses: Piano Works by Christian Wolff, 1976–1983. Mode MO43, Sally Pinkas.

Burdocks; Trio III; Tuba Song. Tzadik 7071, Fred Frith, Joan Jeanrenaud Miya
Masaoka, Gordon Mumma, Bob Ostertag, William Winant, Christian Wolff, The
Other Minds Ensemble.

Christian Wolff: (Re:) Making Music—Works 1962–99. Mode MO133, various artists.

Exercise #2. Artifact Art 016, with works by Wende Bartley and Henry Kucharzyk;
CD *Chaser,* Hemispheres.

Photo Credits

R. Murray Schafer, p. xxx. Photo by André Pierre Leduc.

Robert Normandeau, p. 8. Photo by Alain Taquet.

Chris Paul Harman, p. 14. Photo by Erik Lindala.

Linda Catlin Smith, p. 20. Photo by Rick Sacks.

Alexina Louie, p. 26. Photo by Shin Sugino.

Michael Finnissy, p. 38. Photo by Manfred Melzer.

John Weinzweig, p. 46. Photo by André Pierre Leduc.

Udo Kasemets, p. 56. Photo by John Oswald.

Pierre Boulez, p. 62. Photo by Gabriela Brandenstein, courtesy of Duetsche Grammophon.

Barbara Croall, p. 72. Photo by Richard Moore.

James Rolfe, p. 80. Photo by Vilma Indra Vitols.

John Beckwith, p. 88. Photo by André Pierre Leduc.

George Crumb, p. 106. Photo courtesy of C.F. Peters Corporation.

Peter Hatch, p. 114. Photo by Margaret Toye.

John Oswald, p. 124. Self portrait.

Francis Dhomont, p. 136. Photo by Florence Gonot.

Helmut Lachenmann, p. 160. Photo by Markus Kirchgessner.

Juliet Palmer, p. 170. Photo by Vilma Indra Vitols.

Christian Wolff, p. 180. Photo by C.W. Bratislava.

Mauricio Kagel, p. 188. Photo by Christian Ganet.

John Rea, p. 196. Photo by Bernard Préfontaine.

Gary Kulesha, p. 206. Self portrait.

Howard Bashaw, p. 220. Photo courtesy of Coal Harbour Images.

Christopher Butterfield, p. 230. Photo by Vince Klassen.

Hildegard Westerkamp, p. 240. Photo by Peter Grant.

Keith Hamel, p. 250. Photo by Paul Steenhuisen.

James Harley, p. 268. Photo by Martin Schwalbe.

Index

in electroacoustics, 9-10, 11, 12, 13
of *Patria* series, 3-4.
See also composer-audience
relationship
avant-garde music, 19, 191

Babbitt, Milton, 134
Bach, C.P.E., 172
Bach, J.S., 42, 66, 112, 165, 166
Baden, Mowry, 149
Ballard, J.G., 133
Barenboim, Daniel, 71
Barrault, Jean-Louis, 69
Bartók, Béla, 109-10, 211
Baselitz, Georg, 36
Bashaw, Howard
    connection to interviewer, xxvi
    connection to other composers,
        xxvii, xxviii
    discography, 288
    interview, 221-28
Beatles, 132
beauty, 167-68
Beckwith, John
    connection to interviewer, xxiii
    connection to other composers,
        xxvii
    discography, 288
    interview, xx, 89-95
Beethoven, Ludwig von
    celebrating anniversary of, 48
    and changing perception of
        music, 165, 279
    and humour, 173
    and politics, 113
    use of his music, 41, 132
bells, 252
Benjamin, Walter, 41, 236
Berg, Alban, 53, 75

Berio, Luciano, 71, 129, 215-16, 257, 280
Bernstein, Leonard, 84, 177
Bertolucci, Bernardo, 208
Beuys, Joseph, 238-39
Bihl, Elisabeth, xxiii, 48
Bill, Donald, 91
Birtwistle, Harrison, 270
Boulanger, Nadia, 89
Boulez, Pierre
    connection to interviewer, xxiii-
        xxiv
    connection to other composers,
        xxvii, 189
    discography, 288
    influence of, 85, 121, 134, 213
    interview, xxi, 63-71
Bouliane, Denys, 90
Bowie, David, 282
Brahms, Johannes, 99, 190
Brakhage, Stan, 126, 264
broadcasting of Canadian composers,
    xv-xvi. *See also* CBC
Brown, Earle, 184, 185
Buhr, Glenn, 218
Buñuel, Luis, 209-10
Burroughs, William S., 18
Busoni, Ferruccio B., 212
Butterfield, Christopher
    connection to other composers,
        xxvii
    discography, 288-89
    interview, xx, 231-39

Cage, John
    and C. Wolff, 184, 185
    and E. Satie, 40
    as influence, 162, 184
    and M. Arnold, 153
    and P. Boulez, 66, 69

and U. Kasemets, 57-61

working method of, 234, 273

Canada Council for the Arts, xvi-xvii

Canadian Composers Portraits series,
47, 50

Canadian Creative Music Collective
(CCMC), 127

Canadian League of Composers, xvii,
xxiii

Canadian Music Centre, xii, 48-49

Carpenter, John, 210

Carter, Benny, 208

CBC

and Canadian music, xxviii, 48-50,
55n1

and J. Beckwith, 91-92

and J. Weinzweig, 52, 53

and P. Steenhuisen, xv-xvi, xxviii

CBC Vancouver Radio Orchestra, 55n1

Cernauskas, Kathryn, xxvi

Chabrier, Emmanuel, 40

chant, 24, 77, 210

chaos theory, 272-73

Chardin, Jean Baptiste Siméon, 23

Cherney, Lawrence, 91, 281

Chin, Randy, 177

Chion, Michel, 262

Chopin, Frédéric, 112

Cirque de Soleil, 173

Clapperton, James, xxiii

classical music, 157

Cocteau, Jean, 208

coherence, 154-55

Coleman, Bill, 235-36

commercialism

and Canadian identity, 276

and electroacoustic music, 143-44,
285

and "message" music, 166

and noise, 242-43

and orchestras, 216-18

commissions

between composers, xxiii, xxvi

and G. Kulesha, 210

and J. Beckwith, 91-92

and J. Weinzweig, 49, 50, 52-53

as make up of composers' work,
xvi-xvii, xviii, xix

and R. Murray Schafer, 2

complexity, 277-78

composer-audience relationship

and co-creation, 155

in concert halls, 98-100, 103-04

and frustrating expectation, 172,
174

and listener losing himself, 149

and shock, 118

composer-conductor relationship,
xxviii, 64

composer-performer relationship

B. Croall on, 74

C. Wolff on, 182-83, 184-85, 187

on commissions, xvi

in concert halls, 103-04

in The Flaying of Marsyas, 37

H. Bashaw on, 228

J. Harley on, 275-76

K. Hamel on, 253-54

M. Finnissy on, 44

M. Kagel on, 192-93

Plamondon and Couroux, 101-02

compositional preparation

of C. Butterfield, 234, 238

for electroacoustic music, 143

of H. Bashaw, 224-25, 227-28

of J. Harley, 272, 274

of J. Rea, 200

of K. Hamel, 254, 255-56

and N F B, 52-53
Finnissy, Michael
   and composing time, xvii
   connection to interviewer, xxiii
   connection to other composers,
     xxviii
   discography, 290
   interview, xxi, 39-44
The Flaying of Marsyas, 34-37
folk music
   and G. Crumb, 110-11
   and J. Beckwith, 91
   and J. Rea, 203
   and J. Weinzweig, 54
   and M. Finnissy, 43
   and politics, 195
Ford, Andrew, xii
Forester, Maureen, 91-92
Fox, Christopher, 119
fragmentary structure, 16-17, 19
Freedman, Harry, 47, 52
freedom, 19, 75, 85, 141-42
Freud, Sigmund, 119
Fuller, Buckminster, 61
Fulton, Hamish, 233

Genet, Jean, 71
geometrics, 201, 225, 226
Gershwin, George, 54
Godin, Scott, xxiv
Goethe Institute, 243
Gould, Glenn, 99, 134, 218
Greenaway, Peter, 209
Gregorian chant, 24, 77
Grieg, Edvard, 43
Grisey, Gérard, 257
Gucheng, 175
Guerrero, Alberto, 90

Hamel, Keith
   connection to interviewer, xxvi
   connection to other composers,
     xxvii
   discography, 290
   interview, xx-xxi, 251-59
Handel, Georg Friedrich, 42, 190
Harley, James
   connection to interviewer, xxvi
   connection to other composers,
     xxvii, xxviii
   discography, 290-91
   interview, 269-76
Harman, Chris Paul
   connection to interviewer, xxii,
     xxiii
   discography, 291
   interview, xxi, 15-19
harmony, 66, 67
Hatch, Peter
   connection to interviewer, xxv
   connection to other composers,
     xxvii, xxviii
   discography, 291
   interview, xxi, 115-22
Haydn, Franz Joseph, 173
Heidegger, Martin, 119
Henry, Pierre, 121, 139
Hermannus Contractus, 210
historical perspective, 130-31, 204
Houle, François, 122
Hui, Melissa, xxiii, xxvi
humour
   and A. Louie, 30
   C.P. Harman on, 16, 18
   J. Palmer on, 172-74
   and M. Kagel, 190-91
Hwang, David Henry, 27, 30
hybridization, 199

hyper-instrument, 253

identity
   of Canadian music, 51-52, 90, 91,
      92, 274-76
   for composers, 75-76, 198-99, 218-
      19
   fear of, 71
   of J. Oswald, 134
images, 262-67
improvisation, 126-28, 134
India, 243-45
instrumental music, 138-39, 284-85
instrumental theatre, 118
instruments, invention of, 108-09
international exchanges
   and B. Croall, 74-75
   and C. Butterfield, 235-36
   and G. Crumb, 109
   and G. Kulesha, 215
   and H. Lachenmann, 165
   and J. Rea, 199.
   See also cultural interchange
intuition, 67, 76-77
IRCAM (Institute for the Research
      and Coordination of Acoustics
      and Music), xxiv, 63, 64, 163, 257
irrationality, 194
Ives, C. E., 40, 42, 109, 110, 208

jazz, 53, 54
Joyce, James, 119, 129

Kafka, Franz, 68
Kagel, Mauricio
   connection to interviewer, xxv
   discography, 292
   influence of, 174
   interview, xxi, 189-95

Kappa, 122, 275
Kasemets, Udo
   connection to interviewer, xxiii
   connection to other composers,
      xxvii
   discography, 292
   interview, xx, 57-61
Kembry, Nancy, 23
Klee, Paul, 67
Knussen, Oliver, 207
Komorous, Rudolf, xxvii, 151, 156, 158
Koons, Jeff, 172
Korndorf, Nikolai, 252-53
Kulesha, Gary
   connection to interviewer, xxiv
   discography, 292
   interview, 207-19

labelling music. See titles
Lachenmann, Helmut
   connection to interviewer, xxv
   discography, 293
   interview, xxi, 161-68
language, 166-67
Last Poets, 117
Lee, Dennis, 178
Leggatt, Jacqueline, xxvi
Lesage, Jean, 99
Lescarbot, Marc, 90
Levine, Art, 77
librettos, 27, 28, 30
Ligeti, György Sándor, 71, 189
Lindberg, Magnus, 270
line, 212, 213
Lissajous figures, 264-65
listener, the
   and conventions, 156
   and losing yourself in music, 149,
      150-51

as music maker, 58-59

of plunderphonics, 133-34

sophistication of, 121, 129-30, 192, 193

literature

as base of composition, 232-33, 234, 236

influences from, 22, 68-69, 133, 209

as inspiration for music, 178

live music, 142. *See also* concert halls; orchestras; opera

logic, 67

Louie, Alexina

connection to interviewer, xxiii

discography, 293

interview, 27-31

Lutoslawski, Witold, 211

Mackey, Steve, 173

MacLaren, Norman, 264

Magnanensi, Giorgio, 278

Mahler, Gustav, 75, 109, 110, 112, 280

Mariner, Justin, xxiv

Marinetti, Emilio, 174

marketing, 94-95. *See also* commercialism

Martin, Agnes, 23

Martin, Steve, 154

mash-ups, 129

Mathews, Robin, 91

McCarthy, Cormac, 22

meditation/meditative experience, 25

melodramas, 200

melody, 24

memory, 185-86

Messiaen, Olivier, 66, 77, 150, 237

Michelangelo Buonarroti, 278

Milhaud, Darius, 52, 54, 271

Miller, Paul, 121

mixed media, 284-85

Montaigne, Michel Eyquem de, 68

Montreal Symphony Orchestra, 50, 278-79

mood, 22

Morandi, Giorgio, 23

Morin, Eric, 219n1

Morton, Lawrence, 69

Mott, David, 122

movies. *See* film

Mozart, Wolfgang, 49, 83, 112, 129

Müller, Heiner, 71

multi-sensory performances, 3-4

Murail, Tristan, 257, 285

music, definition of, 58-59

musicals, 85

music criticism, 90

musique concrète, 138, 140, 162

musique concrète instrumentale, 162-63

Mussorgsky, Modest Petrovich, 112

NACO (National Arts Centre Orchestra), 215

narrative

for C. Butterfield, 232-33

for C.P. Harman, 17

in electroacoustic music, 11-12, 266

for J. Piché, 264

for J. Rea, 200-01

for J. Rolfe, 82

for M. Arnold, 154

for R. Komorous, 151

National Arts Centre Orchestra (NACO), 215

National Film Board, 52-53

nationalism, 91-92

nature, love of, 5-6, 23

Neoclassic music, 54

Newman, Barnett, 238
new music, 156-58
New Music Concerts, xviii-xix, 18, 107, 161, 189, 221
noise pollution, 60, 242-43, 244-45
Nono, Luigi, 71, 161, 166
Normandeau, Robert
    connection to interviewer, xxii
    discography, 293-94
    interview, xxi, 9-13
notation
    and H. Bashaw, 228
    and J. Harley, 274
    and K. Hamel, 255-56, 257-58, 259n1
Numan, Gary, 282
NuMuFest, 15

Oesterle, Michael, xxiv-xxv, xxvi, xxviii
Olds, David, xviii
Open Ears festival, 115, 120-21
opera
    confining nature of, 2
    future of, 94-95
    and H. Lachenmann, 166
    and interviews set up, xix
    and J. Rolfe, 81, 82-83, 84, 85
    and P. Boulez, 70-71
    and P. Hatch, 118-19
    The Scarlet Princess, 27-31
    Taptoo!, 89-90, 92-94
    and tradition, 193-94
orchestras
    amplification of, 68, 100-01, 103-04
    and commercialism, 216-18
    composing work for, 68, 275-76
    criticism of, 215-17
    experimentation with, 100-01, 190-91

as formative experience, 155-56
    and G. Kulesha, 212, 214-15
    and interviews set up, xx
    modern problems for, 69-70
    and P. Steenhuisen, 278-80
    and Xenakis, 270, 271.
    See also Esprit Orchestra; Toronto Symphony Orchestra
Orchestre Symphonique de Montréal, 50, 278-79
Oswald, John
    connection to interviewer, xxv
    connection to other composers, xxvii
    discography, 294
    interview, 125-34
Oulipo, 237
Oundjian, Peter, 214-15
outdoor performances, 4-5

painting
    and C. Butterfield, 235
    and cubism, 119
    and H. Bashaw, 224-25
    influence of, 23, 34-35, 36-37, 67, 69, 238-39
    and J. Rea, 201-03
Palmer, Juliet
    connection to interviewer, xxv
    connection to other composers, xxvii, 81
    discography, 294
    interview, 171-78
Papineau-Couture, Jean, 55
Patria series, 1-6
Pauk, Alex, 278
Les Percussions de Strasbourg, 174
Perlman, David, xiii
photography, 128